SHEFFIELD UNIVERSITY ENGLISH LANGUAGE CENTRE

Dear Student

Welcome to the University of Sheffield English Language Teaching Centre (ELTC).

We hope that you find your time with us both instructive and enjoyable.

Our teachers have experience of working with international students in a wide range of locations and situations, both in the UK and overseas. Our teachers and office staff are all here to support you in your studies – please don't be afraid to ask questions if you don't understand anything or you need some help.

At the University of Sheffield you will have the chance to meet students from the UK and all over the world. We hope you will make many friends and will be able to learn about different cultures. Visit our award-winning Students' Union and join some of the fantastic activities they organise.

Most of all we hope that you improve your English during your study with us before you progress onto your academic course or return to your own country.

Richard Simpson

Director, ELTC

ENGLISH LANGUAGE LEARNING OPPORTUNITIES OUTSIDE CLASS

ELTC SOCIAL ACTIVITIES

We have lots of activities outside the class to learn English and make friends. Our full-time Social Organiser is there to help you make the most of your time. Look out for information on the website, posters and from your teachers.

EDUCATIONAL VISITS

During your course (Sept.-June) there are regular visits to places of interest. Learn about the history and culture of the country. Mix with other students and teachers to practise English and learn new vocabulary.

If you want to try something new, make some friends, learn new skills or visit different places, then 'give it a go' is a pretty good place to start. There are regular weekend coach trips to interesting cities too.

http://su.sheffield.ac.uk/get-involved/give-it-a-go

If you want to find out about the 250 societies and committees on offer, you can simply chat to the staff at the Activities Information Desk or check them all out online.

http://su.sheffield.ac.uk/get-involved

Volunteer – for just a few hours, a day or regularly - the best way to discover Sheffield, try something new, develop your skills & have loads of fun. All of our projects are designed with students in mind. With a range of over 200 projects, there are loads for you to choose from so get active and get involved today.

http://su.sheffield.ac.uk/sheffield-volunteering

With 51 sports clubs for you to choose from, Club Sport provides many opportunities for you to enjoy your favourite sports and meet new people. There is also a gym you can join with a swimming pool.

http://www.sport-sheffield.com/

LANGUAGES SHEFFIELD

Languages Sheffield runs a regular Language Exchange evening throughout the academic year. The event is designed for people who wish to share, learn and practise a language with others.

http://www.languages-sheffield.org.uk/about-us/news-events/language-exchange

DAVID COTTON | DAVID FALVEY | SIMON KENT

CONTENTS

Unit	Grammar	Vocabulary	Reading
1 Personality (p6–15)	Question forms, subject & object questions (1.2) Present simple & present continuous (1.3)	Personality adjectives (1.1) Prefixes (1.3) Symbols & abbreviations ; linkers (1.5)	Encyclopedia entry about extroverts & introverts Making connections (1.1) Article about method acting Reacting to a text (1.2) Article about charisma Identifying topic sentences (1.3)
2 Travel (p16–25)	Past simple (2.1) Present perfect simple & past simple (2.3)	Travel expressions (2.1) Phrasal verbs 1 (2.2) Words from the reading (2.3) Time linkers (2.5)	Article about travel & tourism (2.1) Articles about famous explorers; evaluating & justifying (2.2) Article about Wilfred Thesiger; reacting to the topic; extract from Arabian Sands (2.3)
3 Work (p26–35)	Present perfect continuous (3.2) Present perfect simple and continuous (3.3)	Work adjectives; dependent prepositions (3.1) Expressions connected with time & work (3.2)	Adverts for jobs; ranking & justifying choices (3.1) Article about homeworking; evaluating advantages & disadvantages (3.2) Blog comments about work placements; inferring opinion (3.3)
4 Language (p36–45)	Future forms: *will*, *going to*, present continuous (4.2) First conditional (4.3)	Language learning (4.1) Phrasal verbs 2 (4.1) British & American money idioms (4.2) Language style; communication & register (4.3) Percentages & fractions; linkers (4.5)	Advert for a language course; evaluating the success of a text (4.1) Identifying genres; three texts about English & Chinese (4.2) Identifying main ideas; article about avoiding mistakes online (4.3)
5 Advertising (p46–55)	Second conditional (5.2) Comparison, emphasising difference & similarity (5.3)	Advertising adjectives (5.1) Words with a similar meaning connected to 'change' (5.2) Word combinations (5.3) Essay expressions (5.5)	Article about advertising; inferring opinion (5.1) For & Against article about manipulating images; evaluating arguments; text reference (5.2) Newspaper article about advertising to children; responding to the topic (5.3)
6 Education (p56–65)	Defining relative clauses (6.2) Non-defining relative clauses (6.3)	Education & studying (6.1)	Online discussion about single-sex schools (6.1) Article about Maria Montessori; evaluating a summary (6.2) Newspaper editorial about free university education; challenging opinions (6.3)

Listening	Speaking / Pronunciation	Scenario	Study Skills / Writing	Video
Conversation about appearance & personality (1.1) Radio interview with a psychologist (1.2)	Discussing personalities; Word stress (1.1) Discussing personality tests (1.2) Discussing charisma (1.3)	Key language: giving opinions, agreeing & disagreeing, making suggestions Task: choosing a new team member Scenario: choosing a new member	Writing questions (1.2) Study skills: Taking notes while reading Writing skills: A for and against essay	Meet the expert: an interview with Michael Gould, a professional actor, about method acting (1.2)
Questions & answers about travelling abroad; inferring attitude (2.1) Interview about the Universities Explorers Programme (2.3)	Compiling a list of travel tips (2.1) -ed endings; talking about past life events (2.2) Contractions; choosing suitable jobs (2.3)	Key language: discussing advantages & disadvantages, making suggestions Task: organising a study trip Scenario: discussing issues of past study trips and planning a more successful one	Writing travel tips (2.1) Study skills: Taking notes while listening Writing skills: A biographical profile	Study skills video: making notes while listening to a talk about Thor Heyerdahl (2.5)
People talking about homeworking (3.2) Radio interview with three students about their work placements (3.3) Conversation with a careers counsellor; people talking about CVs (3.5)	Discussing jobs (3.1) Discussing what is important in a job (3.1) Discussing ideal working hours (3.2) Discussing work placements (3.3) Correcting politely (3.2)	Key language: asking questions, giving answers Task: taking part in an interview Scenario: conducting and participating in an interview	Writing a job advert (3.1) Study skills: Organising ideas and paragraphs Writing skills: Covering letter & Curriculum Vitae (CV)	Meet the expert: an interview with Caroline Matthews, about her internship in the insurance industry (3.3)
Conversation between two students (4.2) Interview with an expert on communication (4.3)	Discussing language issues (4.1) Debate about British and American English (4.2) Compiling a list of Dos & Don'ts for online communication (4.3)	Key language: accepting & rejecting ideas, considering consequences Task: selecting an English language programme Scenario: discussing proposals and choosing the best one	Study skills: Describing charts & tables Writing skills: A report describing a chart	Meet the expert: interview with Henry Hitchings, author of Language Wars, about English as a global language (4.2)
People talking about adverts (5.1) Conversation about designing a website (5.2) An extract from a lecture on critical thinking (5.5)	Talking about adverts (5.1) Choosing photos for adverts (5.1) Discussing cosmetic surgery (5.2) Group discussion comparing the benefits of different quad bikes (5.3)	Key language: the language of presentations Task: giving a formal presentation Scenario: brainstorming for an advertising campaign and selecting the most effective one	Study skills: Critical thinking Writing skills: An opinion-led essay; planning your essay	Meet the expert: interview with Vena Raffle about the work of the UK Advertising Standards Authority (5.3)
People talking about their education; inferring attitude (5.1) Student describing a teacher (6.1) People talking about their university experience (6.3)	Discussing education (6.1) Timed discussion about educational issues (6.2) Describing & comparing different educational systems (6.3)	Key language: discussing options Task: problem-solving Scenario: looking a problems at a university and finding solutions	Writing your opinion online (6.1) Describing a teacher (6.2) Study skills: Reading strategies: predicting, skimming, scanning, inferring Writing skills: Formal correspondence, correspondence conventions	Meet the expert: interview with Rob Gueterbock, a Montessori teacher, about the Montessori method of education (6.2)

CONTENTS

Unit	Grammar	Vocabulary	Reading
7 Design (p66–75)	Modals (necessity & obligation) (7.2) Modals (present deduction) (7.3)	Word building; design adjectives (7.1) Materials, shapes & texture; abstract nouns (7.2) Words from the reading (7.3) Linkers (7.5)	Introduction from a design book; reacting to the text (7.1) Three articles about design periods; justifying opinions (7.2) Article about Alessi; identifying main ideas (7.3)
8 Business (p76–85)	Past continuous (8.2) Past perfect simple	Business terms & roles (8.1) Collocations 2: business (8.3)	Leaflet for new businesses (8.1) Article about business dilemmas (8.2) Obituaries of business icons; identifying similarities & differences (8.3)
9 Engineering (p86–95)	The passive (9.2) Articles (9.3)	Words from the reading (9.1) Collocations 3 (9.1) Hazards and global threats (9.2) Expressions for managing a discussion (9.5)	Leaflet about women & engineering; identifying genre (9.1) Article about asteroids; identifying facts (9.2) Three articles about superstructures; identifying problems (9.3)
10 Trends (p96–105)	Expressions of quantity (10.2) Infinitives & -ing forms (10.3)	Phrasal verbs 3 (10.1) Fashion (10.2) Describing trends (10.5)	Article about 'the tipping point'; reflecting on the topic (10.1) Article about cultural influences on fashion; identifying examples (10.2) Article about paying for music; reacting to the text (10.3)
11 Arts and Media (p106–115)	Reported speech (11.2) Reported questions (11.3)	Describing books and films; media genre (11.1) Words connected with the arts (11.2) Expressions for a presentation (11.5)	Reviews; inferring the writer's opinion (11.1) Article about media recluses (11.2) Interview with Rageh Omar; identifying topics (11.3)
12 Crime (p116–125)	Third conditional (12.2) Modals (past deduction) (12.3)	Crime (12.1) Collocations 4 (12.2)	Article about stupid criminals; inferring emotions (12.1) Article about the psychology of crime (12.2) News report on a robbery in Sweden; looking at genre (12.3)

Language reference (p126-149) | Meet the Expert (p150-154) | Communication Activities (p155-163)
Audioscripts (p164-175)

Listening	Speaking / Pronunciation	Scenario	Study Skills / Writing	Video
Conversation between two designers (7.2) Conversations at a design museum (7.3) Conversation with a lecturer about written work (7.5)	Word stress; talking about the design of everyday objects (7.1) Designing a new product (7.2) Talking about re-designing an object (7.3)	Key language: describing qualities Task: evaluating designs Scenario: judging products to choose the winning design	Describing a favourite object (7.1) Study skills: Proofreading Writing skills: A product report	Meet the Expert: an interview with Freyja Sewell, a furniture and product designer, about her designs (7.2)
Radio interview with a business advisor; summarising (8.1) Conversation about a business idea (8.1)	Planning a new business (8.1) Reacting to the topic; discussing business dilemmas; weak forms (8.2) Talking about successful people (8.3)	Key language: the language of negotiation Task: negotiating Scenario: negotiating to get the best deal	Describing a memorable event (8.2) Study skills: Recognising formal & informal language; beginning & ending correspondence Writing skills: Formal & informal correspondence	Meet the Expert: an interview with Teresa Le about the Vietnamese food business she set up in London (8.1)
Radio interview with a woman engineer (9.1) Discussion between engineer students (9.5)	Discussing engineering achievements (9.1) Ranking global threats (9.2) Talking about superstructures; weak forms; debate about superstructures (9.3)	Key language: discussing options, making decisions Task: assessing a project Scenario: deciding on a Mega Project	Writing about the greatest engineering achievement (9.1) Study skills: Participating in a group discussion; understanding body language Writing skills: Describing a process using the passive	Study skills video: participating in a group discussion (9.5)
Conversation between a manager and a shop assistant (10.2) People talking about their music habits (10.3) Students talking about vocabulary learning (10.5)	Talking about trends (10.1) Talking about fashion (10.2) Discussing paying for downloads; numbers (10.3)	Key language: raising & responding to issues Task: participating in a meeting Scenario: discussing problems and winning solutions	Describing a recent trend (10.1) Study skills: Recording & learning vocabulary Writing skills: Describing a trend; avoiding repetition	Meet the Expert: an interview with Cate Trotter, a trends consultant, about how understanding trends can help a business (10.1)
Reviews (11.1) Conversation about a job interview (11.3)	Describing a favourite book or film (11.1) Discussing the arts and celebrities; justifying opinions (11.2) Giving a witness report of an imaginary news event (11.3)	Key language: comparing & contrasting Task: choosing a film to produce Scenario: Weighing up the options to reach a group decision	Writing an online review (11.1) Reporting an interview (11.3) Study skills: Delivering a presentation Writing skills: A short formal report; making generalisations	Study skills video: delivering a presentation (11.5)
People talking about their crimes; comparing & contrasting (12.2) People talking about a robbery (12.3) An extract of a lecture on home security; an extract from a lecture on car security (12.5)	Discussing the seriousness of crimes (12.1) Discussing controversial statements (12.2) Solving a crime (12.3)	Key language: reaching a decision Task: discussing court cases Scenario: Looking at court case and agreeing on verdicts	Study skills: Summarising Writing skills: A cause & effect essay	Meet the Expert: an interview with Stefanie Bierwerth, a publisher, about the appeal of crime fiction (12.1)

1 Personality
1.1 PERSONALITY TYPES

IN THIS UNIT

GRAMMAR
- question forms
- present simple and present continuous

VOCABULARY
- personality adjectives
- prefixes

SCENARIO
- giving opinions, agreeing and disagreeing, making suggestions
- choosing a new team member

STUDY SKILLS
- taking notes while reading

WRITING SKILLS
- a for and against essay

'My one regret in life is that I am not someone else.' Woody Allen 1935–, US film-maker, writer and actor

VOCABULARY
PERSONALITY ADJECTIVES

1a Work with a partner to think of as many personality adjectives as you can, e.g. *friendly*, *generous*.

1b Choose three adjectives which you think describe your own personality.

2 Look at these adjectives connected with personality. Which ones are positive, which are negative and which are neutral?

adventurous +	ambitious +	assertive +
bossy −	cautious −	creative +	energetic +
likeable +	moody −	organised +	quiet
reliable +	sensible	sensitive	serious
sociable +	talkative	thoughtful

3 Match words 1–8 with words a–h to make compound adjectives connected with character.

1 easy-   a working
2 open-   b confident
3 even-   c going
4 hard-   d hearted
5 self-   e tempered
6 strong-   f willed
7 warm-   g headed
8 level-   h minded

PRONUNCIATION

4a **1.1** **Word stress** On which part of the compound adjective in Exercise 3 does the stress fall? Listen and check, then repeat the words.

4b Match the meanings below with an adjective from Exercise 3.

A person who …
1 does not easily become angry: *even-tempered*
2 is determined to do what they want: strong willed
3 is not easily upset or annoyed: ~~even tempered~~ easygo[ing]
4 accepts other ideas and opinions: open minded
5 makes a lot of effort: hard woking
6 believes in their own success: self confiden
7 behaves in a calm way even in a difficult situation: even tempore
8 is friendly, kind and generous: warm hearted

4c Think of people you know and one or two adjectives to describe each person. Explain why you describe them like this. Give examples.

LISTENING

5a Look at the people in the photos and discuss. What kind of personality do you think each person has?

5b **1.2** Listen to the three people talking. Was your description of them accurate? A speaks first.

A

B

C

PERSONALITY TYPES 1.1

READING

6a Divide these adjectives into two groups according to personality types.

adventurous   cautious   enthusiastic
quiet   reserved   self-confident
talkative   thoughtful

6b Now divide these jobs into two groups according to personality types. Which adjectives from Exercise 6a do you think go with which jobs? Work with a partner and explain your choices.

artist   salesperson   politician   engineer
teacher   inventor   manager   writer

7a Read the encyclopedia entry quickly and check your ideas in Exercise 6.

7b Read the text again. Are these statements true or false according to the text?
1 Jung thought of the terms extrovert and introvert. F
2 The terms describe a person's way of looking at life. T
3 Extroverts prefer to be surrounded by people rather than be on their own. T
4 Introverts don't think carefully before they do things. F
5 Scientists agree that extroverts are this personality type when they are born. F
6 Introverts tend to be happier than extroverts. T

8 Making connections Work with a partner and choose five jobs. Discuss what personality types the jobs would attract and why. Then discuss your choices with another pair.

computer programmer   musician
tax inspector   fashion model
librarian   film director   police officer
researcher   songwriter   journalist

SPEAKING

9 Work with a partner to discuss the following.
1 In your opinion, how useful do you think the two personality types are for describing personality?
2 What tells you more about a person's personality: their clothes, their body language, their voice, their attitude, their tastes or something else? Which is best in your opinion?

Extroverts and introverts

Everyone has a different personality. It is what makes people individuals and unique. However, there are some shared personality qualities which let us talk about personality 'types'. One of the most basic personality differences is between extroverts and introverts. These terms are used in many theories of personality types. They were made popular by the important Swiss psychiatrist Carl Jung (1875–1961), although he did not invent them. Extroversion and introversion are ways of describing a person's attitude to the world: do they move towards it or away from it?

Extroverts are people who look outwards. They are friendly, sociable, talkative, enthusiastic and self-confident. They are interested in a range of experiences and enjoy spending time with other people. They tend to act first, then think later. When extroverts feel bad, unmotivated or without energy, they look outside themselves. This means they might go shopping, call friends or have a party. Typical extrovert jobs are in politics, sales, teaching and management.

Introverts, on the other hand, look inwards. They feel more comfortable alone and enjoy ideas and thinking. They are reserved, quiet, thoughtful and may be shy. They like to think and consider before taking action, and will often analyse before speaking. In contrast to extroverts they value fewer, but deeper experiences. When feeling bad or stressed, introverts look inside themselves for energy and motivation. Introverts often work as artists, writers, engineers and inventors.

Although the types are different, most people have both extrovert and introvert characteristics in their personality, but often they are more one type than the other. There has been some interesting research into why people are basically extroverts or introverts. Some people say that extroverts and introverts are born not made. Others believe that environment is more important in shaping someone's personality.

Attitudes towards introverts and extroverts vary in different cultures. For example, Americans value extrovert qualities. However, cultures such as those in central Europe and south east Asia regard introvert characteristics more highly. Interestingly, research shows that people who live on islands tend to be more introverted. Studies have also found that extroverts have higher happiness levels than introverts.

1.2 EXPLORING PERSONALITY

LISTENING AND SPEAKING

1 How useful do you think the following are for judging a person's character?

personality tests   handwriting analysis   star signs/horoscopes   interviews

↑ vocab input

2 Have you ever done a personality test? If so, why?

3a **1.3** Listen to an interview with Dr Frank Partridge, an expert in psychometrics (the measurement of intelligence and personal qualities). Tick (✓) the topics covered in the interview.

✓ 1 things that psychometric tests measure (4)
✓ 2 the first tests
  3 problems with personality tests
✓ 4 the Myers–Briggs test
  5 the future of personality tests

3b Complete the questions that the interviewer asks.

1 What exactly _____ psychometrics _____?
2 How _____ psychometric testing _____?
3 _____ useful _____ the tests?
4 _____ they reliable?
5 What _____ personality tests _____ you about a person?
6 _____ you _____ any of these tests yourself?
7 What _____ you _____ on at the moment?

3c Listen again and check your answers to Exercise 3b.

↑ Do handout

GRAMMAR
QUESTION FORMS

4 Look at the questions you completed in Exercise 3b. Which tense is used in each question?

5 Are these statements about question formation true or false? Correct the ones that are false.

1 In questions with the verb *be*, we put the verb before the subject. T
2 In present simple questions (except with *be*), we use the auxiliary verb *do/does*. ~~before~~ T
3 In past simple questions, we use the auxiliary verb *has/have*. did
4 In present continuous questions, we put *do/does* before the subject. is
5 In present perfect questions, we put *has/have* before the subject. T

6 Look at a and b below, then answer questions 1–3.

a Who designed the Stanford–Binet test?
   – Alfred Binet designed it.
b What did Alfred Binet design?
   – Alfred Binet designed the first usable intelligence test.

1 In which question (a or b) is the *wh-* word the subject? (This is a subject question.) a
2 In which question (a or b) is the *wh-* word the object? (This is an object question.) b
3 In which type of question do we form the question with an auxiliary verb, e.g. *do/does, did*? b - object question

→ Language reference and extra practice pages 126–127

METHOD

Some actors believe that they have to 'become' the people they play in order to give a convincing performance. Actors who think and behave in character to prepare for their roles are known as 'method actors'. Two classic examples today of method actors are Daniel Day-Lewis and Johnny Depp.

Daniel Day-Lewis is undoubtedly the greatest method actor of our time. He has won three Oscars for best male actor – more than any other male actor. He works only when it suits him. He does not act for the money. He chooses roles in films that are difficult to play and tries to understand totally the thoughts and emotions of the personalities he portrays.

He prepares thoroughly for roles and finds ways in which he can 'live' in a character. He becomes completely involved in the character. For the film *The Boxer*, he devised a training schedule: twice a day in the gym, seven days a week for three years. He became so fit that he could have entered the ring professionally.

His method acting also appeared when he played the role of Christy Brown, the Irish artist with cerebral palsy, in the film *My Left Foot*. Day-Lewis stayed in a wheelchair while on set, spoke like a person with cerebral palsy, and asked crew members to spoon-feed him and wheel him about. At this time, he taught himself to paint, like Brown, using his toes.

ACTING

One of his most difficult roles was when he played the 16th President of the United States, Abraham Lincoln, in Steven Spielberg's film *Lincoln*. According to one critic, he 'eases into a role of epic difficulty as if it were a coat he had been wearing for years'. He stayed in character during the production, speaking at all times in Lincoln's Kentucky accent.

Another famous method actor is Johnny Depp. He often stays in character during a film. He likes to paint a portrait of a new character to help him find the person's face and personality. For example, he painted the Mad Hatter, for the film *Alice in Wonderland*, with tangerine hair. One of his best known roles is as Edward Scissorhands. *Edward Scissorhands* is a film about an artificial man named Edward who has scissors for hands. Depp was so committed to the role that he passed out from heat exhaustion in one scene.

Johnny Depp has described his feelings after finishing the film: 'I can remember when I finished *Edward Scissorhands* looking in the mirror as the girl was doing my make-up for the last time and thinking, "Wow, this is it. I'm saying goodbye to Edward Scissorhands." You know it was kind of sad. But in fact, I think they're all still somehow in there … With any part you play, there is a certain amount of yourself in it. There has to be, otherwise, it's just not acting. It's lying.'

EXPLORING PERSONALITY 1.2

7a Put the words in the right order to make questions from a personality test.
1 do / ever / you / get / worried / ?
2 you / are / a / confident / person / ?
3 you / do / make / easily / friends / ?
4 makes / happy / what / you / ?
5 who / you / phone / do / when / you / worried / are / ?
6 in your life / influence / who / the / biggest / is / ?
7 test / you / a / ever / have / personality / taken / ?
8 worry / about / do / what / you / the / most / ?
9 influenced / you / at / school / most / who / the / ?
10 best / advice / gives / you / who / the / ?

7b Work with a partner to ask and answer the questions.

8 Work with a partner to complete a text about Sigmund Freud. Take turns to ask and answer questions. Prepare your questions first.

Student A: turn to page 163.
Student B: turn to page 157.

A: *Who was born on 6th May 1856?*
B: *Sigmund Freud.*

READING

9 Look at the photos of two actors. What do you know about them and their style of acting?

10a Read the first paragraph of the article. What is 'method acting'?

10b You are going to read an article about two method actors and how they prepare for a character. Scan the article and name three films that Daniel Day-Lewis appeared in and two films that Johnny Depp appeared in.

10c Read the article again. Find examples of how the two actors were committed to the roles they played in each of the films mentioned.

10d Reacting to the text Read the final paragraph again. Work with a partner and talk about the film character you have found most difficult to say goodbye to, and why.

11 Discuss these questions in groups.
1 Which actor would you most like to meet, and why?
2 Do you know any other films that these actors appeared in? What did you think of those films?
3 Do you know of any other method actors?

WRITING

12 Imagine you are going to meet a famous person, dead or alive (e.g. a famous leader in history, a film star, a pop star, a character in a book). Write down five questions you would like to ask this person. Then compare your questions with a partner.

▶ **MEET THE EXPERT**

Watch an interview with Michael Gould, a professional actor, about method acting.
Turn to page 150 for video activities.

1.3 CHARISMA

READING

1 Look at the photos of famous people. Work with a partner to discuss the following.
1 What do you know about the people in the photos on this page?
2 Think of three qualities which you associate with each person.

2a Scan the article quickly and answer the questions.
1 Which people are mentioned in the article?
2 What do (or did) they do to earn a living?

2b Identifying topic sentences Read the article again and put the first sentence of each paragraph in the correct gap.
a Unfortunately, we can also find examples of people who have abused their charisma.
b Is charisma dangerous?
c Most people will recognise the woman in this photo.
d Most of us expect our leaders to have charisma.
e Nowadays, psychologists are taking a greater interest in charisma and want to redefine its meaning.

IN FOCUS | CHARISMA

Charisma:
A KIND OF MAGIC?

1 _____ She is Michelle Obama, the wife of Barack Obama. In the photo, she is greeting children of her employees who have come to the White House for a 'Bring your children to work day'. Michelle Obama regularly gives talks all over the world to young people. She tells them that anything can happen if they work hard and never give up on their dream. She is currently working on a project which encourages young people to eat more healthily. She inspires young people because she has a special quality – charisma.

2 _____ They point out that people often misunderstand what charisma is and think of it as a kind of fame, but it is not the same as the celebrity of overrated pop stars. Charisma is a kind of magic and is relatively rare. Charismatic personalities are able to draw people to them, and they succeed in getting others to see them as a leader.

3 _____ We want them to inspire us and offer us a vision of a better future. But is charisma a good or bad thing? There are many examples of people who use charisma in a positive way.

Martin Luther King was one of the leaders of the Civil Rights movement in the United States. He was a charismatic speaker who used non-violent methods to bring about equality between black and white people. Nelson Mandela and Aung San Suu Kyi are two other examples of charismatic political leaders who share the qualities of self-sacrifice and personal courage.

4 _____ In the business world, many top business executives have misused their charisma and acted in a way that greatly damaged their companies. Some, like the Canadian ex-tycoon Conrad Black, have served prison sentences. Far more seriously, we can all think of famous military and political leaders who have destroyed their countries and caused great harm to their people.

5 _____ It certainly is when it causes us to lose our critical judgement, and this is frequently the case. When we choose our leaders, it is vital to consider whether they have the knowledge, wisdom and experience to do a good job. That is what really matters.

CHARISMA

2c Answer these questions about the article.
1. Why is Michelle Obama so good at giving talks?
2. What mistake do people make about charisma?
3. What special ability do charismatic people have?
4. What was Martin Luther King trying to achieve?
5. Why does the writer mention Conrad Black?
6. What is the writer's opinion about charisma?

VOCABULARY
PREFIXES

3a Find words in the article that mean the following.
1. describe something again, and in a better way (para 2)
2. not understand correctly (para 2)
3. not as good as some people think or say (para 2)
4. used something in the wrong way or for a wrong purpose (para 4)
5. a person who used to be very successful and powerful in business (para 4)

3b Underline the prefixes in the words you found. Match each prefix with one of these meanings.

| incorrect | former | again | too much |

4a Look at the words below. What do the underlined prefixes mean?
1. <u>bi</u>cycle
2. <u>anti</u>social
3. <u>mono</u>rail
4. <u>out</u>perform
5. <u>semi</u>circle
6. <u>dis</u>comfort

4b Think of a word with a prefix that means the same as the underlined words in these sentences.
1. He was always <u>too confident</u>.
2. His team <u>played much better than</u> the other team.
3. She asked her <u>former boss</u> for advice.
4. His mother's French and his father's Italian, so he's <u>able to speak two languages fluently</u>.
5. He told me to <u>write</u> the essay <u>again</u>.
6. His ability was <u>not as great as people believed</u>.
7. She <u>did not correctly understand</u> the lecturer.
8. I <u>don't like</u> people who don't listen when I'm talking.

SPEAKING

5 Work with a partner to discuss the following.
1. If you were choosing photographs of people for an article about charismatic people, who would you choose?
2. Is charisma the most important quality to possess if you want to be successful in your career? If not, what other qualities are important?
3. Are charismatic people dangerous?
4. Can charisma be taught?

GRAMMAR
PRESENT SIMPLE AND PRESENT CONTINUOUS

6a Look at the highlighted phrases in the article and Exercise 2b. Mark them *PS* for present simple and *PC* for present continuous.

6b Look at the uses a–d of the present simple and present continuous. Match each use to one of the phrases in the article. Then write the correct tense in the gaps.

a   an action happening around now (often temporary): _____
b   a regular or habitual action: _____
c   a fact or general truth: _____
d   a trend or a changing situation: _____

GRAMMAR TIP

We often use these verbs to talk about trends: *grow, increase, decrease, change, rise, fall*

The number of people researching the power of charisma is increasing.

➥ Language reference and extra practice pages 126–127

7a Look at these sentences and choose the correct answer.
1. Dr Partridge *regularly gives / is regularly giving* talks about personality.
2. The professor *interviews / is interviewing* a candidate at the moment and can't come to the phone.
3. The number of companies using personality tests *grows / is growing*.
4. I do lots of different research, but today *I carry out / I'm carrying out* research into the personalities of twins.
5. He *drives / is driving* to work every day.
6. People *become / are becoming* very interested in how personalities develop over time.
7. A psychologist *studies / is studying* the way people's minds work.
8. The doctor's practice *is / is being* in Harley Street.
9. I *read / am reading* an interesting book on psychology at the moment.
10. The survey found that most people feel that modern life *becomes / is becoming* more difficult.

7b Match the sentences in Exercise 7a with the uses in Exercise 6b.

8a Use the following prompts to write questions in the present simple or present continuous.
1. make friends / easily?
2. what / usually / do / weekend?
3. what / read / at the moment?
4. enjoy / art and music?
5. prefer / extroverts or introverts?
6. work / on any new projects now?
7. do / anything interesting / at the moment?
8. lose temper / easily?

8b With a partner, add two more questions and then take turns to ask and answer the questions. Tell the class one interesting fact about your partner.

1.4 SCENARIO
PERSONALITY CLASH

SITUATION

1 Read the situation below. What problems might the new assistant have working for two bosses?

Sydney GKNX, an Australian company, has a small office in Sydney which sells television and radio programmes. The office staff consist of Chris Morton (television), Jodie Walker (radio) and two secretaries Georgia and Debbie. The office needs a new assistant who will work for both Chris and Jodie.

2a 1.4 Listen to Chris and Jodie talking. What is the main problem they must solve? Did you think of it in Exercise 1?

2b Listen again and note the good and bad points about Chris and Jodie's personalities. Compare your answers with a partner.

Chris		Jodie	
+	–	+	–
ambitious		sociable	

KEY LANGUAGE
GIVING OPINIONS, AGREEING AND DISAGREEING, MAKING SUGGESTIONS

3a Listen again and complete the extracts.
1 CHRIS: It's not our fault, is it?
   JODIE: ____ ____. I suppose we are difficult at times.
2 CHRIS: Mmm, ____ ____, I do have a bad temper at times.
3 CHRIS: That's the kind of person I want to employ here.
   JODIE: Sorry, I ____ ____ with you about Barbara. ____ ____ ____, she was a really hard worker.
4 JODIE: Louise was jealous of my relationship with Georgia.
   CHRIS: I ____ ____.
5 JODIE: Why don't we go for a man this time?
   CHRIS: No, that's ____ ____ ____ ____.
6 CHRIS: We want someone, male or female, who'll fit in here. I ____ we contact the agency again. …
   JODIE: OK, ____ ____ you phoning them this time? I'm really busy, …

3b Look at the words and phrases you put in the gaps in Exercise 3a. In each case was the speaker:
a giving an opinion?   c disagreeing?
b agreeing?   d suggesting?

3c Look at Audio script 1.4 on page 164. Work with a partner to find other examples of the language functions in Exercise 3b.

1.4

PERSONALITY CLASH

4 Chris and Jodie send an email to Recruitment Associates, an employment agency in Sydney. Read this extract from the email and answer the questions.

1 Discuss the qualities that Chris and Jodie are looking for. Are some of the qualities more important than others? If so, what are they?
2 What other qualities, not mentioned in the email, do you think the assistant needs?

From   Chris.Smith.@my:emails.au
To   enquiry@Recruitment.Associates.au

We are looking for someone who is:
- lively and sociable; able to get on with men and women.
- mature, open-minded, not over-sensitive.
- self-confident, with a strong personality.
- hard-working; able to work under pressure.
- flexible and with a good sense of humour.
- very smartly dressed.
- man or woman, any nationality.

You know us both well and you have the job description. Please note what we say above, but also use your own judgement to find a suitable candidate for us.

Best wishes
Chris and Jodie

TASK
CHOOSING A NEW TEAM MEMBER

5a Work with a partner. You work for Recruitment Associates. You are going to choose a suitable candidate for the job.

Student A: read the profiles of Elayne and Daniela below.
Student B: read the profiles of Rashid and Mitsuo on page 159.

Underline the good points of your candidates and put a cross against the bad points.

5b Share information about the personalities of the candidates you studied. Discuss the good and bad points of each one.

5c Rank the candidates in order of suitability (1 = most suitable, 4 = least suitable).

6 As a class, choose the best candidate to be Chris and Jodie's new assistant.

Elayne: Australian, aged 22

Comes from a large family (two older brothers, three sisters). Smiles a lot, has a sunny personality. Speaks in a loud voice. Very self-confident. Maybe over-confident?

Your three best qualities? 'extrovert, energetic, cooperative – willing to do any task, even if it's boring'
Your worst quality? 'I am strong-willed and don't like to be criticised.'
Your ideal boss? 'Someone who gives clear instructions, so I know what to do.'
Why choose her? 'I'm popular wherever I work because I'm even-tempered and reliable.'
Doesn't smoke. Thinks smoking should not be allowed in any place of entertainment, e.g. a café, bar or sports ground.
Interests: basketball, hiking and dancing (rock and jive). Interested in fashion.
Dressed in a smart business suit for the interview.

Daniela: Italian, aged 30

An only child. Confident and sensible. A good sense of humour. Laughs a lot. Speaks English with a strong Italian accent.

Your three best qualities? 'responsible, open-minded, flexible'
Your worst quality? 'I can be moody at times.'
Your ideal boss? 'Someone who lets you do your duties your own way and doesn't interfere too much.'
Why choose her? 'I don't need a boss to tell me what to do all the time. I can work independently and under pressure.'
Smokes a lot. Life-long vegetarian. Has strong views about people who eat meat.
Interests: reading, cinema, going to restaurants with friends.
Dressed casually in a white jumper and black skirt.

1.5 STUDY AND WRITING SKILLS

STUDY SKILLS
MAKING NOTES WHILE READING

1 Work with a partner to discuss the following.
1 When do you need to make notes?
2 What techniques do you use when you make notes?
3 Which sources do you trust more when reading – books or online sources?

2a Read the essay below. Which statements in the essay do you disagree with?

2b Note-taking Read the essay again and complete the notes. Use one or two words in each gap.

PARAGRAPH 2 NOTES

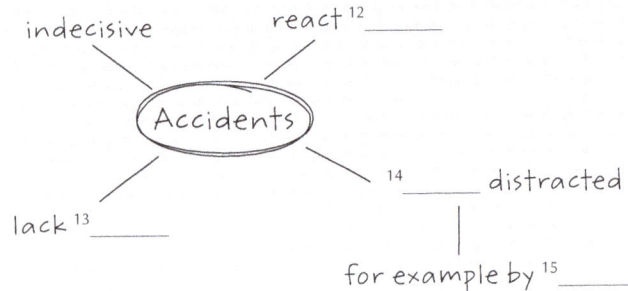

PARAGRAPH 3 NOTES
Women drivers

2c Which style of note-taking in Exercise 2b – bulleted notes or word webs – do you prefer? Which do you think is most effective for understanding and processing a text?

Are women better drivers than men?

1 Some people believe that women are better drivers than men. However, others think that women make worse drivers. In one survey of 3,000 male drivers in the UK, most felt they were better drivers than the women in their lives. The idea that women make worse drivers is a stereotype. It comes from a time when women drove less than men, and driving was seen as a man's responsibility. There are certainly different views on this controversial question, although there are a number of reasons why a woman's personality makes her a more competent driver.

2 Firstly, women are more patient and polite towards other road users, such as pedestrians and cyclists. In stressful situations they are more likely to stay calm, and less likely to be involved in 'road rage' incidents. Secondly, female drivers are more cautious and therefore take fewer risks, for instance when overtaking. Thirdly, they are more responsible so they tend not to drive when tired or after drinking alcohol.

3 On the other hand, many people argue that women cause accidents because they can be indecisive or react slowly because they lack confidence. In addition, they are easily distracted, for example, by children in the car, scenery or other drivers. Research also shows that women find map reading more difficult than men, and can have problems with the difference between left and right. Despite the fact that women have more accidents, insurance is often cheaper for them because the accidents tend to be minor. In particular, women have more accidents when parking. This is because women often have poor spatial awareness. In contrast, men tend to have more serious accidents.

4 To sum up, it can be seen that women make safer drivers than men because of their personality. This is supported by the fact that women have fewer serious accidents and pay lower insurance premiums than men. Overall, it is clear that women are less competitive and aggressive than men behind the wheel and therefore better drivers.

STUDY AND WRITING SKILLS 1.5

3a **Symbols and abbreviations** Have you thought about using symbols and abbreviations? Match the common symbols and abbreviations below with their meaning. Can you add any others?

1	&	a	this leads to / causes
2	+	b	male / man
3	>	c	greater / more than / better than
4	<	d	female / woman
5	e.g.	e	smaller / less than
6	♂	f	is not equal to / the opposite
7	♀	g	that is / this means
8	→	h	and
9	=	i	is the same as / equals
10	∴	j	for example
11	i.e.	k	plus / in addition to
12	≠	l	therefore

3b Look again at the notes in Exercise 2b and change them using some of the above symbols and abbreviations.

WRITING SKILLS
A FOR AND AGAINST ESSAY

4 Look again at the essay *Are women better drivers than men?* Match ideas a–d with each paragraph.
a conclusion
b arguments for
c introduce the topic / state the proposition
d arguments against

5a **Linkers** Look at the highlighted phrases in the text. Decide which of them are used to do the following.
1 list/add points   3 show contrast
2 introduce examples 4 introduce a conclusion

5b Look at the structures that are used with the linkers for contrast. Which linkers need a new sentence? Which linkers always need two clauses?

6a Combine these two sentences using the five phrases for showing contrast in Exercise 5a.

He is patient and careful at work. He is impatient and aggressive when he drives.

He is patient and careful at work. However, he is impatient and aggressive when he drives.

6b Complete the sentences in an appropriate way.
1 He was slow and often late for work. However, …
2 Although the twins looked the same, …
3 Despite the fact that he was shy, …
4 Children find learning languages easy. Adults, on the other hand, …

7a Work in groups. Choose an essay title from the following.

Are men/women better _____ than women/men?

managers   politicians   teachers   doctors   lawyers

7b In your groups, brainstorm the qualities you think you need to do the jobs.

7c Look at the statements 1–13 below and do the following tasks.
a Decide which of the statements below apply more to men and which to women.
b Add two more statements of your own.
c Select some to include in your essay. Remember to have some to show the other side of the argument.
d Think of examples to support the statements you have included.

1 _____ are good at listening.
2 _____ find it easier to deal with people.
3 _____ have more authority.
4 _____ are more sympathetic to others.
5 _____ are better organisers.
6 _____ pay more attention to detail.
7 _____ stay calm in stressful situations.
8 _____ are good at getting the best out of people.
9 _____ are energetic and enthusiastic.
10 _____ work better in a single-sex team.
11 _____ are better at public speaking.
12 _____ are more inspiring.
13 _____ take decisions quickly.

8 Write your essay. Use the structure of the essay on the left as a model. You can have a neutral conclusion.

9a Read your partner's essay and take notes.

9b Tell another student about your partner's essay.

2 Travel
2.1 TOURISM AND TRAVELLING

IN THIS UNIT

GRAMMAR
- past simple
- present perfect and past simple

VOCABULARY
- travel expressions
- phrasal verbs (1)

SCENARIO
- discussing advantages and disadvantages, making suggestions
- organising a study trip

STUDY SKILLS
- making notes while listening

WRITING SKILLS
- a biographical profile

Travel makes a wise man better, but a fool worse. Thomas Fuller 1608–1661 English historian

LISTENING AND VOCABULARY
TRAVEL EXPRESSIONS

1a Complete the questions with the words in the box.

destinations   travel   journey   abroad   trip   package   ~~home~~

✓ 1 What's the furthest you have travelled from *home*?
  2 Have you ever been _____? Where did you go to?
  3 Have you ever been on a business _____? Where to?
  4 Do you like _____ holidays where everything is arranged for you? Why?/Why not?
✓ 5 What is the longest _____ you have been on?   4mins x 3
✓ 6 What are the most popular _____ for people from your country?
✓ 7 Do you think that _____ broadens the mind? Why?/Why not?

1b In pairs or small groups, ask each other the questions.

2a 🔊 2.1 Listen to Nadia, a Swedish student who has travelled a lot. Tick (✓) the questions in Exercise 1a which she answers.

2b Listen again and make notes on her answers to the questions in Exercise 1a. Are they similar to your answers?

3a Complete the reasons for travelling with the words in the box. Look at Audio script 2.1 on pages 164–165 and check your answers.

broaden   experience   explore   find   get   meet   learn (x2)   see   become (x2)   do   study   escape   earn

People travel in order to …

1 *get* away from it all.
2 _____ new sights.
3 _____ new places.
4 _____ new people.
5 _____ different cultures.
6 _____ new skills.
7 _____ voluntary work.
8 _____ more self-confident.
9 _____ a new language.
10 _____ money
11 _____ themselves.
12 _____ more independent.
13 _____ their horizons.
14 _____ for qualifications abroad.
15 _____ poverty.

3b Inferring attitude Listen again. How do you think Nadia feels about the different reasons for travel? Is she positive (+), negative (–) or neutral (+/–) about each one?

1 get away from it all +/–

3c Work with a partner. How important are the different reasons, do you think? Why? Can you add any others?

TOURISM AND TRAVELLING 2.1

READING

4 Work with a partner to discuss the following.
1. What's the difference between a tourist and a traveller?
2. How much of your own country have you visited?
3. Is it possible to travel without leaving home?

5a Read the article quickly and choose the most suitable heading for each paragraph. (There are two extra headings.)

3 a Virtual tourism
1 b Tourist or traveller?
  c Most popular destinations
2 d Holiday at home
  e Holiday problems

5b Read the article again and answer the questions.
1. How is a traveller different from a tourist? Give three examples.
2. How did tourism start?
3. What does the text say about people who live in large countries?
4. What is an 'armchair traveller'?
5. How has television affected attitudes to travel?
6. How might travel change or develop in the future?
7. Do you agree that travel is no longer necessary?

SPEAKING AND WRITING

6 What are the most interesting places you have visited in your own country and abroad? Where else would you like to visit?

7 Complete these travel tips with the words in the box.

accommodation   be   customs   documents   find out
vaccinations   insurance   read   respect   take

1. _____ about local laws and customs.
2. _____ aware of people acting suspiciously.
3. Obtain comprehensive travel _____.
4. Check what _____ and healthcare you need.
5. Make copies of _____, e.g. tickets, passport, insurance policy, and leave one copy at home.
6. _____ enough money.
7. _____ about local tricks used on tourists.
8. Never carry packages through _____ for others.
9. _____ local dress codes; think about what you wear.
10. Stay in locally-owned _____ and try to eat in locally-owned restaurants.

8 Work with a partner. Think of as many travel tips for someone visiting or coming to live/work in your country as you can, and write the five most important.

Think for a minute
TRAVEL AND TOURISM

Getting away from it all?

1 _____

What's the difference between travel and tourism? Well, being a traveller is more than just being a holidaymaker. A holiday is just a short time away, and it normally involves relaxation. Tourists stay in holiday resorts, not travellers. Travellers go for the experience, and their journeys are usually much longer and more challenging. For example, travellers tend to avoid tourist traps and like to go off the beaten track to discover new places. Travel is an age-old phenomenon, but tourism is a relatively recent invention. Thomas Cook is often described as the first travel agent because he arranged the first 'package tour': a 19-kilometre trip for 500 people, in 1841.

2 _____

Going overseas in order to experience a different way of life is what many people think of as travel, but travel does not necessarily mean going abroad. How many people can say they have visited every part of their own country? Many people who live in vast countries such as Russia and the USA have only visited a small part of their own country, and so domestic travel is also very exciting. It's a surprising fact that about 75 percent of US citizens do not own a passport, so travelling does not mean leaving the country for them.

'How many people can say they have visited every part of their own country?'

3 _____

Some people can't travel or don't like the physical reality of travelling to faraway destinations. These days it is easy to be an 'armchair traveller'. People can visit distant corners of the world or even little known parts of their own country without leaving their living rooms by using Google Earth. Television documentaries and the internet make the world a small place, and some people argue that travel is no longer necessary. Many people already use interactive computer programmes, and virtual travel will become increasingly common. Enthusiasts argue that by doing this we will have all the benefits of travel without the inconvenience.

Next week: Tea and coffee

2.2 EXPLORERS

READING

1 What do you know about the people in the pictures? Who are they? What did they do?

2a Work in groups of three. Read about one explorer each and complete the chart for that explorer.

2b In your groups, summarise the key facts so that others in your group can complete the chart.

	Ibn Battuta	Cousteau	Tereshkova
Nationality			
When born			
Job/work			
Travelled to			
Length of journey			
Greatest achievement			
What they were called			
When died			

2c According to the texts, which explorer:
1. became interested in the sea at an early age?
2. studied his religion?
3. had a name related to a seabird?
4. went on a holy journey?
5. received an important award?
6. had a relationship with someone who did the same job?
7. told his stories about his journeys in a book?
8. cared for the environment?

2d Evaluating and justifying Which of these explorers do you think achieved the most? Think of three reasons to justify your opinion.

VOCABULARY
PHRASAL VERBS (1)

3a Look at these eight phrasal verbs. Which six verbs are in the texts? Find and underline them.

break down	get back	stop off	check in	lift off
set out	carry on	look around		

Ibn Battuta
early traveller

Ibn Battuta was born in Tangier, Morocco in 1304. He was an Islamic scholar and was an explorer known for his extensive travels.

He set out, aged 21, on a hajj, or pilgrimage to Mecca. He travelled more than 75,000 miles and over a period of 30 years he travelled through most of the Islamic world. He visited all the Arab lands and stopped off in Spain, Russia and Turkey. He carried on to India before he got to China.

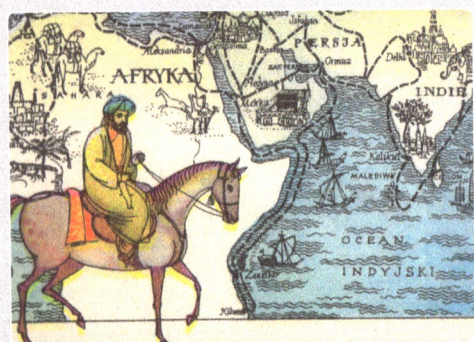

When he got back to his native city, he dictated an account of his journeys to Ibn Juzayy and called it the *rihla*, or *The Journey*.

He was called 'the traveller of the age' and is now considered one of the greatest travellers of all time. He died in 1369. The Ibn Battuta Mall in Dubai, UAE, was inspired by his travels and a film about him called *Journey to Mecca* came out in 2009.

Jacques Cousteau
underwater explorer

Jacques Cousteau was a French undersea explorer, environmentalist and inventor. He was born in France in 1910. When he was young, he became fascinated by the sea, machines and film-making.

In the French navy, Cousteau began exploring underwater and worked on a special breathing machine which allowed divers to stay underwater for several hours. This gave them time to really look around under the ocean. In 1943, he and engineer Emile Gagnan invented the aqualung – the very first scuba diving equipment.

In 1948, Cousteau began travelling the world's oceans in his research ship *Calypso*. Cousteau produced many films and books about his underwater adventures, including the TV series *The Undersea World of Jacques Cousteau*, which introduced the public to the world of sharks, whales, dolphins, treasure and coral reefs.

Cousteau started the Cousteau Society to protect ocean life. In 1989, he received a great honour: he was made a member of the French Academy. Finally, after a long and varied life, Cousteau died on 25 June 1997.

EXPLORERS

2.2

3b Match the phrasal verbs in Exercise 3a with their meanings below.
1 start/begin a journey
2 make a short visit to a place while you are going somewhere else
3 return
4 explore
5 continue
6 rise into the air
7 go to the desk at an airport or hotel
8 stop working

3c Complete the text with the phrasal verbs in the correct form.

We ¹_____ very early, before dawn, and drove south. We ²_____ at a service station for petrol and a coffee. After this we ³_____ driving for another three hours. There were a lot of delays and hold-ups. We finally arrived at the aircraft museum at 2 p.m., and ⁴_____ the main sights. We didn't ⁵_____ until midnight. It was a very tiring day.

Valentina Tereshkova
space pioneer

Valentina Tereshkova parachuted out of over 125 aircraft before she jumped out of the spacecraft Vostok 6. This unusual hobby led to her selection for cosmonaut training and her achievement of becoming the first woman in space.

Tereshkova was born on 6 March 1937, in western Russia. As a teenager she worked in a textile plant and took up parachuting in her spare time.

When Tereshkova was selected for the Soviet space programme in 1962 because of her parachuting skills, she became the first recruit without experience as a test pilot. Tereshkova was chosen to be the pilot of the Vostok 6 mission. The pilots called her *Chaika*, Russian for 'seagull'.

The spacecraft lifted off from Tyuratam Launch Centre on 16 June 1963. It re-entered the Earth's atmosphere on 19 June and Tereshkova parachuted to the ground, landing near Kazakhstan in central Asia. On 3 November 1963, Tereshkova married another cosmonaut. They had a daughter, Elena – the first child born to parents who both went into space.

GRAMMAR
PAST SIMPLE

4 Underline all the past simple verbs in the three texts. Which are regular and which are irregular?

5 Which two statements about the past simple are not true?
1 We use the past simple for finished actions that are in the past.
2 We use the past simple with the following time expressions: *never, all my life, ever, yet.*
3 We often say the exact time of the action.
4 We use time expressions like: *yesterday, last week, in 1999, ago, when I was young.*
5 We use *did/didn't* + the infinitive in questions and negatives.
6 We normally use *did* and *didn't* with the verb *be*.

→ Language reference and extra practice pages 128–129

PRONUNCIATION

6a 2.2 *-ed endings* Listen to the sentences containing these verbs. Do the verbs end in the sounds /d/, /t/ or /ɪd/?

travelled   visited   stopped   invented   produced
worked   lifted

6b Listen again and practise saying the words.

7 Complete the facts below with the past simple of the verbs in the box.

photograph   lead   hit   study   pilot   die   fly (x2)
sail   bring   explore   find   discover   not return

1 Louise Boyd (1887–1972) _____ and _____ the Arctic Ocean. She also _____ over the North Pole.
2 Ferdinand Magellan _____ the first expedition that _____ around the Earth, between 1519 and 1522.
3 Sir Walter Raleigh (1554–1618) _____ potatoes and tobacco from America to Europe.
4 When _____ Ranulph Fiennes _____ the legendary Lost City of Ubor in the desert of Oman?
5 Vasco da Gama _____ in India in 1524. He _____ an ocean route from Portugal to the East.
6 Alan Shepard _____ America's first manned space mission. He briefly _____ into space on 5 May 1961. In a later mission he _____ golf balls on the Moon.
7 Ibn Battuta _____ _____ _____ to his home town, Tangier, for many years.
8 When he was young, Ibn Battuta _____ Islamic laws.

SPEAKING

8 Write down the dates or years of six important events in your past. Give your list to a partner. Ask each other questions to find out what the dates represent.

2001
Did you start primary school then?

2.3 THE EMPTY QUARTER

READING

1 Work with a partner to discuss the following.
1 Make a list of six words you associate with deserts. Compare your list with another pair.
2 What might attract people to life in a desert?

Wilfred Thesiger

Explorer of the 'Empty Quarter'

1 Wilfred Thesiger was one of the greatest explorers and travel writers of the 20th century. He died in 2003. His books, which describe his journeys in Africa, Asia and the Middle East, have won many literary prizes. His best known book is *Arabian Sands*, which is about two journeys through Arabia. People have praised his description in the book of the 'Empty Quarter', a vast, waterless desert stretching between Saudi Arabia, Yemen and Oman. He spent five years travelling in the 'Empty Quarter', often accompanied by the Bedu, the fierce tribespeople living in the area.

Photo of Salim bin Kabina, a Bedouin companion, by Wilfred Thesiger

2 Thesiger fell in love with the desert. He enjoyed the 'sense of space, the silence, and the crisp clearness of the sand'. It was a place where he found peace and friendship. He also learned to love the Bedu, and they learned to respect him. He shot lions to protect his companions, and he became a competent amateur doctor. He chose the 'Empty Quarter' for his journeys because it was 'one of the very few places where I could satisfy an urge to go where others had not been'.

2a Read the article about the explorer Wilfred Thesiger. What attracted him to life in a desert?

2b Underline the parts of the article which tell you:
1 that Thesiger was well-known in the 20th century.
2 that his books were popular.
3 that it was difficult to travel in the 'Empty Quarter'.
4 who the Bedu were.
5 what kind of relationship Thesiger had with the Bedu.

3 Read an extract from *Arabian Sands*. Are these statements true or false?
1 The camels began to rest at sunset.
2 Thesiger was happy because he thought the difficult journey was over.
3 The most difficult journey was the one for the next day.
4 When the travellers stopped the first time, they were near the Uruq al Shaiba.
5 The Uruq al Shaiba are bigger and higher than the Himalayas.

1 To rest the camels we stopped for four hours in the late afternoon on a long gentle slope which stretched down to another salt-flat. There was no vegetation on it and no salt-bushes bordered the plain below us. Al Auf announced that we would go on again at sunset. While we were feeding I said to him cheerfully, 'Anyway the worst should be over now that we are across the Uruq al Shaiba.' He looked at me for a moment and then answered, 'If we go well tonight we should reach them tomorrow.' I said, 'Reach what?' and he replied, 'The Uruq al Shaiba. Did you think what we crossed today was the Uruq al Shaiba? That was only a dune. You will see them tomorrow.' For a moment I thought he was joking, and then I realised that he was serious, that the worst of the journey which I had thought was behind us was still ahead.

2 It was midnight when at last al Auf said, 'Let's stop here. We will get some sleep and give the camels a rest. The Uruq al Shaiba are not far away now.' In my dreams that night they towered above us higher than the Himalayas.

4 Find words in the texts that mean the following.
1 said good things about something (article, para 1)
2 extremely large (article, para 1)
3 looking very aggressive or violent (article, para 1)
4 have a good opinion of (article, para 2)
5 a strong wish (article, para 2)
6 formed the edge of (extract, para 1)
7 a hill of sand (extract, para 1)

5 Reacting to the topic In groups, discuss the following.
1 Are you interested in travel writing?
2 Have you ever read a travel book about a) your own country and b) a country you would like to visit?
3 Is it more interesting to read about 'exotic' places and people or ordinary places and people?

A B C D

LISTENING

6a You are going to listen to Martin Wells being interviewed for a magazine and he mentions the following places. Match the places with the photos. Do you know which countries they are in?
1 the Amazon River Basin
2 the ice-cut fjords of the South Island
3 the Himalayas
4 Hoi Anh

6b 2.3 Listen to the first part of the interview and check your answers.

7a 2.4 Listen to the second part of the interview. Take notes under the following headings.
1 The Salween River
2 Difficulties and dangers of the journey
3 What Martin learnt from the travel experience

7b Work with a partner and compare your notes. Correct or add to them if necessary. Then check the accuracy of your notes by looking at Audio script 2.4 on page 165.

PRONUNCIATION

8a 2.5 Contractions Listen to the sentences and underline what the speaker says.
1 I just returned / I've just returned from the forests.
2 I had / I've had the most amazing year.
3 Last year in January, I won / I've won a scholarship.
4 Then I raised / I've raised a large sum of money.
5 And then I started / I've started travelling.
6 I climbed / I've climbed the Himalayas in Nepal.

8b Listen again and repeat the sentences.

GRAMMAR
PRESENT PERFECT AND PAST SIMPLE

9a Choose the correct tense in these sentences.
1 I've never driven / I didn't drive before.
2 I left / have left school when I was 16.
3 I already visited / have already visited a foreign country.
4 I finished / haven't finished my university studies yet.
5 I've known / I knew my best friend for the last ten years.
6 I've never been / I never went on a plane.

9b Complete the rules with *present perfect* or *past simple*.
1 We use the _____ to talk about finished actions in a time period that continues up to now (with time expressions such as *this week*, *for the last five years*).
2 We use the _____ to talk about finished actions at a specific past time (with time expressions such as *yesterday*, *last year*, *in 1999*, *when I was 9*).
3 We use the _____ to talk about experiences in our lives, but we don't say when they happened (with adverbs such as *never*, *ever*, *already*, *yet*).

10a Underline the sentences in Audio script 2.5 on page 165 that contain *already* and *yet*. Answer the questions.
1 Which adverb do we use in negative sentences?
2 Does *already* come before or after the main verb?
3 Where does *yet* come in the sentence?

→ Language reference and extra practice pages 128–129

10b Look at the sentences below. Each has a mistake with an adverb or time expression. Replace the wrong word/phrase with words from the box.

already   before   never   this week   yet

1 Martin has yet climbed Mont Blanc twice.
2 We've interviewed five people for this expedition so far last week.
3 We've ever been to the Himalayas.
4 The students haven't passed the course already.
5 Mark and Susanna have been on a climbing expedition once yet.

SPEAKING

11a Look at these travel-related jobs. What experience do you need for each one?
1 Tour assistant – Paris, London, Rome
2 Mountain expedition assistant – Himalayas
3 Field trip volunteer – Amazon
4 Assistant travel agent – busy travel agency

11b Work with a partner. You are going to see if you are suitable for the jobs in Exercise 11a.

Student A: turn to page 155.
Student B: turn to page 161.

Which of the four jobs would suit you best?

21

2.4 SCENARIO
A STUDY TRIP

SITUATION

1 Read the situation below. What kind of things can go wrong on a trip like this, do you think?

Westlake is an American university. Two years ago, the university organised a study trip to Poland and the Czech Republic, so that students could learn about the countries' culture and history. Unfortunately, the organisers made many mistakes and the trip was not successful. This year, they will take another group of students (aged 18–21) to the same area. They want to avoid the mistakes they made in the past.

2a Read the notes written by one of the organisers about the previous trip. Which problems, if any, did you discuss in Exercise 1?

2b Match each problem in the notes with one of these categories. You can use each category more than once.

theft	money	information
communication		climate
misbehaviour	organisation	

3 In small groups, discuss these questions. Compare your answers with another group.
1. Which were the most serious problems? Rank them in order of seriousness (1 = most serious, 6 = least serious).
2. Which of the following do you blame for each problem?

| the organisers | the students |
| bad luck | none of the above |

4a [2.6] Listen to a conversation between Douglas and Karen, two organisers of the previous trip. Which problems from the notes do they talk about?

4b Listen again. Make notes on the topics they discuss. Use these headings.
- Student relations
- Hotels
- Student behaviour
- Free time

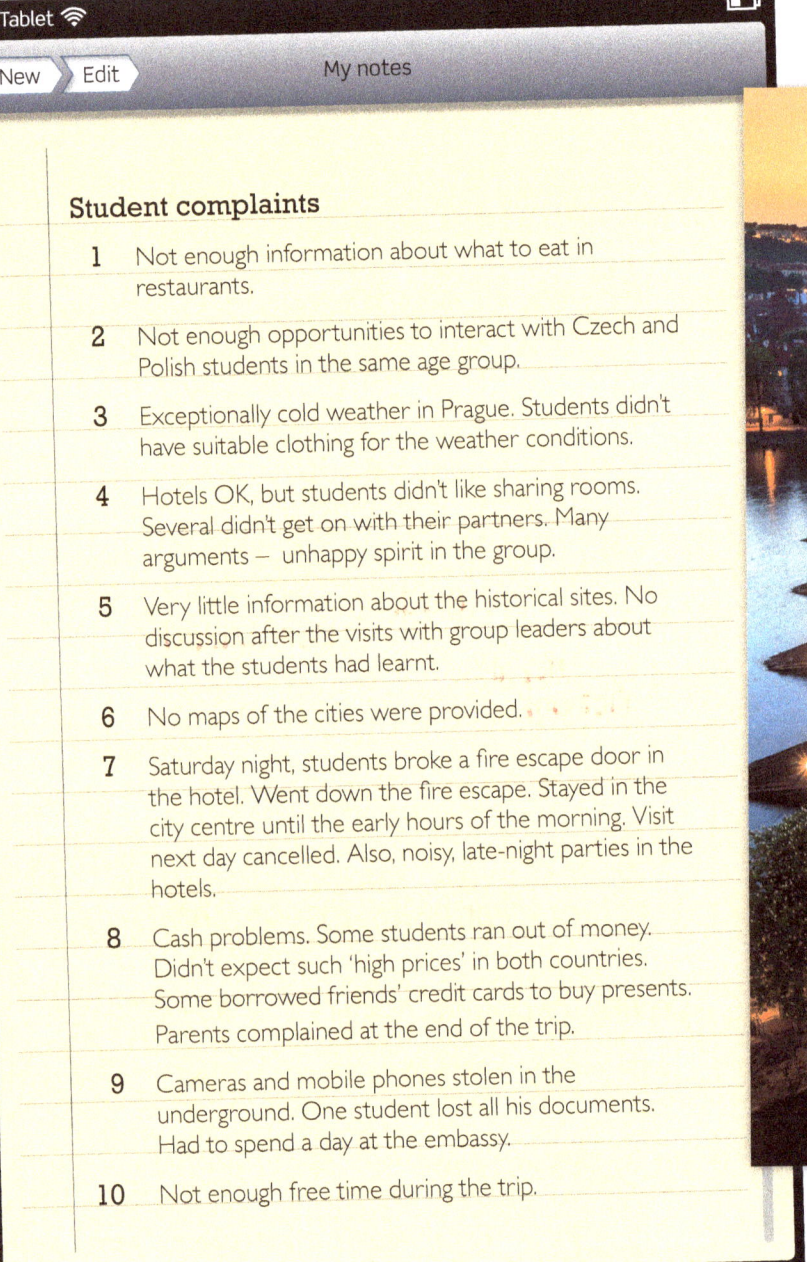

MyTablet

New | Edit | My notes

Student complaints

1. Not enough information about what to eat in restaurants.
2. Not enough opportunities to interact with Czech and Polish students in the same age group.
3. Exceptionally cold weather in Prague. Students didn't have suitable clothing for the weather conditions.
4. Hotels OK, but students didn't like sharing rooms. Several didn't get on with their partners. Many arguments – unhappy spirit in the group.
5. Very little information about the historical sites. No discussion after the visits with group leaders about what the students had learnt.
6. No maps of the cities were provided.
7. Saturday night, students broke a fire escape door in the hotel. Went down the fire escape. Stayed in the city centre until the early hours of the morning. Visit next day cancelled. Also, noisy, late-night parties in the hotels.
8. Cash problems. Some students ran out of money. Didn't expect such 'high prices' in both countries. Some borrowed friends' credit cards to buy presents. Parents complained at the end of the trip.
9. Cameras and mobile phones stolen in the underground. One student lost all his documents. Had to spend a day at the embassy.
10. Not enough free time during the trip.

2.4 A STUDY TRIP

KEY LANGUAGE
DISCUSSING ADVANTAGES AND DISADVANTAGES, MAKING SUGGESTIONS

5 Listen again and complete the two extracts.

Extract 1

KAREN: I think we talked about this before the trip. There are ¹_____ _____ and ²_____ _____, aren't there? On the one hand, it's good to give them free time, they get a chance to explore places. ³_____ _____ _____ _____, if you give them too much free time, they say we haven't organised enough trips for them. You just can't win.

DOUGLAS: True, and don't forget, Karen, ⁴_____ _____ _____ giving them a lot of free time is that they get into trouble.

Extract 2

KAREN: How could I forget that! Actually, I've got a few suggestions for this next trip.

DOUGLAS: Me too.

KAREN: Good. Well, I think we should have more meetings with students before they leave. The ⁵_____ _____ about this is they'd get to know each other better.

DOUGLAS: Yeah. That's true. Also, it'd be a ⁶_____ _____ to give students maps of the cities they visit. I suggest contacting the tourist boards and asking them to send us some.

KAREN: And how about showing them some restaurant menus before they leave? That'd be a big ⁷_____ for them.

6 Work with a partner. Discuss the advantages and disadvantages of giving young people a lot of free time during a study trip.

TASK
ORGANISING A STUDY TRIP

7a You are a member of the organising committee for the next trip to Poland and the Czech Republic. Discuss the advantages and disadvantages of these suggestions for the next trip.

- Students must be in their hotel rooms by 11 p.m. each night.
- They should all take the same amount of spending money.
- They should keep a diary each day of their impressions. The diary will be given a grade at the end of the trip.
- No student should explore areas by themselves.

7b Add five suggestions of your own which will make the next trip more successful. Think about the problems in the notes and conversation.

7c Compare your suggestions with another group. Decide on the best five.

2.5 STUDY AND WRITING SKILLS

STUDY SKILLS
MAKING NOTES WHILE LISTENING TO A TALK

1a Work with a partner. Discuss these ideas for how to make notes while listening. Which do you agree with? Why?

- Before you start, have some key questions you want the answers to, for example *Who? What? When? Why?*
- Listen for structuring language, e.g. *firstly, secondly,* etc.
- Listen carefully for phrases which tell you important information is coming, e.g. *Now, let's move on to …*
- Wait until the end and write down what you can remember.
- Use a numbering system for your notes.
- Try to write down as much as you can.
- Use abbreviations where possible. (See Lesson 1.5.)
- Focus on verbs and nouns – leave out articles, pronouns, conjunctions, etc.
- Write in complete sentences.
- Use diagrams and word webs.

1b Can you add any other ideas that work for you?

2 Look at the man on the first slide from a talk. What sort of person do you think he is?

Slide 1 Thor Heyerdahl

3 ▶2.1 Watch the first part of the talk and choose the most suitable heading for Slide 2 from the list below.

a Career and travels
b Travels in Polynesia
c Publications and awards
d Greatest achievement
e Early life
f Books

Slide 2 _____

- born Larvik, S. Norway, 1914
- studied Zoology & Geography @ Oslo Uni
- 1st exped → Polynesia 1937–1938
- was interested in how islands 1st inhabited
- died 2002 at home in Italy

4 ▶2.2 Watch the second part of the talk and complete the notes 1–10 in Slide 3. Use one word, number or date in each gap. Compare your answers with a partner.

5 ▶2.3 Watch the third part of the talk and make your own notes. Work with a partner and compare the style of your notes.

6 Choose the most suitable headings from Exercise 3 for Slides 3–5. (There are two extra headings.)

Slide 3 _____

^{1}_____ – built raft (Kon-Tiki) – crossed Peru → Polynesia in ^{2}_____ days wanted to prove ancient cultures connected by ^{3}_____ who crossed ^{4}_____

^{5}_____ Norwegian archaeological expedition → Galapagos Islands, ^{6}_____

led Easter ^{7}_____ expedition, 1955–1956

1969–70 ^{8}_____ 2 rafts (Ra *1* & Ra *2*) across ^{9}_____ to show possible ancient Egyptian contact with S. ^{10}_____

Slide 4 _____

Slide 5 _____

STUDY AND WRITING SKILLS 2.5

Amelia Earhart (1897–1937) Aviation pioneer

1 Amelia Earhart was born in Kansas, USA, in 1897 and moved to Chicago in 1914 when her father was fired from the Rock Island Railroad. After graduating from high school in 1915, she went to Canada where she trained as a nurse's aide. In 1919 she attended Columbia University but gave up after a year to join her parents in California.

2 In 1920 Earhart went to her first air show and was hooked. She took flying lessons and bought her first plane, which she flew to a height of 14,000 feet in October 1922, a women's world record. In 1925 she moved to Boston and got a job as a social worker. During that time, she also wrote local newspaper columns on flying.

3 Earhart will be principally remembered for being the first woman to fly solo non-stop across the Atlantic. On 20 May 1932, she took off from New Brunswick. She wanted to fly to Paris, but poor weather conditions and mechanical problems forced her to land in Derry, Northern Ireland.

4 It was inevitable that Earhart would attempt a round-the-world flight, and she left Miami on 1 June 1937. After stopping in South America, Africa, the Indian subcontinent and south east Asia, she arrived in New Guinea on 29 June. She left on 27 July, but while she was crossing the Pacific, contact was lost. The US government spent $4m looking for her, but she was never found. In 2012 a new expedition tried to prove that she survived a crash landing but died a little while later on a small island, very close to the original rescue search.

5 Earhart published two books about her flying experiences: *20 Hours 40 Minutes* and *The Fun of It*, but she went missing before her third book was published. She was awarded the Distinguished Flying Cross by Congress and the Cross of Knight of the Legion of Honour by the French government. In 2009 a film was made of her life starring the Hollywood actress Hilary Swank.

WRITING SKILLS
A BIOGRAPHICAL PROFILE

7 Read the biography of Amelia Earhart. Match each paragraph with one of these topics.
a the end of her life
b her early life and education
c her early career
d publications, awards and prizes
e her greatest achievement

8 Find verbs in the text that mean the following.
1 be dismissed from a job (para 1)
2 finish high school or university (para 1)
3 learn a particular job (para 1)
4 go to (school or university) (para 1)
5 stop doing something (para 1)
6 go to a new place to live (para 2)
7 write and print something for sale (para 5)
8 be given a prize, honour or money (para 5)

9 **Time linkers** Look at the text and underline five different time linkers, e.g. *after*.

10 Match these sentence halves and join them in an appropriate way using the time linkers.
1 Heyerdahl received a number of awards
2 Heyerdahl went to the Galapagos Islands
3 Heyerdahl became curious about how the islands were inhabited
4 He set out to prove his theories

a leading an expedition to Easter Island.
b his lifetime.
c he was staying in Polynesia.
d giving up his study of Geography.

11 Write a biographical profile of Thor Heyerdahl. Use the notes you made in the Study Skills lesson. Use the text about Amelia Earhart and the time linkers from Exercise 9 to help you.

25

3 Work

3.1 JOBS

IN THIS UNIT

GRAMMAR
- present perfect continuous
- present perfect simple and present perfect continuous

VOCABULARY
- work adjectives
- dependent prepositions
- expressions connected with time and work

SCENARIO
- asking questions, giving answers
- taking part in an interview

STUDY SKILLS
- organising ideas

WRITING SKILLS
- covering letter and curriculum vitae (CV)

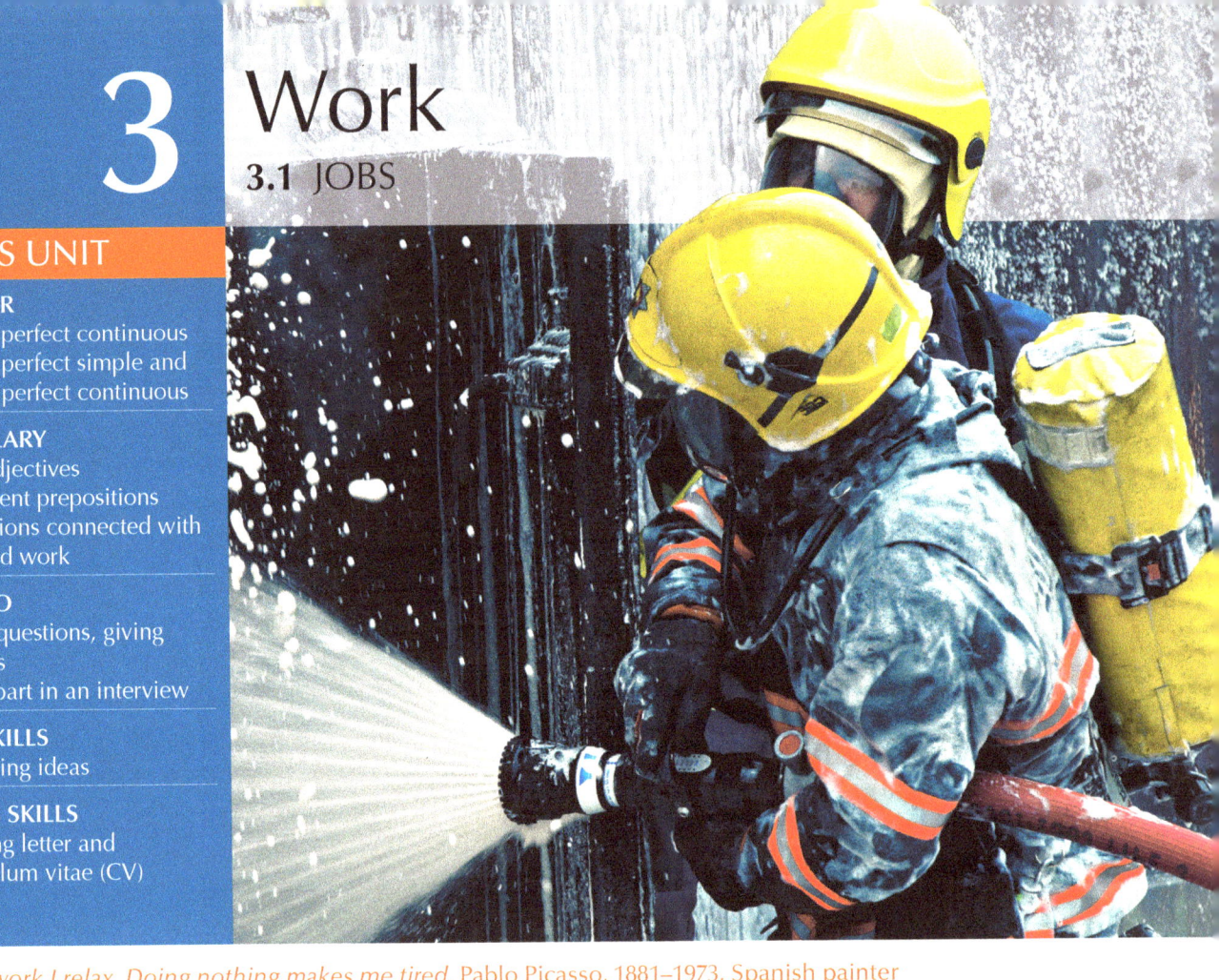

When I work I relax. Doing nothing makes me tired. Pablo Picasso, 1881–1973, Spanish painter

SPEAKING

1 Look at the jobs below and discuss the questions.

nurse   politician   model   journalist   firefighter   lawyer
professional footballer   teacher   shop assistant   police officer
TV presenter   personal assistant   sales manager

1 How important/useful do you think they are?
2 How much status do these jobs have in your country?
3 About how much are people paid for these jobs in your country?
4 Do you think they should be paid more or less money? Why?

LISTENING AND VOCABULARY
WORK ADJECTIVES

2a 3.1 Listen to five people talking about their jobs. Match each speaker to a job from Exercise 1. What are the key words which tell you the jobs?

1 *shifts, patients, …*

2b Listen again. What aspects of their jobs does each person say they like/dislike?

3a Add the missing letters to the adjectives below. Which adjectives would you use to describe the jobs from Exercise 1?

1 r_w_rdng
2 ch_ll_ng_ng
3 gl_m_r_ _s
4 str_ssf_l
5 t_d_o_s
6 r_p_t_t_v_
7 s_t_sfy_ng
8 st_m_l_t_ng
9 fl_x_bl_
10 m_n_tn_ _s

3b Which of the jobs in Exercise 1 would you like to do? Which wouldn't you like to do? Why? Use the words from Exercise 3a in your discussion.

READING AND VOCABULARY
DEPENDENT PREPOSITIONS

4 Read the job advertisements and match them with statements 1–8 below.

1 The company is the most important one in its area of business.
2 You will need to work by yourself.
3 The company offers the chance to work in their offices abroad.
4 You will not work at the same time every week.
5 The company offers extra money once a year for good work.
6 There are opportunities for promotion.
7 You will be in charge of a number of staff.
8 The company wants people who are relaxed in stressful situations.

26

JOBS

3.1

5 Match the words with the correct preposition from the box. Check your answers in the adverts.

on	to	for	of	in	by

1 looking
2 experience
3 depend
4 responsible
5 expected
6 knowledge
7 motivated
8 report
9 prospects
10 fluency
11 ability
12 suitable

6 Which job in the adverts would you apply for? Why?

7 Ranking and justifying choices Look back at the four jobs in the adverts and rank them from 1–4 (highest to lowest) under the following categories.

a level of interest   c pay/benefits
b status   d suitability for a woman (or a man)

Explain your ideas to a partner. Give your reasons.

WRITING

8 Work with a partner. Write a short job advertisement using some of the collocations in Exercise 5. Include the job title, salary and details of the positions.

SPEAKING

9a What is most important to you in a job? Choose the five most important things for you from the list. Then discuss your ideas with a partner.

- long holidays
- friendly colleagues
- short travelling time
- competitive salary
- opportunity for promotion
- pleasant working environment
- other benefits (e.g. company car, mobile phone)
- regular bonus
- good pension
- flexible hours
- foreign travel
- prestigious company

9b What would your dream job be?

A

Marketing Executive

Competitive Salary + Car + Pension Scheme

Jakarta, the country's leading sports shoe manufacturer, is looking for an ambitious marketing executive to join our busy marketing department. You will have experience of designing and coordinating large advertising campaigns. Candidates should be prepared to spend time at our overseas branches in Rome and Berlin. Fluency in a European language would be an advantage. This is a very exciting opportunity for the right candidate. Salary will depend on experience.

JAKARTA

B

SALES MANAGER

Excellent Benefits + Annual Bonus

Broadgate PLC is one of the largest suppliers of office equipment in the country. The successful candidate will be a dynamic person with excellent organisational skills. You will be responsible for leading and motivating a sales team. You are expected to develop new market opportunities as part of Broadgate's continuing programme of expansion. A knowledge of the office equipment market is desirable, but not essential. This is a challenging opportunity with one of the country's most respected employers.

Broadgate PLC

C

Receptionist

The prestigious Belnet hotel group is seeking a lively and enthusiastic person to join its City branch. The ideal candidate is someone motivated by working in a small team in a high pressure environment.

You will report to the head of reception services. The post will include shift work (including some nights and weekends). Experience of reception work preferred. There are excellent prospects for rapid career progress in the company. This is a very satisfying and rewarding job for the right person.

Excellent salary and benefits

Go to www.belnetjobsrec1.co.uk for full details and application procedure

Belnet

D

Cantro Tours

Tour managers/guides (London and worldwide)

Cantro Tours is an international travel organisation providing travel packages to a wide range of clients.

Energetic, self-confident young people with fluency in English and one other language are needed to work with groups of travellers to a variety of UK and overseas destinations. You will act as an expert on the area you take groups to, so a knowledge of the local culture and language is required. The ability to work alone and under pressure is essential. Previous experience is not necessary as full training is given. The posts are suitable for recent graduates or students on summer vacation.

Industry competitive salary and travel benefits.
For more info go to www.cantrotours.co.uk/jobs

3.2 HOMEWORKING

Working from home on the rise

1 Sunjit Patel is a graphic designer with a well-known publishing company. He has lived in south London since he was five, and for the last three years he has been working from home. He prefers working from home because he can spend more time with his family and have a better work-life balance. Sunjit is just one example of a worldwide, upward trend towards working from home, and according to a study by the International Labour Organisation, 'The expansion of teleworking … is likely to further accelerate in the years to come.'

2 What are the reasons for the rise of homeworking? Technology has been a key factor. Fast broadband connections have provided people with a quick way of receiving and sending data from home. People can now do most of the work at home that they did previously in an office. Other reasons for the rise of homeworking are that it lowers costs for companies and homeworkers tend to be more productive and take fewer sick days than office workers.

3 In recent years, a large number of companies have been offering employees more flexible ways of working. British Telecom was one of the pioneers of home working. In fact, it has been offering a telework scheme since 1986, which has paved the way for others. It says that homeworkers save the company an average of £6,000 per person, annually.

4 Homeworking brings many benefits to employers and employees. Office space is costly, so if a company can reduce its workstations, it may be able to move to a smaller site. Homeworking employees will no longer be commuting daily to work, which is time-consuming and stressful. They can plan their own work schedule and develop good time management skills.

5 There are, however, disadvantages of homeworking. For some people the office provides a break from the family, colleagues to talk to and a creative environment. There are many jobs too in which people have to work closely in teams and brainstorm ideas. Homeworking is not really suitable for that kind of activity. It is also not suitable for people who have got a very young family and nowhere separate to work.

6 Whatever the pros and cons, teleworking is here to stay. For Sunjit Patel it is only good: 'For someone like me, who has a family and the time management skills to work well on their own, homeworking is a no-brainer. I'm much happier with my life since I quit the office.'

READING

1 Work with a partner to discuss these questions.
1 Would you like to work from home? What would be the advantages/disadvantages for you?
2 Homeworking is generally on the increase. Why do you think that is?

2a Read the first three paragraphs of the article quickly and check your answer to the second question in Exercise 1.

2b Read the first three paragraphs again and find the following information.
1 how long Sunjit has lived in London
2 how long Sunjit has been working at home
3 the name of a company that was one of the first to introduce homeworking

3 Read the rest of the article and list the advantages and disadvantages of homeworking.

4a Think of some more advantages and disadvantages of homeworking and add them to your list from Exercise 3.

4b Evaluating advantages and disadvantages In groups, compare your ideas and discuss whether the advantages of homeworking outweigh the disadvantages.

VOCABULARY
EXPRESSIONS CONNECTED WITH TIME AND WORK

5a Match the expressions with their meanings.
1 time-consuming
2 time management
3 workstation
4 work–life balance
5 spend time

a organising your time effectively
b taking up a lot of time
c how much time you spend at work and home
d use or pass time doing a particular thing
e the place in an office where a person works, especially with a computer

HOMEWORKING

3.2

5b Complete the text with the words and expressions from Exercise 5a.

I've got a full-time job and I'm tired all the time. I don't need to improve my ¹_____ skills as I organise my time efficiently. But I do have to ²_____ a lot of commuting to work, and it's very ³_____. One way I could save time would be to look at homeworking. My boss might like that as she could reduce the number of ⁴_____. I could stay in touch with the office by email and phone. I'm not a workaholic. What I want is a better ⁵_____ so I can be with my family more of the time.

GRAMMAR
PRESENT PERFECT CONTINUOUS

6a Look at the three highlighted phrases in the text. Which of these statements about the present perfect continuous are true?

1 It is formed with *have/has* + *been* + *-ing*. T
2 It is used to talk about an action that finished a long time ago. F – ongoing
3 It is used to talk about an action that continues to the present. T
4 It is often used with the time expressions *since* and *for*. T
5 It is often used to focus on the duration of an action (e.g. in answer to the question *How long?*). T

6b Look again at the highlighted phrases. Complete the rule with *for* or *since*. make list on board

We use _____ + a point in time (when the activity started) and _____ + a period of time.

GRAMMAR TIP

Remember that we do not usually use state verbs in the continuous form, e.g.

be   know   understand   feel   unless action

→ Language reference and extra practice pages 130–131

6c Write sentences using the present perfect continuous where possible. If it is not possible to use the verb in the continuous, use the present perfect simple. Use *since* and *for* when appropriate.

1 Cristina / work as a designer / she graduated.
   Cristina has been working as a designer since she graduated.
2 I / know Yukiyo / six months.
3 How long / Mohammed / study engineering at university?
4 Fuat / live in Istanbul / he got a job there.
5 Marianna / work at home / two years.
6 I / not live here / very long.
7 Ji Hyun / feel sick / yesterday morning.
8 Mark and Julie / teach / same college / a year?

6d Which of the following phrases go with *for* and which go with *since*?

just a few days   Monday   hours   we moved
two weeks   2011   8 o'clock

7 Work with a partner. Talk about things you've been doing for some time, using *since* and *for*.

I've been revising for my exams since Monday, and I haven't been sleeping properly. I'm really tired at the moment. So far, I've revised English and Arabic.

LISTENING

1. 2 years – translation
2. 18 hours – writer – lonely
3. design – not comput
4. 6 y – run a business – job

8a 3.2 Listen to four people talking about working from home. What is each person's job?

8b Listen again. How long has each person been working from home? Do they like it? What reasons do they give?

9 Complete the extracts with the present perfect simple or present perfect continuous of the verbs in the box.

be⁵   take⁷   learn⁶   live²   work³   not work
translate¹   pay   ⁸

1 I _____ from Italian to English for most of my career.
2 We _____ in Milan for nearly five years.
3 How long _____ you _____ from home for?
4 I _____ a lot more for heating.
5 I _____ never *been* a morning person.
6 I've been a new language since January.
7 I've been lessons for the last six months. having
8 He hasn't at home much recently. been

PRONUNCIATION

10a 3.3 Correcting politely Listen to this short dialogue. Underline the main stress in what B says.

A: So, you've been working from home for eight years?
B: No, actually I've been working from home for six years.

10b Listen again and repeat the dialogue with a partner. Then practise some more dialogues.

Student A: turn to page 155.
Student B: turn to page 163.

SPEAKING

11 Work with a partner to discuss this question.

What would be your ideal pattern of working hours?

I'd love to work long shifts for six months of the year and then travel for the other six.

I can't get up in the mornings, so I'd like to work from after lunch till 8 p.m.

3.3 WORK PLACEMENTS

READING & vocabulary

1 Read this description of work placements. Then work with a partner and discuss the questions.

> Work placements and internships are usually done by young people as part of their college studies or afterwards to get into a work sector. They give people experience of work. They can be paid or unpaid. They are different from apprenticeships, which are for more practical jobs.

1 What are work placements called in your country?
2 Are they common?
3 Are they generally paid or unpaid?
4 Do you know anyone who has done a work placement?

2a Read Sachiko Suzuki's blog which includes four comments about work placements and answer the questions.
1 Which two are the most balanced and considered? C D
2 Who is the most positive?
3 Who is the most negative?

2b *Inferring opinion* Read the blog again and decide who is the most likely to say the following: Azra (A), Tom (T), Sabrina (S) or Charlotte (C).
1 'Work placements exploit young people.' T
2 'You need to make sure you get enough training before you take on responsible roles.' S
3 'I would recommend work placements to people without question.' A
4 'Basically, some work placements are good, and some are bad.' C
5 'Work placements can be a good way to find out which area of the business you would like to work in.' S
6 'Work placements are good for people who want to improve their confidence.' A
7 'I would not recommend work placements to anyone.' T
8 'The most important thing is to get a placement that gives you a role with some responsibility.' C

3 Which comment do you most agree with and why? Compare your choice with a partner.

LISTENING

4a 3.4 Listen to three university students talking on the radio about their work placements. For each student, find out the following information.
1 name
2 the country they are from
3 what they are studying
4 the city where they are doing their work placement

4b Work in groups of three and choose one student each. Listen again and take notes on what your student has been doing recently and why they had a good work placement.

4c In your groups, summarise the information from your notes.
Recently Jan has been doing a work placement …

GRAMMAR
PRESENT PERFECT SIMPLE AND PRESENT PERFECT CONTINUOUS

5 Look at these sentences from the blog and then complete the statements with *present perfect simple* or *present perfect continuous*.
1 I've just completed a work placement.
2 I've been looking for a job since January.
3 I've already sent off two applications this morning.
4 For the last month I've been working very long hours.
a The _pps_ focuses more on the completed result (sometimes with a focus on number).
b The _ppc_ focuses more on the activity itself and its duration (sometimes with a focus on time).

6 Work with a partner and look at Audio script 3.4 on page 166. Underline all the examples of the present perfect simple and present perfect continuous. Note the question forms and negative forms. Find two examples to illustrate each of the statements in Exercise 5.

7 Complete the sentences with the present perfect simple or continuous forms of the verbs in brackets. Sometimes both are correct.
1 I _____ for a work placement in a hotel for some time. (look)
2 I _____ Japanese since May. (learn)
3 The boss _____ ill this week. (be)
4 The intern _____ me in reception since Monday. (help)
5 Maria _____ in São Paulo since May. She's moving to Rio in August. (work)
6 I _____ in Moscow all my life. (work)
7 My mother _____ here for 25 years. (work)
8 Patricia _____ her job recently (not enjoy)
9 What _____ at work recently? (you / do)
10 We _____ ten people for the job. (interview)

8 Work with a partner and ask each other these questions.
1 What have you been doing to improve your English?
2 What have you been doing at college/work recently?

SPEAKING choose / write one progress

9a Work with a partner. Make a list together of at least three arguments against each of the following statements.
Work placements exploit young people.
Work placements should always be paid.
Only the rich and the privileged can afford to work for free.
Work placements benefit the employers more than the employees.

9b In your pairs, discuss what makes a good work placement.

▶ **MEET THE EXPERT**

Watch an interview with Caroline Matthews about her internship in the insurance industry.
Turn to page 150 for video activities.

WORK PLACEMENTS 3.3

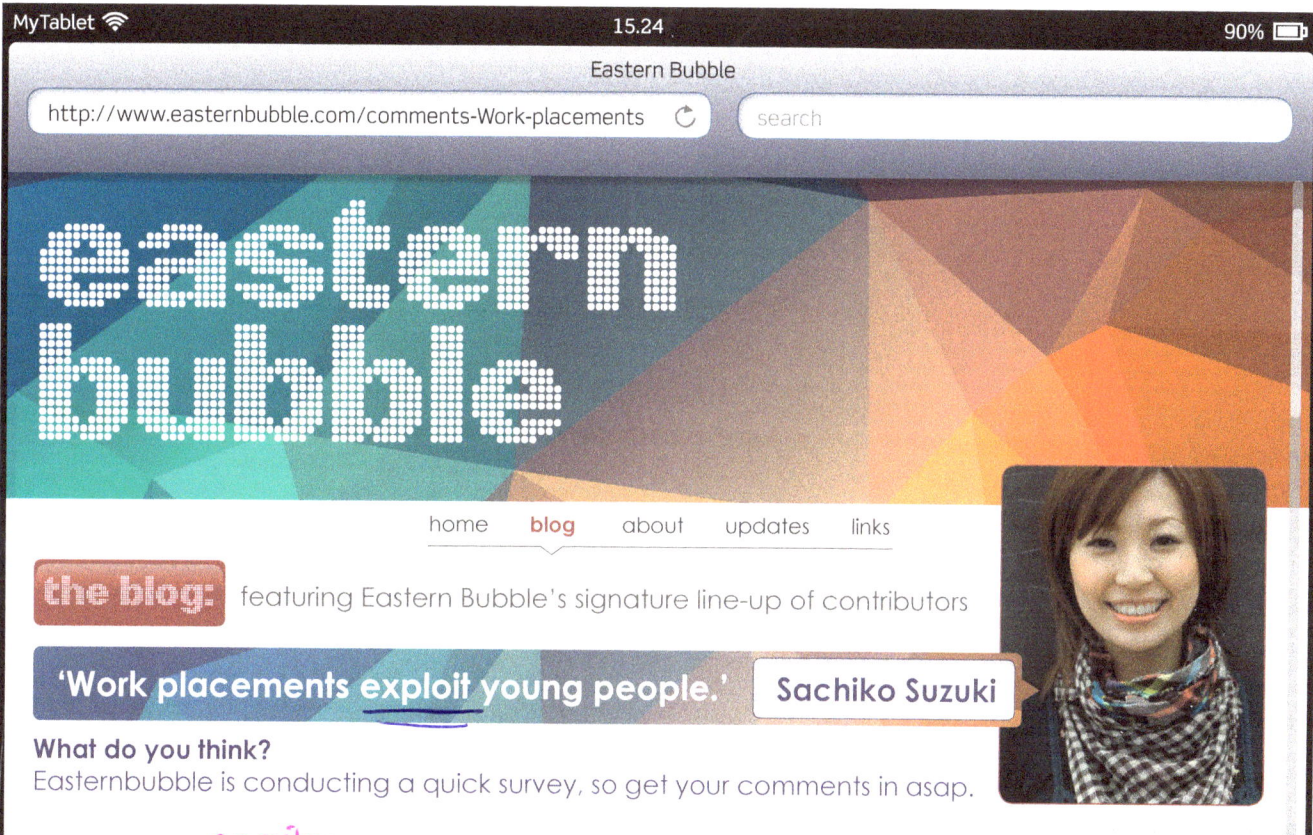

'Work placements exploit young people.' — Sachiko Suzuki

What do you think?
Easternbubble is conducting a quick survey, so get your comments in asap.

AZRA AYDIN — positive

I have to disagree. I've just completed a work placement, and I really have a sense of having achieved something. I come from Izmir in Turkey, and I was quite nervous about studying abroad. I did my work placement at a famous events company in Paris. They contacted me as a result of a networking event my university had set up. The placement taught me everything I now know and opened so many doors. I also won an award for the best work placement in France. As a result, I've had eight job offers without even applying. Best of all, the company I did my placement at has just offered me a job. The great thing about them was the support and training they gave me, and they gave me a lot of confidence.

TOM BLISSETT — negative

I totally agree with the statement. Basically, people on work placements should always be paid. It's only rich privileged people who can afford to work for free. Unpaid placements only benefit the companies. I couldn't get a job after university, so I did an unpaid placement for six months. I wasn't given any responsibility and ended up just washing pots and pans in the basement. I didn't get to meet the customers. What a waste of time! And they didn't even give me a job at the end. I've been looking for a job since January and I've already sent off 2 applications this morning. I'm looking for an apprenticeship now.

SABRINA PEISSL — balanced

I've been doing a work placement for the last nine months in a major bank in Zurich. I've worked in many different departments so I've had the chance to see which department I really like. They are paying me a good salary. On the other hand, I've had too much responsibility without enough training. I've opened accounts, I've organised credit and debit cards and I've dealt with client complaints without much supervision. And for the last month I've been working very long hours. Overall, it's been a good work placement, but I would have liked more training.

CHARLOTTE HAWKINS — balanced

I have been looking for a job in TV for some time, and I've done A LOT of internships. My first internship was at the BBC, and it was brilliant. They immediately gave me lots of responsibility, and I learnt so much. They didn't pay me though. I enjoyed being an intern at Al Jazeera, who gave me a lot of support. However, I have also done some terrible internships. I spent whole days (unpaid) filing paperwork at one production company. To get the best out of an internship, convince the company to give you proper work to do.

3.4 SCENARIO
SITUATION VACANT

SITUATION

1 Read the situation below. Do you think you would like this sort of work experience?

Jade Gyms is a famous American health club chain. It is opening a number of branches in London. The club is about to invite applications for some internships. These are aimed at students and recent graduates and will be both challenging and rewarding.

At the moment, the senior managers are discussing the advert for the positions and are considering what skills and personal qualities the successful people should have.

2 List the skills and personal qualities you think the ideal candidates should have.

3a 3.5 Listen to two senior managers from Jade Gyms, Harry and Marta. Which skills and qualities do they say are important?

3b Compare the skills/qualities they have chosen with the ones you discussed in Exercise 2. Are any the same?

KEY LANGUAGE
ASKING QUESTIONS, GIVING ANSWERS

During interviews, framing expressions can be very helpful. Framing expressions for questions help to show another question is coming. Framing expressions before answers help to avoid silence and give candidates time to think.

4a 3.6 Listen and complete the extracts from the interviewer at a job interview.

1 Now, looking at your CV. I ____ ____ ____ ____ what you feel you learnt in your last placement?
2 I'm also ____ ____ ____ your reasons for applying to our company.
3 Now, ____ ____ ____ ____ ____ ____ all our candidates. What are your strong points?
4 OK. Thank you. A ____ ____ ____ your computer skills. What software are you familiar with?
5 Right, thank you. Moving on. ____ ____ ____ ____ what you think the growth areas in the leisure industry are?
6 OK. ____ ____ ____ question. Where do you think you'll be in five years' time?

3.4 SITUATION VACANT

4b Listen again and complete the extracts from the candidate at the interview.

1. I'm ____ ____ ____ me that because I feel I developed some important skills while I was there.
2. That's a ____ ____ ____. Basically, because it is such a respected and famous organisation.
3. Well, without going into ____ ____ ____, I have very good people skills.
4. I thought you might ____ ____ ____ ____ that. Well, what I can say is, I have a good knowledge of Excel and Word, and can prepare excellent Powerpoint presentations.
5. Well, ____ ____ ____ ____, but I think the boom in fitness centres will continue in the next few years.
6. Let me just ____ ____ that for a moment. Well, I hope to be working for your company in a senior position.

4c Look at Audio script 3.6 on pages 166–167 and check your answers to Exercises 4a and 4b.

5 Work with a partner to practise the questions and answers in Exercise 4.

6 Think about the new internship positions at Jade Gyms. Write down three questions the interviewer might ask. With a partner, practise asking and answering the questions using framing language. You may invent any information you wish. You could ask about:

- foreign languages
- good/bad qualities
- opinions about travel for work
- education
- skills

TASK
TAKING PART IN AN INTERVIEW

7a Work in groups, Student As and Student Bs. You are going to prepare for and take part in an interview for a work placement.

Student As (interviewers): Turn to page 163 and prepare for the interview together.

Student Bs (candidates): Turn to page 157 and prepare for the interview together.

7b Now work in pairs of A/B and do the interview. (A is the interviewer, B is the candidate.)

8 Student A turn to page 156. Student B turn to page 155. Complete the evaluation sheet about your partner. Discuss the results and if necessary explain the scores to your partner.

9 Return to your group and explain how successful you think the interview was.

USEFUL PHRASES

Thank you for coming in today.
Please take a seat.
Are there any questions you'd like to ask us?
It's been a pleasure meeting you.
We'll let you know shortly.

3.5 STUDY AND WRITING SKILLS

STUDY SKILLS
ORGANISING IDEAS

1a Paragraphs Complete the text about paragraphing with the words in the box.

| information | link | texts | logically | main |

It is common to divide writing into paragraphs. A paragraph contains sentences, and these all ¹_____ to the ²_____ idea contained in the key sentence. This is called the topic sentence. It is usually the first one but can come later in the paragraph. The other sentences support it by giving more ³_____ or examples. A paragraph will have a final sentence which usually signals what will come next or summarises information which was in the paragraph. Most written ⁴_____ have several paragraphs which connect ⁵_____ to each other.

1b Why do we divide texts into paragraphs?

2 Organising a paragraph Read this paragraph from an application letter. It was sent by a candidate who applied to Jade Gyms for a job. Work with a partner to discuss the following.
1 Which is the topic sentence?
2 Which sentences support the main idea?
3 Why is the final sentence not suitable for this paragraph?

I have been interested in healthy living and fitness for many years. This is why I chose to study for a degree in Sports Management at my local university. I have had excellent grades throughout my studies and expect to graduate in a few weeks' time. After this, I am thinking of going on to do a part-time Master's degree in Business Administration. I am a member of the university debating society and enjoy dancing to South American music.

3 The following sentences are from another paragraph in the letter. Put the sentences in the correct order and underline the topic sentence.
a For example, I am captain of the university debating team.
b One of my strongest points is my personality. I am a confident person, very outgoing and sociable.
c I believe the qualities that I have mentioned are important for a fitness instructor.
d Because of this, I have many friends and am a member of several clubs.

4a Look again at the job adverts on page 27. Which advert interests you the most? Think about these questions.
1 Why do you want to apply for the position?
2 What skills and qualities do you have to offer the organisation?

4b Complete this first paragraph of your application letter for the job. Then write two paragraphs, explaining your reasons for applying and describing your skills and qualities.

I am writing to apply for the position of _____, which you advertised in today's Jobsonline.com. I am very excited by the opportunity you offer and believe that I have the personality and qualifications you are looking for.

WRITING SKILLS
COVERING LETTER AND CURRICULUM VITAE (CV)

5 What is the difference, if any, between a CV, a resumé and a covering letter?

6a 3.7 **Covering letter** Listen to a careers counsellor answering questions from a student about covering letters. What three things does the student ask about?

6b Listen again. What are the counsellor's answers to the questions? Make notes next to the questions you wrote in Exercise 6a.

7 Denise Martin is applying for a job as an instructor at the London branch of Jade Gyms (see page 32). Read her covering letter and complete it with the words and phrases in the box.

| work placement   available for interview   skills
| look forward   degree   delighted   position |

Dear Ms Khan,   25 September
Re: Fitness Instructor

I am a student studying Sports Management at the University of Surrey. I am writing to apply for the ¹_____ of Fitness Instructor, which you advertised in today's KeepFitOnline.com.

I have been interested in healthy living and fitness for many years, which is why I chose to study for a ²_____ in Sports Science at my local university. I graduate in three months' time and would like to work in a Health and Fitness club. I was ³_____ to see your advert because your clubs have an excellent reputation.

I am an outgoing, confident person and believe that I have good communication ⁴_____. I speak French fluently and German to an intermediate level. Last summer, I worked with a dietician at a hospital and gained useful knowledge of health foods. I also had a two-month ⁵_____ with a sports goods company. In my spare time, I run an aerobics class every Monday evening.

I am ⁶_____ at any time convenient to you. I ⁷_____ to hearing from you soon.

Yours sincerely,

Denise Martin

STUDY AND WRITING SKILLS 3.5

8 Curriculum Vitae (CV) Work in small groups to discuss the following.
1. What is more common nowadays in your country: sending a CV or filling in an online application?
2. Should you use the same CV for all applications?
3. What headings do you normally find in a CV?
4. Should you include a photo of yourself with your CV?
5. Should you always tell the truth in a CV?
6. Do you agree that the best CV is no more than one page long?
7. If you were an employer, how would you feel about a CV which had spelling mistakes?

9a [3.8] Listen to six people giving their opinion about writing CVs. Make notes about what they say.

9b Work with a partner to discuss what each person said. Do you agree with them?

10 Look at Monique Lepine's CV. Fill the gaps with these extracts. There is one extra extract that you do not need to use.
a Cycle regularly. Play tennis in a local club.
b Diploma
c Work placement
d graduate
e Graduate trainee
f numerate
g Good at teamwork
h fast-expanding
i Voluntary

11 Jade Gyms have vacancies in administration, sales, personnel and finance. Apply to their Head Office in London for any position. Write a covering letter and a CV.

Curriculum Vitae: Monique Lepine

Profile

I am a highly-motivated ¹_____ in Commerce with a strong desire to succeed in my chosen career. I am interested in working for a ²_____ company in the leisure industry, which will appreciate my qualities. I am bright, articulate and ³_____, with excellent communication skills.

Education

2011–2012	Postgraduate ⁴_____ in Marketing
2008–2011	Diploma in Commerce, University of Provence
2006 (June)	Baccalauréat Series B (Economics)

Work Experience

2013–present	Euromarché, Paris, ⁵_____
2012–2013	⁶_____ work overseas
2011 (summer)	Part-time work at Tennis Championship (Roland Garros, Paris)
2010 (summer)	Sales Assistant, Carrefour Store, Nice, South of France.
2009 (summer)	⁷_____ (two months), Kopcea, Paris

Key skills

Fluent in English, French and German
IT-literate; working knowledge of Microsoft Office package
Fast typing – 80 words a minute

Interests

⁸_____

4 Language

4.1 LEARNING LANGUAGES

IN THIS UNIT

GRAMMAR
- future forms
- first conditional

VOCABULARY
- language learning
- phrasal verbs (2)
- British and American money idioms
- language style

SCENARIO
- accepting and rejecting ideas, considering consequences
- selecting an English language programme

STUDY SKILLS
- describing tables and charts

WRITING SKILLS
- a report

A different language is a different vision of life. Federico Fellini, 1920–1992, Italian film-maker

VOCABULARY
LANGUAGE LEARNING

1 Work with a partner. Discuss how similar you think these activities are to learning a language.

driving a car
playing a musical instrument
playing/doing a dangerous sport
painting/drawing
dancing the tango, waltz, etc.
playing a board game (e.g. backgammon, chess, Monopoly)

Learning to drive is similar because you need to practise a lot.

2 What sort of people do you think make the best language learners?

3 Complete the statements with the words in the box. Which ideas do you agree with?

bilingual   native   slang   accent   second   grammar
dialects   false friends   pronunciation

1   Organised and logical people find it easy to learn _____ rules.
2   Musical people find it easy to develop accurate _____ and a good _____.
3   Extroverts find it easy to communicate in their _____ language and so often find it easy to learn to speak a _____ language fluently.
4   Flexible people can adapt to different _____. (The way a language is spoken in different areas.)
5   People who are _____ already know two languages so learning one more is very easy.
6   Learners of languages should make an effort to learn informal phrases, everyday expressions and even _____.
7   Words that look the same or familiar in different languages but have different meanings are called _____. This makes learning to use them properly very difficult.

READING

4a Look at the text. Where does it come from? What is its purpose?

4b Read the text quickly. Who is it aimed at?
a   foreign language speakers
b   native English speakers
c   people who want to speak English as a foreign language
d   business people

36

LEARNING LANGUAGES 4.1

4c Read the text again. Are these sentences true, false or not given?
1. You will receive a certificate at the end of the course.
2. There are tests to check your progress during the course.
3. English is one of the languages offered.
4. You will become fluent in six weeks.
5. There are support materials in English.

5 *Evaluating the success of a text* How effective do you think the text is in achieving its aim? Would you sign up for a course? If not, how could you improve the text to make the courses sound more attractive?

VOCABULARY
PHRASAL VERBS (2)

6a Look at the phrasal verbs highlighted in the text and match them with their meanings below.
1. make as much progress as others — keep up with
2. learn easily — pick up
3. understand — catch on
4. make less progress than other people — fall behind
5. survive — get by
6. disappoint/fail — let down
7. start doing something, e.g. a new activity — take up
8. become successful very fast — take off
9. give benefits — pay off

6b Complete the sentences about your English studies. Then compare your answers with a partner.
1. I can get by in _____ (language) when I am abroad.
2. I would like to stop learning English and take up _____.
3. I catch on quickly when my teacher _____.
4. It took me _____ (weeks/months/years) to pick up the basics of _____.
5. I find it difficult to keep up with my work/homework because _____.
6. The aspect of my English which lets me down is _____.
7. I'm falling behind in _____. I'm going to have to work hard to catch up.
8. One thing I can do to help my level of English really take off is _____.
9. Learning English will pay off for me when _____.

SPEAKING

7 Work in small groups to discuss the following.
1. English is an international language because it is easy to learn.
2. Language is the most important part of cultural identity.
3. Everyone should learn at least one foreign language.
4. A government has a duty to protect its country's language.
5. The world would be a better place if everyone spoke the same language.

Not Only English Spoken Here!

- Do your foreign language skills **let you down** when you travel abroad?
- Are you **falling behind** in your career?
- Would you like to make new friends?
- Do you want to learn about other cultures?

If you answered 'yes' to any of the above, then you need *Learn Fast*, the all-inclusive foreign language course.

At school you may have found foreign language learning confusing, but don't worry – our fully-supported courses will teach you the language you need for every situation. Our accelerated learning system means that we can guarantee that within six weeks you will **pick up** the basics of any language you choose. Pretty soon you will be able to do much more than just **get by**. You will become fluent and able to hold intelligent conversations with native speakers. Soon your language level will really **take off** as you begin to master the language.

All aspects of the language are covered – reading and listening, grammar and vocabulary development and pronunciation work to perfect your accent. An online tutor and workbook will answer your grammar questions, and there are also regular tests as part of the course.

Slow to **catch on**? Not with our special system which is designed with the non-language learner in mind. We offer a series of online resources and apps for mobile learning, together with a writing skills support package. Extensive notes in English make learning easier and faster.

Now, more than ever is the time to **take up** a new language. It will open up a new world for you and help you **keep up with** the bilingual high flyers. This is an investment which will **pay off** immediately and for the rest of your life.

Don't delay ... Do it today!
Choose from the following: French, Spanish, German, Italian, Portuguese, Polish, Russian, Arabic, Japanese, Chinese.
All levels from beginner to advanced.

For more information visit our website at:
www.learnfast.edu

4.2 THE FUTURE OF ENGLISH

LISTENING

1 Which variety of English is more popular in your country, British or American English, or another variety? Which variety of English would you prefer to learn?

2a 4.1 Listen to two friends at university, Henri and Fabio, talking on the phone. What is the reason for the phone call?

2b Listen again and complete the sentences. Use the word in brackets to help you.
1 Fabio is going to finish his essay _____. (when?)
2 Henri is going to finish his essay _____. (when?)
3 Fabio is going to the cinema with _____. (who?)
4 Fabio is going to the cinema on _____. (when?)
5 Henri's presentation is on _____. (when?)
6 Henri and Fabio will see each other at the lecture _____. (when?)

GRAMMAR
FUTURE FORMS

3a Look at Audio script 4.1 on page 167. Underline all the ways of expressing the future that you can find.

3b Look at your underlined examples in the Audio script and find an example of:
1 a prediction about the future
2 a decision made at the time of speaking
3 an intention for the future
4 a fixed arrangement, plan or programme

3c Complete the rules with *will*, *going to* or the present continuous.
1 We use _____ to talk about unplanned decisions and promises that we make at the time of speaking, and to make predictions about the future.
2 We use _____ to talk about fixed future arrangements, usually involving other people.
3 We use _____ to talk about plans or intentions (something which you have already decided).

→ Language reference and extra practice pages 132–133

4 Work with a partner. Look at part of another conversation between Henri and Fabio. Choose the best answer and discuss the reasons for your choice.

FABIO: I've made a decision. ¹*I'm going to take / I'll take* a Master's Course in Communication. The course ²*will challenge / is challenging* me, but I think I can manage it. What about you?

HENRI: Not sure. I haven't made any arrangements yet, but I think ³*I'm taking / I'll take* a postgraduate course. ⁴*I'm not knowing / I won't know* my exam results till the end of August. ⁵*I'm probably deciding / I'll probably decide* then.

FABIO: Sounds good. Oh, I've arranged to meet Richard on Wednesday for band practice. ⁶*We're meeting / We'll meet* at 5 p.m. Do you want to join us?

HENRI: Sorry, but ⁷*I'm playing / I'm going to play* tennis with Fran then.

FABIO: OK, how about going for a coffee now?

HENRI: Sorry, I'm so tired. I think ⁸*I'll go / I'm going* home now.

READING

5a Identifying genres Quickly read the texts and match them to the following genres.
a an online university prospectus/brochure
b an online debate
c a factual newspaper article

5b Read the three texts again and match the following endings to the texts. What helped you make your decision?
a I think the differences in spellings, dialects and regional idioms increase the beauty of the language. We cannot regulate English. It is constantly evolving.
b Our lively Chinese language club celebrates the Chinese New Year and is one of the most active student clubs on campus.
c And, perhaps a little less glamorously, it is the official language of air safety instructions and air traffic control.

5c Answer these questions about the texts.
1 What do the following numbers refer to: 400m, 600m, 2bn, 1bn, 19?
2 What areas does English dominate?
3 Why should you study Chinese?
4 Why does the first writer in the debate want American English to be adopted?
5 Why does the second writer in the debate prefer British English?

---

1 English is the native language of about 400m people and is spoken, with some degree of fluency, by perhaps another 600m.

The number actively engaged in learning it is rapidly heading towards 2bn. And though there are more people on the planet who speak no English than there will be fluent speakers, the vitality of the language seems obvious.

There are certain inescapable facts about the global role of English. It dominates diplomacy, trade and shipping, as well as the entertainment industry and youth culture. It is the lingua franca of computing and technology, of science and medicine, and it is prominent in international business and academia. It is the working language of the United Nations.

by Henry Hitchings

Department of Oriental Studies

About us | Degree | Academic | How to apply | Alumni

Why study Chinese?

为什么学习中文和中国文化？

China has the longest continuous culture surviving from ancient times and will soon become the largest economy in the world. China is the world's largest nation and Mandarin Chinese is spoken by over one billion people, making it the most widely-spoken first language in the world.

Mandarin Chinese is not only spoken in the People's Republic of China and Taiwan. It is also spoken in the Chinese communities of Brunei, Indonesia, Malaysia, Mongolia, the Philippines, Singapore and Thailand.

Our Chinese Studies degree will give you a broad understanding of Chinese culture through study of its language, history and literature, and includes a year at a top Chinese university in Beijing or Shanghai.

EF English Forum

This month's online debate:

Motion: The English-speaking world should adopt American English

Comments from the floor:

Look at the influence of American English in films, TV, music, the web and advertising. There are advantages to standardising international communication. It is time for American English to be adopted by the English-speaking world. This would make communication easier.

I love the sound of the English spoken on the BBC. I want to learn British English because my favourite authors are the 19th century British writers. I also love Shakespeare.

British and American English are not the only varieties of English out there. What about all the Australians, Canadians, South Africans, Irish and New Zealanders? I think some form of Indian English will almost definitely become the most spoken version of English soon.

THE FUTURE OF ENGLISH 4.2

VOCABULARY
BRITISH AND AMERICAN MONEY IDIOMS

6a Complete the idioms with the words in the box.

broke   pass   rip   tighten   million   splash   spending   cheapskate

1. If you _____ the buck, you make someone else responsible for something you should deal with.
2. If you are _____, it means you have no money.
3. If you look like a _____ dollars, you look wonderful.
4. If you are a _____, you do not like spending money.
5. If you go on a _____ spree, you spend a lot of money in a short time.
6. If you _____ out on something, you spend a lot of money on something.
7. If you _____ your belt, you spend less money than you used to.
8. If you _____ someone off, you charge them too much money.

6b 4.2 Listen to the sentences above and check your answers.

7 Work with a partner and ask and answer these questions.

1. When was the last time you went on a spending spree?
2. When was the last time you looked like a million dollars?
3. What was the last thing you splashed out on?
4. Have you ever been broke?
5. Why are tourists sometimes ripped off?
6. Is it always a bad thing to pass the buck?
7. Would you keep a friend if they were a cheapskate?
8. If you had to tighten your belt, what could you give up?

SPEAKING

8a You are going to hold a debate about British and American English. This is the motion:

The English-speaking world should adopt American English.

Divide into two groups to prepare the arguments.
Group A: look at page 156 and prepare arguments for the motion.
Group B: look at page 159 and prepare arguments against the motion.

8b Now hold the debate. Follow the debate procedure.

1. The spokesperson from Group A speaks for the motion.
2. The spokesperson for Group B speaks against the motion.
3. Other people from both groups can speak and give their opinions for or against.

8c Now vote on the motion (for or against) and decide which group has won the debate.

▶ MEET THE EXPERT

Watch an interview with Henry Hitchings, author of *Language Wars*, about English as a global language.
Turn to page 151 for video activities.

4.3 AVOIDING ONLINE MISTAKES

LISTENING

1a 4.3 Richard Falvey works at the British Council and is talking about using correct and appropriate language online and face-to-face. Listen to the first part of the interview and answer the questions.

1 What is the British Council?
2 Complete the following list of organisations that Richard develops partnerships with:
charities, non-governmental organisations, educational institutions, _____, _____.
3 What two things are key to building trust?

1b 4.4 Listen to the second part of the interview and complete these extracts.

1 Firstly, Who's your _____?
2 Secondly, how well do you _____ them?
3 Thirdly, how much do they know about the _____?
4 And finally, what is the _____ you want? What do you want them to do as a result of your _____?

1c 4.5 Listen to the third part of the interview and make notes. Give at least one example of each of the following.

1 how to avoid confusion
2 how to avoid losing trust
3 how to get the register right

2 Work with a partner to discuss these questions.

1 Have you ever upset anyone by your use of language (face to face or online)? What happened?
2 Has anyone upset you by their use of language? How did you feel?

VOCABULARY
LANGUAGE STYLE

3a Look at Audio script 4.5 on pages 167–168 and find these words. Then match them with their meanings.

1 formal
2 informal
3 register
4 context
5 appropriate
6 humorous
7 polite
8 familiar
9 medium

a friendly
b speaking in a way that shows respect for other people
c a way of communicating information or ideas
d funny
e situation
f suitable for a particular time or situation
g suitable for ordinary and relaxed situations
h suitable for serious occasions
i a way of speaking or writing which you use when you are in a particular situation

3b Work with a partner and use some of the words in Exercise 3a to talk about the language you use and how you talk to the following people.

- very close friends
- colleagues
- your parents
- a school principal / your boss

READING

4 *Identifying main ideas* Read the list of tips on how to avoid mistakes online and choose the most suitable heading for each tip.

a Watch your language
b Use secure passwords
c Don't share personal information
d Use privacy settings
e Reply to all?
f Keep all tagged photos private

5 Read the text again and match the mistakes to Tips 1–6. There are two extra mistakes.

Someone:
a sent a tweet using abusive language.
b included someone on an email that they should not have.
c posted too frequently on Facebook.
d posted embarrassing photos.
e included their boss on their LinkedIn site.
f made a spelling mistake on a job application.
g used their birthday as a password.
h gave too much personal information.

6 Work with a partner to discuss these questions.

1 Have you ever done anything online that you have regretted?
2 How many social media sites do you use regularly?
3 How worried are you about how the information about you online might be used?
4 Should you always use correct spelling and grammar in emails, Facebook, Twitter and texts?
5 What do you think of people who post all the time on Facebook?

40

AVOIDING ONLINE MISTAKES 4.3

How to avoid MISTAKES ONLINE

TIP 1 _____
Remember that if you post personal information online, you could lose control of it. A friend of mine posted photos of us on holiday. He put them on Facebook with some inappropriate comments, and they were very embarrassing. I'm friends with my boss and she saw them. She was not impressed at all. A lot of young people post embarrassing pictures for fun, but I know someone who lost their job because of this.

TIP 2 _____
My son was not careful about posting and sharing personal information. He revealed his date and place of birth, phone number and home address. He even told his friend where the spare set of keys were hidden. Needless to say, our home was broken into! If you share personal information online, be careful and don't share information that can help people steal your identity or find out where you live. Don't accept every request to become a friend.

TIP 3 _____
Be careful when you click 'Reply to all'. If you reply to everyone in a message group, then everyone in that group will read that email. This is quite a common mistake and can ruin relationships with friends and colleagues. I once included my boss on an email she should not have seen. So, take extra care when you respond, and on Facebook do not get confused between posting on a wall and sending a private message.

TIP 4 _____
Every site allows you to choose your privacy settings. Decide how visible you want your profile, contacts, photos and videos to be and then learn how to set the the right level of control. Familiarise yourself with the sites' policies about information you post. My sister had her boss on her LinkedIn site but showed herself as LOOKING FOR WORK on the site. Her boss was not impressed.

TIP 5 _____
If you include letters, numbers and punctuation in a password, it will be hard to break. Use different passwords for different accounts and don't choose your birthday like my friend did. Never share your password with anyone. If someone wants to steal your identity, they might look at your social media pages. So do not post a picture with your pet's name on your Facebook page if this is a secret word you share with your bank.

TIP 6 _____
If you want to create a good impression, proofread your writing. Even better, get someone else to check what you have written. There's nothing worse than a silly spelling or grammar mistake. And check that your language is appropriate. I usually reject candidates if they make spelling mistakes on their job applications.

GRAMMAR
FIRST CONDITIONAL

7 Look at the highlighted first conditional sentences in the text. Complete these statements about the first conditional using the words in the box.

will   present simple   imperative   real   could   might

1 We use the first conditional to talk about _____ possibilities in the future.
2 In the *if*-clause we can use the _____.
3 In the main clause we can use modals like _____, _____ and _____, but we can also use the _____ to give advice.

8 Complete these sentences using your own ideas.
1 If I pass my exams, _____.
2 If I show you how to use Twitter, _____?
3 What _____ if I press this key?
4 If it's nice weather, _____.
5 If it rains, _____.
6 If I go to London, _____.
7 _____, we will miss the plane.
8 If my computer crashes, _____?

→ Language reference and extra practice pages 132–133

9a Write a list of tips on how to avoid making mistakes online. Use the first conditional beginning with *if* and an imperative.

If you share personal information, be careful.

9b Compare your list with a partner.

SPEAKING

10a Work with a partner and choose a topic from the following list: social network sites, email, instant messaging, texting. Make a list of Dos and Don'ts. For example, here is a list for emails:

DOS	DON'TS
• Get to the point quickly.	• Use poor grammar and spelling.
• Fill in the subject line.	• Reply to all without checking.
• Use appropriate language.	• Use all capital letters for a word. (It reads like you're 'shouting'.)

10b Now swap your list with another pair and evaluate their list. Which Dos and Don'ts do you think are the most useful?

4.4 SCENARIO

LANGUAGE TRAINING

SITUATION

1 Read the situation below and answer the questions.
1. Why does IMA need an English language programme?
2. Which staff will it focus on in its language training?

International Medi-Aid (IMA), based in Florence, Italy, is a charity which provides medical aid to many countries. Recently the management decided that English will be the working language of the organisation. The Human Resources department of IMA will start by organising English language training for 200 staff at Head Office. It will prioritise those who are in most need of training.

2a Read the extract from a report from a member of the HR department at IMA. What are the two problems concerning the language programme?

2b In small groups, discuss and make notes on the advantages and disadvantages of each proposal, from the point of view of both the staff and the charity.

3a [4.6] Listen to three members of the HR department, Claire, Frank and Sophia, talking about the English language training programme. What three topics do they discuss?

3b Listen again and answer the questions.
1. What will the HR members do before deciding about one-to-one classes and British and American English?
2. Why do they decide to run classes for Administrative staff?

REPORT: RESULTS

Here are the results of the survey of the staff's English language ability that I carried out recently.

NUMBER	ENGLISH LANGUAGE ABILITY			
	EXCELLENT	GOOD	FAIR	POOR
Directors (14)	4	2	2	6
Senior staff (26)	8	6	5	7
Fundraisers (30)	6	2	10	12
Medical staff (32)	10	7	3	12
Administrative staff (98)	36	15	25	22

We need to keep any training costs low as the budget for language training for the first year is only €150,000. There are five possible ways of providing English language training. However, we do not agree on the best programme. These are the proposals, with estimated costs.

- **Proposal 1:** Send staff to a language school close to Head Office.
  Cost: 10 participants on a four-week course (20 hours a week) = €20,000.

- **Proposal 2:** Hire two English language instructors to give courses at Head Office.
  Cost: 10 participants on a four-week course (20 hours a week) = €8,000.

- **Proposal 3:** Hire a language expert to plan and set up courses online for staff.
  Cost: no information at present, but this could be expensive – at least €40,000

- **Proposal 4:** Send groups of staff to the UK or USA for a crash course.
  Cost: for a two-week course (30 hours per week) + air fare + accommodation = €5,000 per employee for the UK, €7,000 for the US

- **Proposal 5:** Provide one-to-one English language training at Head Office. **Cost:** €80 per hour

4.4 LANGUAGE TRAINING

KEY LANGUAGE
ACCEPTING AND REJECTING IDEAS, CONSIDERING CONSEQUENCES

4a Look at the expressions below and match each group to one of these headings: Accepting ideas, Rejecting ideas, Considering consequences.

Group 1: _____
Let's think this through.
If we do that, what will happen?
What will the effects be?

Group 2: _____
I think you're right.
It's an interesting thought.
That's a great idea.

Group 3: _____
Mmm, I don't know about that.
I'm afraid I don't like the idea.
I'm not in favour of it.

4b Listen again and tick (✓) the expressions you hear. Then look at Audio script 4.6 on page 168 and find one other expression for each category.

TASK
SELECTING AN ENGLISH LANGUAGE PROGRAMME

5a Work in groups of four. You are members of the Human Resources department of IMA and are going to decide on the English language programme.

Student A: turn to page 156.
Student B: turn to page 161.
Student C: turn to page 163.
Student D: turn to page 155.

Follow this procedure.
1. Discuss the options for English language training. Try to persuade the members of your group that your option is the best. You want the charity to spend most of the budget on your option.
2. Listen to all the arguments. Then, as a group, agree on the English language programme for the first year.

5b Present your group's programme to the class. Then vote on the best as a class.

4.5 STUDY AND WRITING SKILLS

STUDY SKILLS
DESCRIBING CHARTS AND TABLES

1 Where do you usually see charts and tables in your everyday life? How often do you need to look at or use them? For what reasons?

2 Match the percentages and the fractions.

1. 67%
2. 32%
3. 75%
4. 23%
5. 52%
6. 48%
7. 80%
8. 74.5%

a just under a quarter
b just over two thirds
c slightly less than a third
d just over half
e (exactly) three quarters
f more than three quarters
g approximately three quarters
h almost half

3 Answer the questions.
1. Which of the following is a *majority*?
   a 32% b 24% c 77%
2. Which of the following is a *minority*?
   a 21% b 83% c 91%

4 Look at the table showing results from 100 student questionnaires at a university language centre last year and this year on student satisfaction in two areas: teaching and facilities (buildings, rooms, equipment).

	Teaching		Facilities	
	Last year	This year	Last year	This year
Very satisfied	51	65	32	10
Satisfied	24	24	38	52
Quite satisfied	10	6	20	25
Not satisfied	12	2	8	12
No opinion	3	3	2	1

Look at the results for last year. Are these statements true or false? Correct the false statements.
1. Approximately half the students were very satisfied with the teaching. T
2. Ten percent of the students were quite satisfied with the facilities. F 20
3. Just under two thirds of the students were very satisfied with the facilities. F 43
4. Almost a quarter of the students were satisfied with the facilities. F 38%
5. The majority was very satisfied or satisfied with teaching and facilities. T
6. A small minority had no opinion about teaching and facilities. T
7. More than a quarter weren't satisfied with the teaching and facilities. F less

5 Look at the results for this year. Work with a partner and write some true/false statements like in Exercise 4. Give them to another pair to answer, then check their answers.

This year almost two thirds of students were very satisfied with the teaching.

6 Look at the chart below for 20 seconds and choose the best summary.
a This chart shows the number of native and second language speakers of some different languages.
b This chart shows the percentage of speakers of a number of different languages over some years.
c This chart compares the number of native speakers of important world languages at two different points in time.
d This chart shows some changes in eight languages and the number of native speakers from fifty years ago and now.

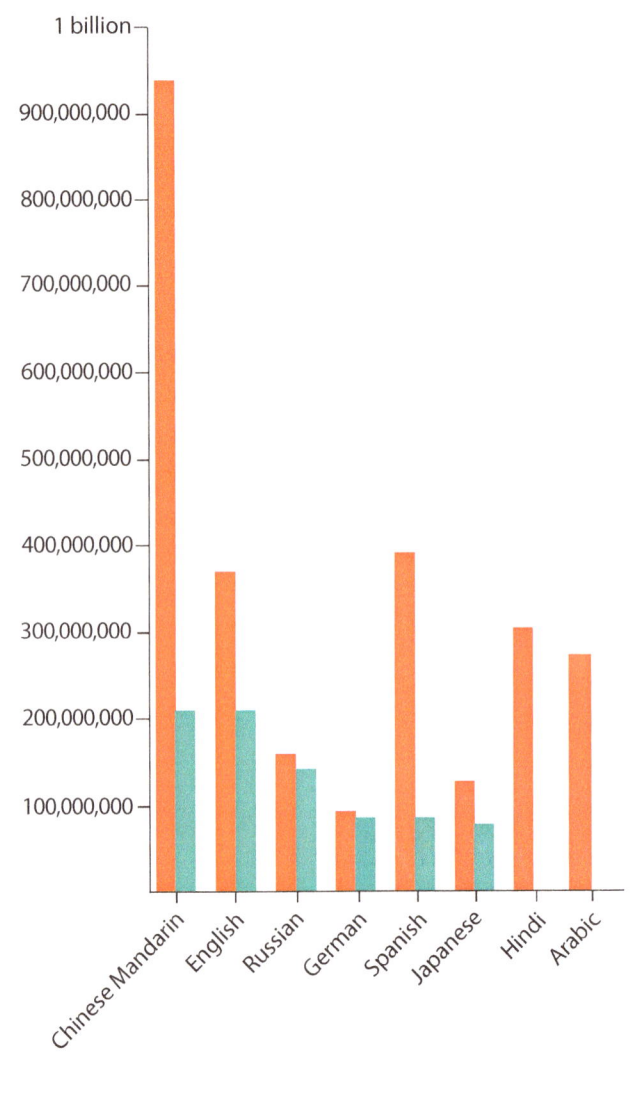

Approximate number of native speakers of languages 50 years ago and today

44

STUDY AND WRITING SKILLS 4.5

7 Complete the report with the words and phrases a–g.
a   the approximate number
b   approximately
c   a significant increase
d   there were no figures given
e   however
f   over the period
g   overall

The bar chart shows ¹ _a_ of speakers of different languages in the world now and fifty years ago. ² _g_, the chart demonstrates that the number of speakers of all languages have increased over the period.

Fifty years ago there were ³ _b_ 200 million speakers of Chinese. This has increased to the present figure of almost a billion. There were also 200 million speakers of English fifty years ago, but this figure has only increased to 370 million.

In addition, there has been ⁴ _c_ in the number of Spanish speakers from 100 million fifty years ago to around 400 million today. Similarly, there were increases in the number of Russian and Japanese speakers. In contrast, there were 100 million speakers of German fifty years ago, but this figure has remained almost the same ⁵ _f_.

⁶ _d_ for speakers of Hindi and Arabic fifty years ago. ⁷ _e_, at present there are about 300 million speakers of Hindi and 280 million speakers of Arabic.

WRITING SKILLS
A REPORT

8a You have been asked to write a report for a university lecturer describing the information shown in the chart on the right. In pairs or small groups, answer these questions.
1   What percentage of the population of Australia uses English as a first language?
2   Which country has the highest percentage that uses English as a second language?
3   Which country in the chart has the highest combined percentage of speakers of English?

8b Look at the other countries in the chart and make statements about their use of English as a first and second language.

9a Look at the chart again and complete the sentences.
☐   In Malaysia almost a third of the population …
[9] There were no figures given for …
☐   Overall, the chart demonstrates that six countries in the chart have a majority of …
[1] This chart shows the percentage of people from a number of countries who …
☐   The country with the lowest percentage of speakers of English as a first language …
☐   In South Africa, just under a quarter of …
☐   It is also interesting that in Barbados and New Zealand …
☐   Compared to the 97% of speakers of English as a first language in the UK, in the USA the percentage …
☐   The percentage of speakers of English as a second language in the USA is approximately the same as …

9b Put the sentences in a logical order. The first and last have been numbered.

10 Look back at the report in Exercise 7. Underline the linkers (e.g. *however*).

11 Write a report about the information in the chart in Exercise 8. Use your sentences from Exercise 9 and link them where you can. Use the report in Exercise 7 as a model.

Percentage of population using English as a first or second language

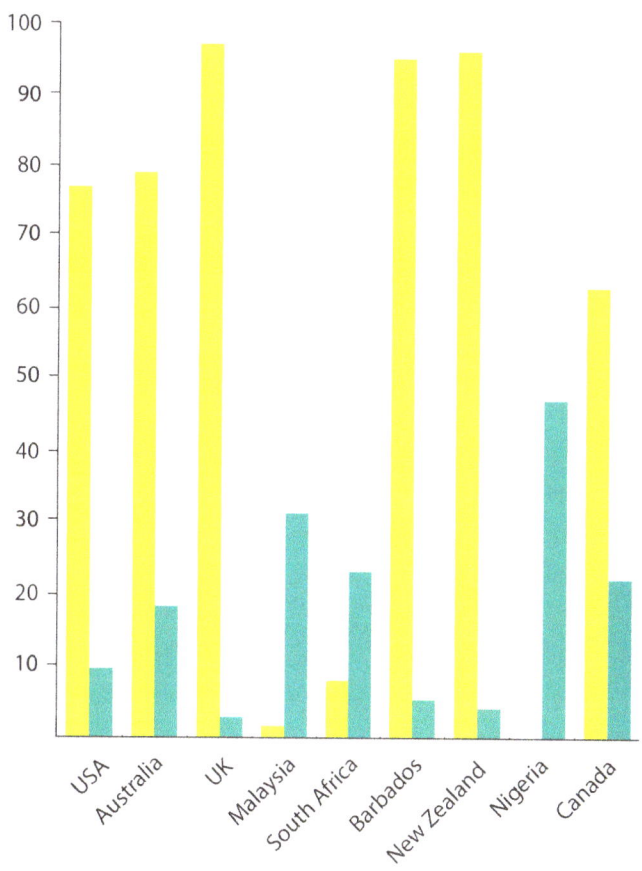

■ English as a first language   ■ English as a second language

homework?

45

5 Advertising
5.1 WHAT MAKES A GOOD ADVERT?

IN THIS UNIT

GRAMMAR
- second conditional
- comparison

VOCABULARY
- adjectives
- advertising
- words with a similar meaning
- word combinations

SCENARIO
- the language of presentations
- giving a presentation

STUDY SKILLS
- critical thinking

WRITING SKILLS
- an opinion-led essay

You can tell the ideals of a nation by its advertising. Norman Douglas, 1868–1952, Scottish writer

SPEAKING

1 Work with a partner to discuss the following.

1. Have you ever bought something just because of an advert? When?
2. Are there any adverts which you particularly dislike? Which one(s)? Why?
3. Think of a memorable advert. Describe it.

READING

2a Read three opinions about advertising. Are these statements true, false or partly true?

1. Michael Hamilton says that adverts must attract attention and be colourful.
2. He also states that an advert should encourage us to do something.
3. Miranda Hoyles states that adverts nowadays do more than in the past.
4. Hoyles also says people like adverts that reflect everyday life.
5. Christie Peterson focuses on company names, slogans and logos.
6. She says that mystery in an advert is more important than learning the product or company name.

> First of all, an advert has to be attention-grabbing and powerful. You need a strong image that is eye-catching, a catchy slogan, a joke or something shocking. In advertising, we talk about the AIDA formula. A is for attention. I is for interest. D is for desire. A is for action. An ad needs to do more than get our attention. It also has to be effective and persuasive. It must get us interested, make us want the product and motivate us to go out and buy it.
>
> **Michael Hamilton, advertising executive**

> Advertising has changed over the years. Adverts are no longer purely informative and focused on the product. Many of the adverts that we see today are short stories telling inspirational tales that are often witty, humorous and sophisticated. People do not want to remember that life can be dull. They want to see something original and creative. The adverts take away the ordinariness of everyday life and take us to somewhere exotic or romantic.
>
> **Miranda Hoyles, head of US advertising agency**

> Many people talk about advertisements that are exciting and intriguing. But for me, an instantly recognisable logo is really important. Good logos have been built up so they are recognisable. Part of what makes a good advert is a clear symbol that people immediately identify with the company. A good slogan also helps you make a connection. 'The real thing' makes you think of Coca-Cola immediately. It's also important that your slogan does not become irritating.
>
> **Christie Peterson, illustrator**

2b *Inferring opinion* Work with a partner to discuss the following. Which of the people in the text do you think would agree with or say the following? Why?
1 Advertising helps people to escape from reality.
2 Strong symbols and carefully chosen words are the key to good advertising.
3 Impact is the most important aspect of advertising.
4 Being too repetitive in an advert can be dangerous.

2c Which opinion do you agree with the most?

VOCABULARY
ADJECTIVES, ADVERTISING

3 Find adjectives in the first two texts in Exercise 2a which mean the following.
1 attracting your attention easily
2 unusual, attractive and noticeable
3 amusing and enjoyable, easy to remember
4 very surprising
5 works well and produces the results you want
6 able to make people do or believe something
7 funny and clever
8 not interesting or exciting
9 imaginative, using completely new and different ideas
10 unusual and exciting because it comes from a distant country

4 Match the words connected with advertising with their meanings.

| sponsorship | commercial (n) | promote | jingle |
| misleading | slogan | endorse | logo |

1 an advert on TV or radio
2 financial support a company gives in order to get publicity for themselves
3 a short phrase that is easy to remember
4 to say publicly that you support or approve of something
5 giving the wrong idea or impression
6 special design/symbol that a company puts on all its products or adverts
7 to help to sell something, especially by advertising
8 a short, easy to remember phrase with music

WHAT MAKES A GOOD ADVERT?   5.1

5a Choose the correct words.
A: OK, let's brainstorm how we're going to ¹*promote/endorse* this product.
B: Well, we could get a famous celebrity, like an actor or sports star to endorse it.
A: I think that would be much too expensive. ²*Commercial/Sponsorship* of a TV programme would also cost a lot. And a TV ³*logo/commercial* is out of the question for the same reason. I've seen some great TV spots which are visually beautiful and really ⁴*eye-catching/shocking*, often set in romantic or ⁵*dull/exotic* locations. But I don't think they've been very ⁶*effective/witty* as people can't remember the product they're advertising.
B: I agree, but we don't want something ⁷*catchy/dull* and boring. How about advertising on the internet? Would the budget run to that?
A: Yes, we could stretch to that.
B: And would you like something mysterious and clever or witty and with a(n) ⁸*eye-catching/catchy* jingle?
A: Maybe. What I really want is something new and ⁹*dull/original*. But most importantly, it must be ¹⁰*persuasive/misleading*. It must get people to buy the product.

5b 🔊 5.1 Listen and check your answers.

LISTENING

6a 🔊 5.2 Listen to three people talking about different adverts and answer the questions for each extract.
a What is the type of product?
b What is the brand?
c Did the speaker like the advert?

6b Listen again and note down the adjectives that each speaker uses to describe the advert.

6c Which advert was the most effective? Why?

SPEAKING

7a You are going to discuss some photos for use in adverts. Work in groups of four, two As and two Bs.
Student As: Look at the two photos on page 156.
Student Bs: Look at the two photos on page 158.

With your partner, discuss the following.
1 Which product(s) you could use them for.
2 How you would use them for advertising.
3 What slogans you would choose.

7b Now work in new pairs, A and B. Explain your advertising ideas to your new partner.

47

5.2 MANIPULATING IMAGES

IS IT ACCEPTABLE TO MANIPULATE IMAGES IN ADVERTISING?

FOR

In recent years, digitally manipulating images, or 'photoshopping', has become increasingly common, particularly in the advertising industry. It is now usual practice for the photos of celebrities and models to be retouched and altered to make them look more physically 'perfect' than they really are. Photoshopping has caused a great deal of controversy over the years, with those against it arguing that it promotes an unrealistic and distorted image of what people, particularly women, look like.

But is photoshopping as bad as many people believe? An expert on fashion, Amanda Fortini, certainly does not think so. She writes articles on fashion and popular culture for the *New York Times* and has come out strongly in defence of photoshopping images. She argues that adult women and men are well aware that images of celebrities are retouched. She quotes Christine Loiritz, editor of French *Marie Claire*, to support her opinion, 'Our readers are not idiots, especially when they see those celebrities who are 50 and look 23.' Her point is that young people have seen programmes about airbrushing on television and in the newspapers. They are not without knowledge of the techniques advertisers use.

Fortini also points out that images of famous people have been altered and exaggerated for many years – this technique is not new. Ever since advertising began, images of a beautiful, wealthy and youthful world have been used to sell products. We should accept that airbrushed images are a fiction, a fantasy. We should enjoy them, not criticise them.

Manipulated images are powerful. Some are subtle and others are instantly recognisable as fakes. Many are witty. We want to manipulate the world in which we live and this is reflected in our willingness to produce and consume those images. Advertisers should be free to produce whatever images they think are beautiful and will help sell their products.

So is it acceptable to manipulate images? Of course it is. Amanda Fortini is right. We know what images are fake, and we should use our critical skills when viewing images. As she says, 'The problem isn't altered photos, it's our failure to alter our expectations of them.'

READING

1 Work with a partner to discuss the following.
1 What do you think of the two photos of the same person in the article?
2 Is it acceptable to manipulate images of people in advertising?

2 You are going to read a FOR and AGAINST article in a magazine on the above topic. Work in pairs.
Student A: Read the FOR text on this page.
Student B: Read the AGAINST text on page 158.

Scan your texts and find out what it says about these people. Then share your information with your partner.
1 Amanda Fortini
2 Julia Roberts
3 Kate Winslet
4 Britney Spears
5 Christine Loiritz
6 Brad Pitt
7 Chuck Close

3a Read your text again and make notes on the key points.

3b Work with your partner. Using only your notes, summarise your text for your partner.

4 Evaluating arguments Which arguments do you think are stronger – FOR or AGAINST? Why?

5 Text reference Look at the FOR text again and decide who or what the highlighted words refer to.

VOCABULARY
WORDS WITH A SIMILAR MEANING

6a Look at these verbs from the texts connected to 'change'. Match them to their meanings below.

alter	enhance	manipulate	distort	exaggerate

1 to improve something
2 to skilfully control or move something
3 to change
4 to change the shape or sound of something
5 to make something seem better, larger, worse, etc. than it really is

6b Complete the sentences with an appropriate form of the verbs in Exercise 6a. Use each verb only once.
1 Her face had not _____ much over the years.
2 You can _____ photos using various software programmes.
3 Tall buildings can _____ radio signals.
4 Benitez said everyone hated him, but he was _____.
5 Salt _____ the flavour of food.

MANIPULATING IMAGES   5.2

LISTENING

7a [5.3] Listen to a conversation between a web designer and two photographers and answer the questions.
1 What kind of photographs do they take?
2 Where do they take their photographs?
3 Do the photographers have a website at the moment?

7b Listen again and complete the sentences.
1 If we _____ an invitation to a ceremony in Papua New Guinea, we'll go there right away for a great shoot.
2 We'd design the website ourselves if we _____ enough time.
3 If we _____ quickly, we'll limit the damage.
4 If we make the sea bluer, the picture _____ look even better.
5 If I _____ you, I'd use this photo as your main image.
6 If I had the couple's number on me, I _____ give them a call now.
7 What _____ you do if you had an unlimited budget?

7c In groups, discuss how you would design the photographers' website.

GRAMMAR
SECOND CONDITIONAL

8a Look at these sentences from the conversation.
1 If we act quickly, we'll limit the damage.
2 We'd design the website ourselves if we had enough time.

Now complete the statements below using the words in the box.

| will | present simple | unlikely | would | likely | past simple |

1 We use the first conditional to talk about things that are **likely** to happen.
2 We use the second conditional to talk about things that are **unlikely** to happen.
3 We form the first conditional with: if + **past**, **will** + infinitive.
4 We form the second conditional with: if + **past**, **would** + infinitive.

8b Look at the sentences in Exercise 7b and find an example of the following.
1 if + past simple + modal
2 a set phrase with If I were you + would

8c Look at the sentences in Exercise 7b again and choose the correct words in these statements.
1 It is **likely** / unlikely they will get an invitation to Papua New Guinea.
2 They **have** / don't have enough time.
3 It is **likely** / unlikely they will act quickly.
4 It is **likely** / unlikely they will make the sea bluer.
5 This phrase is **used** / not used to give advice.
6 The speaker has / **does not** have the phone number.
7 The speaker has / **does not** have an unlimited budget.

→ Language reference and extra practice pages 134–135

GRAMMAR TIP

In second conditional sentences, *would* can be replaced with *could* to mean 'would be able to'.

9 Discuss these questions in groups.
1 Would you be offended if someone photoshopped you?
2 Who would you most like to look like, if you could?
3 What is the first thing you would change about your life if you had a lot of money?
4 Who would you most like to meet if you could meet anyone?
5 Who would you most like to help if you had a lot of money?
6 If you could go (or go back) to university, what would you study?
7 What would you have for dinner today if you could choose anything you wanted?

SPEAKING

10 In small groups, discuss this question.

Should cosmetic surgery on people under the age of twenty-one be made illegal?

49

5.3 ADVERTISING AND CHILDREN

READING

1 What products are most commonly featured in adverts for children? How are they advertised?

2a Read the article quickly and say which of the following are *not* mentioned in the text.
1 the time children spend watching television
2 the ways in which advertisers can reach children
3 the dangers of advertising to children
4 how different countries control advertising
5 products that are not allowed to be advertised in different countries

2b Read the article again and find the following.
1 three examples of ways in which advertisers reach children
2 three serious problems with advertising for children
3 four countries that impose controls on advertising for children
4 three countries that used to have no governmental controls on advertising to children
5 three examples of how countries approach the control of advertising to children differently

3 Responding to the topic Work with a partner to discuss the following.
1 Do you agree that advertising should not be aimed at children? Why?/Why not?
2 In the text there are a number of approaches to controlling advertising for children. Which is the best?
3 In your opinion should some products not be advertised at all? If so, which?

VOCABULARY
WORD COMBINATIONS

4 Look at the article again and find the words below. Which other words do they combine with? Is each combination adjective + noun or noun + noun?
1 managers (line 2)
2 target (line 5)
3 commercials (line 13)
4 cartoons (line 18)
5 message (line 27)
6 sums (line 31)
7 food (line 31)
8 products (line 34)
9 websites (line 40)

5 Complete the sentences so they are true for you.
1 I think advertising managers should …
2 I think junk food is …
3 I like/don't like TV commercials that …
4 Companies should not spend vast sums of money on …

Advertisers targeting young people
Paul Johnson reports

A new report has concluded that advertising managers are becoming increasingly interested in children. Studies show that children influence about 50 percent of things that families buy, so they are
5 an attractive target for advertisers. Unfortunately, some companies have increased their advertising to children for many of their least nutritious products.

John Taylor, the author of the report and a lecturer at the Department of Media and Communications at
10 the University of West London, says: 'Advertisers can reach their target in many ways. They can, for example, show an advert many times during school holidays, they can make the TV commercials a little louder than the programmes to attract attention,
15 or they can sponsor programmes and show their commercials just before the programme begins.'

Most advertisements aimed at children are short, imaginative and often in the form of animated cartoons. 'Children love the adverts and watch them in the same
20 way as any entertainment programme,' Taylor says.

There are concerns about advertising aimed at young people. The concerns are shared by Sarah Durham, a writer and journalist specialising in media analysis. 'The most worrying thing is that children do not think
25 carefully when they see television advertisements. They are less critical than adults and do not usually realise that the advert has a persuasive message, to encourage them or their parents to spend as much money as possible on the product or service,' she says.

30 There are also concerns over the vast sums of money that junk food manufacturers spend on advertising to persuade children to buy their food products. Many advertisements,
35 argues Durham, promote food that is a lot higher in fat, salt and sugar than healthier alternatives. 'Many companies target children with offers of free toys, models of cartoon characters, gimmicky
40 packaging and interactive websites. In most western countries, there are a lot more adverts during children's TV for food than any other type of product, and these are mainly for confectionery,
45 sweetened breakfast cereals and fast food restaurants.'

Government approaches to controlling advertising to children vary. In Sweden, one of the strictest
50 countries where advertising is concerned, TV advertising to children under the age of 12 is banned. Greece bans television advertisements for children's toys between 7 a.m. and
55 10 p.m. Other countries, such as Denmark and the Netherlands, also have strict legal controls.

Some countries are not as certain as the Swedes that advertising to children
60 is harmful. For example, the French have argued that children need to see many advertisements so that they can develop their ability to think as they grow up. The belief is that advertising
65 will help children to be more aware of its persuasive power. However, even countries who have in the past preferred not to have legal controls, are now getting tougher. France has
70 banned adverts for mobile phones to the under 12s. The UK has now banned junk food adverts in shows aimed at children under 15, and Germany has banned adverts making 'direct offers'
75 to children.

This all means that there is little hope that the situation will be resolved by any kind of cross-European regulations. 'Because some countries are much more
80 relaxed than others about advertising to children, the European Union is unable at present to have a common approach to the problem. Until the majority of member states are as sure as the Swedes
85 of the harmful nature of advertising, the current indecision will continue,' concludes Taylor.

ADVERTISING AND CHILDREN 5.3

GRAMMAR
COMPARISON

6 Look at the comparative forms highlighted in the text. Complete these statements using the words in the box.

| a little | most | as (x3) | less | a lot | -est | more |
| -er | not as | much more | least | | | |

1 We make the comparative of one-syllable adjectives by adding _____ to the adjective. With most longer adjectives we put _____ before the adjective.
2 We make the superlative of one-syllable adjectives by adding _____ to the adjective. With most longer adjectives we put _____ before the adjective.
3 We use _more_ or _much_ to emphasise a large difference.
4 We use _est_ to emphasise a small difference.
5 We use _as_ + adjective + _as_ to say there is no difference.
6 We use _not as_ + adjective + _as_ to say there is a difference.
7 We use _a little_ to make an adjective weaker.
8 We use (the) _least_ + adjective to show the smallest amount (the opposite of _most_).

➜ Language reference and extra practice pages 134–135

7 Correct the mistakes in the sentences.
1 Coca-Cola is the most biggest seller of soft drinks to children.
2 Children's teeth are a much more bad than they were ten years ago.
3 This computer game is so expensive as that one.
4 These trainers are much more better than those ones.
5 The new ZX radio-controlled car is lot faster that the 2012 version.
6 Coffee is just as tastier as tea.
7 When it comes to children, health is the more important thing in the world.
8 Children like the cereals that are the less healthy for them.
9 The ad wasn't as good I expected.

SPEAKING

8a Work in groups of three. You are a family (mother, father, son) and you want to buy a quad bike (a motorbike with four wheels) for the 16-year-old son.

Student A (father): Turn to page 156.
Student B (mother): Turn to page 158.
Student C (son): Turn to page 160.

8b Look at the table on page 159, which has information about four different quad bikes. As a family, compare the four bikes, talking about the small and big differences and the things that are the same. Try to agree on which bike to buy.

▶ MEET THE EXPERT

Watch an interview with Vena Raffle about the work of the UK Advertising Standards Authority.
Turn to page 151 for video activities.

5.4 SCENARIO
B-KOOL SOFT DRINKS

SITUATION

1 Read the situation below. Work with a partner and look at this list. Which factors do you think B-Kool should use to choose the advertising agency? Rank them in order of importance (1 = most important, 5 = least important).
- how good the presentation by the agency is
- how good their ideas are for the advertising
- how enthusiastic they seem to be about the drink
- how much the agency will charge for the campaign
- how well known the agency is

B-Kool is a soft drinks manufacturer, based in New Orleans, USA. The company is going to introduce a new drink to the market soon, which will appeal to the eight to fourteen-year-old age group. The drink is made from a mixture of exotic fruits. When it was tested, young people used three words to describe its qualities: fresh, delicious, healthy. There will be an international advertising campaign to launch the new product. The marketing department has asked three advertising agencies to present their ideas for the campaign. B-Kool will choose one of the agencies to plan and carry out the campaign.

2a **5.4** Listen to the Marketing Director, Amy Chen, talking to Larissa Klein, head of an advertising agency. What five points does Amy Chen want the agency to cover in their presentation?

2b Listen again. Complete the notes that Larissa Klein made during the conversation. Use one or two words in each gap.

> Points to cover in the presentation
>
> - Name of drink?
> - Slogan?
> - Packaging: Can or bottle? Design, ¹_____ and ²_____?
> - How to advertise? ³_____ during children's television? Children's magazines? Use the ⁴_____? One TV commercial or ⁵_____, one for each country? ⁶_____ spots? If yes, what time of day? What sort of programme to ⁷_____?
> - Ideas for promoting the drink, e.g. ⁸_____ in schools or offer ⁹_____ with the logo on them?

5.4 B-KOOL SOFT DRINKS

KEY LANGUAGE
THE LANGUAGE OF PRESENTATIONS

3a 5.5 Larissa Klein and two colleagues make a presentation to the marketing department of B-Kool. Listen to the beginning of the presentation and complete the phrases.

Beginning a presentation:
1. I'd like to _____ _____ _____ Emilio Sanchez on my left, and next to him, Karl Reiner.
2. Our _____ _____ is to present some ideas for your new product.
3. Our presentation _____ _____ _____ three parts.
4. If you _____ _____ _____, we'll be pleased to answer them at the end of our presentation.

3b 5.6 Listen to the next part of the presentation and complete the phrases.

Talking about a different subject:
1. Moving _____ _____ _____ the design of the can.

Referring to an illustration:
2. Please _____ _____ _____ _____.

3c 5.7 Listen to the end of the presentation and complete the phrases.

Ending a presentation:
1. Now, let me _____ _____ _____ points.
2. Thank you very much _____ _____ _____ _____.
3. Are there _____ _____?

3d In which section of the presentation would you expect to find the following? Match the phrases to the headings in Exercises 3a–c.
1. Now, I'll sum up.
2. I'm going to talk to you about our advertising campaign.
3. Hello everyone, thanks for coming to my presentation.
4. That's all I have to say. Emilio will now show another design for the can.
5. This brings me to my next point.
6. Karl will now talk about our promotions.
7. This is how I'd like to organise my talk.
8. Thanks for listening to my talk.

TASK
GIVING A FORMAL PRESENTATION

4a Work in small groups. Each group represents an advertising agency. Choose a name for your agency, then discuss your ideas for an advertising campaign to launch the new drink.

4b Make your presentation to the other groups. Each person in your group should present one part of the presentation. Use the following structure for your presentation.
- name of the new drink
- slogan for the drink
- design of the packaging
- how to advertise the drink – what media to use
- special promotions

5 As a class, discuss the presentations. Which one was the most interesting/creative/persuasive?

5.5 STUDY AND WRITING SKILLS

STUDY SKILLS
CRITICAL THINKING

1a [5.8] Listen to an expert talking about critical thinking. Make notes under these headings.
- What is critical thinking?
- What do critical thinkers do?
- Why is critical thinking important for academic studies?
- Why is it an important skill for everyone?

1b Work with a partner and summarise what you've heard.

2 Work with your partner and decide under which heading the following statements belong.
CRITICAL THINKERS DO ...
CRITICAL THINKERS DON'T ...

1. identify a writer's purpose and opinion.
2. question every statement or fact in a text.
3. question beliefs, opinions and ideas which are in a text.
4. think that Wikipedia is the most reliable online source of information.
5. distinguish between facts and opinions.
6. look for evidence which supports arguments or opinions.
7. always keep the same opinion when reading a text.
8. always read a text to find opinions that are the same as their own.
9. look for the main argument and key ideas in a text.
10. pay careful attention to the style and tone of a text.
11. believe that their own beliefs and values are always right.
12. accept a writer's ideas just because he or she is well known.

3 You are going to critically read an essay. Before doing so, decide what you think about the topic. Discuss this question in small groups.

Should TV advertisements for unhealthy products be banned?

4 Quickly read the essay. On first impression, do you generally agree or disagree with the writer?

Should TV advertisements for unhealthy products be banned?

¹ In many countries, there are already laws which do not allow advertising for tobacco products. Some people now want to go further and ban advertisements for other unhealthy products such as alcohol and junk food. This is undoubtedly the right way forward for governments. There are strong arguments for banning TV advertising of these products. The benefits of doing this greatly outweigh the disadvantages.

² It is clearly desirable to limit TV advertisements of fast food. It is widely known that the rate of obesity has increased significantly in western countries. For example, obesity is second only to smoking as a cause of death in the United States. In that country, the food industry spends over $33 billion per year to advertise food products that are considered to be junk food. Drinking alcohol is also very unhealthy. It results in a wide range of diseases. If children see fewer adverts on TV of people doing these activities, they are much less likely to try to imitate their behaviour.

³ Opponents of banning advertising argue that people know what they must do to be healthy. In a free society, people must be able to choose whether to buy a product. They say that if a product is legal, businesses should be able to sell and advertise it. However, it is the government which has to deal with the consequences of people buying unhealthy products. The cost of healthcare for those who have unhealthy habits, such as smoking, drinking alcohol and eating junk food is enormous. Therefore, it is clearly the duty of a government to prevent the behaviour by banning television commercials of such products.

⁴ Another reason why people are against banning TV advertisements for unhealthy products is that manufacturing the products creates jobs and brings in large amounts of tax for governments. However, surely this is a false argument. The money invested in making these unhealthy products could be used for more worthwhile businesses such as those which improve our environment. Furthermore, it is not right for governments to make money from activities which harm its citizens.

⁵ To conclude, it is the responsibility of governments to prevent people from damaging their health. Laws to ban TV advertisements of unhealthy products are beneficial to society. They help to save lives and improve the health of a nation.

STUDY AND WRITING SKILLS 5.5

5a You are now going to practise 'thinking critically' about a text. Read the essay again and answer the questions below.

Looking at the text:
1. Identify and underline the main opinion of the writer.
2. What facts (things that cannot be debated) does the writer use to support his opinion?
3. What statements, if any, in paragraph 2 do you question?
4. Identify and underline opinions of people who do not agree with the writer. Why does the writer mention these?
5. What is the style and tone of this article? Is it persuasive, objective, biased or critical?
6. Find words or phrases in the text that the writer uses to persuade you to accept his point of view, e.g. *undoubtedly* (para 1, line 5).

Thinking about the topic:
7. Do you agree with the writer or with people who are against banning unhealthy products?
8. What other products (if any) do you think should not be shown in TV adverts?

5b Work in small groups to compare and discuss your answers to Exercise 5a.

WRITING SKILLS
AN OPINION-LED ESSAY

6 Complete the description below with the words in the box.

| weaknesses | disadvantages | correct | opinion | persuasive |

There are two common kinds of discursive essay. The first kind of essay does not generally include a strong ¹_____. It presents the advantages and ²_____ of an action or contains different ideas and facts about a topic.

It is called a 'for and against' essay. The second type of essay is an 'opinion-led' essay. The writer expresses his or her opinion strongly on a controversial topic. He or she argues strongly that their opinion is ³_____, and the style and tone of the text is ⁴_____. In an opinion-led essay, the writer may introduce opposing opinions, but this is usually to show their ⁵_____.

7 Read the statements about opinion-led essays. Which two statements are NOT generally considered good practice?
1. In your first paragraph, you may rephrase the essay question.
2. It is a good idea to copy several phrases from the essay question.
3. After the first paragraph, you use some paragraphs to give reasons for your opinions.
4. It is not necessary to give evidence for your statements, for example by quoting people or referring to surveys.
5. You present arguments, showing that you disagree with something or question whether it is right.
6. In your last paragraph, you restate your opinion, so it links with the opening paragraph.

8 Look at the essay again and find an expression to add to the groups below.

Giving an opinion
In my opinion …
Personally I think …
I feel strongly that …
_____(para 1)

Giving facts
There is/are definitely…
It is well known that …
It is true that …
_____(para 2)

Giving reasons and results
This is because …
As a result, …
_____(para 3)

Adding a surprising fact / an opposing argument
Nevertheless …
On the other hand …
_____(para 3 & 4)

Using persuasive language
clearly …
undoubtedly …
_____(para 4)

Adding information
What's more …
In addition …
Moreover …
_____(para 4)

Concluding
In conclusion, …
It is clear that …
_____(para 5)

9a **Planning your essay** Choose one of the topics for an opinion-led essay. Decide what your opinion is. Note your reasons for your opinion and any evidence to support your point of view. Think of arguments against your opinion.

- To what extent do you think people are influenced by TV advertisements?
- There are too many unacceptable methods in advertising today.
- Businesses should not be allowed to advertise on social networks.

9b Use the following structure to plan your essay. Write a maximum of 300 words.

- Introduction (Introduce the subject and your opinion.)
- Main body of the essay – reasons and evidence (Most important ideas come first. Mention opposing opinions, but attack them!)
- Conclusion (Summarise and restat your opinion.)

6 Education

6.1 EDUCATION ISSUES

IN THIS UNIT

GRAMMAR
- defining relative clauses
- non-defining relative clauses

VOCABULARY
- education and studying

SCENARIO
- discussing options
- problem-solving

STUDY SKILLS
- reading strategies

WRITING SKILLS
- a formal letter

Education's purpose is to replace an empty mind with an open one. Malcolm Forbes, 1919–1990, US magazine publisher

VOCABULARY AND LISTENING
EDUCATION AND STUDYING

1 Work with a partner to discuss these questions about education in your country. Check that you know all the words in *italics*.

1. What age do children usually start *primary* (or *elementary*) school?
2. What age do children usually start and leave *secondary* school?
3. What age does *compulsory education* start? At what age does it finish? Do you think these are the correct ages?
4. Is there both *state* (public) *education* and *private education*? Which is better? Why?
5. Do most people go on to *higher education*? Why?/Why not? Do they have to pay?
6. Are *exams* or *continuous assessment* more common? Which is the better way of monitoring progress? Why?
7. Do many students start and then *drop out of* courses in your country?

2 Look at the phrases below. Which two nouns in each group are correct? Cross out the incorrect noun and write the correct collocation for this noun. You may need to change the verb or the preposition.

1. **go to** school / ~~a place at university~~ / college
   get a place at university
2. **revise for** an exam / ~~a subject~~ / a test
3. **graduate from** university / ~~primary school~~ / high school
4. **get** a degree / a good grade / ~~an exam~~
5. **take/retake** ~~homework~~ / an exam / a course
6. **pass/fail** an exam / a course / a ~~good result~~
7. **hand in** an essay / ~~a seminar~~ / an assignment
8. **do** ~~progress~~ / coursework / your best
9. **make** mistakes / progress / ~~homework~~
10. **study** ~~an exam~~ / a subject / a language

3a [6.1] **Inferring attitude** Listen to three people talking about their education experiences. Is each person positive, negative or neutral?

3b Listen again and tick (✓) the collocations in Exercise 2 you hear.

3c In small groups, ask and answer questions using the collocations above.

How do/did you revise for exams?

56

EDUCATION ISSUES   6.1

READING

4a Read the comments from an online discussion. Which comments are for mixed-sex schools, which are against, and which are neither for nor against?

4b Read the comments again and find nouns which mean the following.
1. sets of numbers which represent a fact (comment 2)
2. the subjects at a school, college, etc. (comment 4)
3. staying away from school without permission (comment 4)
4. upsetting and frightening someone smaller and weaker, especially in a school situation (comment 5)

4c Match the people in the discussion to the following. Which person believes:
1. that mixed schools are less competitive? 5
2. that there is proof that single-sex schools are more successful? 2
3. that school should be the same as real life? 4
4. that the problem isn't whether a school is single sex or mixed? 1
5. that single-sex education caters for girls and boys better? 3

5 Which of the opinions in the discussion do you agree with? Which do you disagree with? Why?

SPEAKING AND WRITING

6 Work in groups to discuss the following.
1. Schools should spend more time teaching the skills people need to get a job.
2. Education is basically a social experience. The atmosphere is the most important thing.
3. There should be no private education. All children should attend state schools/universities.
4. The purpose of secondary education is to prepare you for life.
5. Examination results are the most important aspect of education.
6. Academic achievement depends mainly on your teacher.
7. Teachers should be paid according to the exam results of their students.
8. Sport is the most important subject at school.

7 Write a comment giving your opinion on one of the statements in Exercise 6 for the *Newsline* website.

MyTablet

Newsline: the online news service

SIGN IN / REGISTER

DISCUSSION: Single-sex schools are better than mixed schools

Comment 1
POSTED BY JANE, AMSTERDAM

I think mixed-sex schools are the only way for children to learn, because it's natural. In higher education and their working life, they will be mixed so it makes sense for them to be mixed at school. School should reflect the real world.

Comment 2
POSTED BY HANS, GERMANY

My reaction to this is very clear. For me, single-sex schools are much better, and the statistics show that they get better exam results, particularly at secondary level. Anything which helps children pass exams must be a good thing.

Comment 3
POSTED BY BILL, USA

Boys and girls learn in very different ways. I feel that they should be educated separately so teachers can focus on their different needs. The way I see it is that if you have a zoo, you don't put the lions in with the zebras!

Comment 4
POSTED BY MARTIN, LONDON

My view on this is that it doesn't really matter. What is important is the curriculum and keeping students interested. I was a teacher, and we had a lot of truancy to deal with and problems with students missing lessons because they found them boring. Never have a timetable with Maths as the first class on Monday morning!

Comment 5
POSTED BY EMILY, SYDNEY

Mixed schools are better, there's no question. There is too much competition at single-sex schools, which often means that students don't make enough progress. I also think there is more bullying at single-sex schools, where children are picked on because of the increased competition. Single-sex schools lead to a 'dog eat dog' situation.

Comments 1-5 of 5

6.2 MONTESSORI

LISTENING AND WRITING

1a 🔊 6.2 Listen to a university student talking about a teacher. Does he say the teacher was good or bad?

1b Look at the adjectives in the box. Then listen again and tick (✓) the ones he uses to describe the teacher.

friendly informal easy-going strict punctual
late formal well-prepared interesting

2 Find the words below in Audio script 6.2 on page 169 and underline the phrase they appear in. Try to work out the meaning from the context. Use your dictionary to find the meanings of any you do not know.

criticise unique approach pace method environment

3 Tell your partner about your favourite/worst teacher at school. Write a short profile (80–100 words) of him or her. Use Audio script 6.2 on page 169 to help you.

READING

4a Read the article and say what the following dates refer to.

a 1870
b 1952
c 1896
d 1912
e 1936

4b Evaluating a summary Read the article again and correct the four mistakes in this summary.

Maria Montessori pioneered a new teaching method after she graduated as a nurse in 1896, and taught deprived children. She tried to use everyday objects in the class, and she wanted the children to develop social skills with each other and learn to be competitive. She taught children to experiment and to depend on the teacher, so that the main role of a teacher is to lead children. Through her book and her teacher training centres, she helped spread the method, and today there are many Montessori schools in Europe and North America.

---

article discussion edit this page history

Maria Montessori

Maria Montessori (1870–1952) is a famous Italian educationalist whose method of teaching has influenced people all over the world.

Born in the province of Ancona, Italy, in 1870, Montessori became the first female doctor in her country after she graduated from medical school in 1896. Later, working with deprived children, she set up a 'Children's House' (Casa dei Bambini) in Rome. This was the place where she developed the Montessori Method, an educational system that encourages an informal style of teaching. Children learn from handling everyday materials, and they develop at their own pace. The Montessori philosophy is simple.

Children are unique individuals who must be free to learn without being criticised or restricted. It is the child that controls the pace, topic and lessons, not the rest of the class or the teacher. As a result, children enjoy learning, and this gives them confidence and makes them happy.

The Montessori Method also teaches children skills to help them become independent. Very young children learn to dress themselves, to cook and to put their toys and clothes away. Children are encouraged to repeat activities as often as they wish, and they develop their observation skills by doing different activities.

A Montessori teacher observes children closely in order to provide them with individual learning programmes. The teacher is a guide, not a leader of the classroom, helping to open students' eyes to the wonders around them.

Maria Montessori wanted to free children's minds so that they would learn by self-teaching and self-correction. It is an approach to teaching which encourages children to learn by doing and experimenting.

A typical room in a Montessori school has many things children can use, for example, books, objects and games.

The furniture is light so they can arrange it as they wish, and the cabinets are low, so the children can reach them. Because the environment offers a range of activities, children like to work together, and they develop a social life based on cooperation rather than competition.

Maria Montessori travelled all over the world, training teachers to use her method, but it was only in her final years when she established the teacher-training centres that would take her work forward. There are now many schools in Europe and North America which use the Montessori curriculum and methods.

She wrote *The Montessori Method* in 1912 and *The Secret of Childhood* in 1936.

MONTESSORI 6.2

4c Answer these questions about the article.
1. What is the main role of the children in the Montessori approach? *independent*
2. Why did Montessori want to open the minds of her students? *guide*
3. How have the furniture and cabinets been designed in a Montessori classroom and why? *light, low*
4. What point does the writer make about the children's social life? *cooperate*

5 Work in pairs to discuss the following.
1. How does the Montessori approach compare with the way you were educated?
2. 'Children are unique individuals who must be free to learn without being criticised or restricted.' Do you agree? Why?/Why not?

GRAMMAR
DEFINING RELATIVE CLAUSES

6a Look at the following sentence from the text. The words in bold are a defining relative clause.

*It is an approach to teaching **which encourages children** …*

Now find and underline the relative clauses in the text that contain the following relative pronouns and adverbs.

who	that	which	whose	where	when
				time	*place*

6b Which relative pronouns or adverbs do we use to talk about the things below?

people	things or ideas	places	time
who	*that*	*where*	*when*
people + possessions/ideas	*whose*		

→ Language reference and extra practice pages 136–137

7 Match the sentence halves and join them using *who, that, which, whose, where* or *when*.
1. A professor in a British university is someone *who* b
2. A university is an institution *where* d
3. A thesis is a long piece of writing *which/that* c
4. A seminar is a class at university/college *where* f
5. An academic is someone *who* e
6. A vacation is a period of the year *when* a

a. universities or colleges are officially closed.
b. has the highest rank of the teachers in a department.
c. you do as part of a university degree.
d. students study for degrees and academic research is done.
e. teaches and does research in a college or university.
f. the teacher and students discuss a particular topic.

GRAMMAR TIP
We can leave out the relative pronoun (e.g. *that*) if the verb in the relative clause has a subject (in this case *children*).

A typical room in a Montessori school has many things **that** **children** can use.
A typical room in a Montessori school has many things **children** can use. *object pronoun*

8 Underline the subject and object in the following sentences. Then cross out the relative pronoun where possible. *subject pronoun*
1. Students who enter university may face a number of problems.
2. Is your degree worth the paper ~~that~~ it is written on?
3. There are university tutors ~~who~~ you can phone if you have a problem.
4. The university ~~which~~ I go to is very good.
5. People who have degrees have a better chance at interviews.

9 Complete the following sentences.
1. The person who influenced me most at school was …
2. A day when my life changed was …
3. The subject at school which I hated the most was …
4. I dislike people who …
5. I like days when …
6. I like teachers who …
7. I like films which …
8. I like lessons in which …

SPEAKING

10 Timed discussion In small groups, take it in turns to choose a topic from below and lead the discussion on that topic for three minutes.
- Children should be allowed to choose what they are going to do in school.
- Children need to learn facts, not play games.
- Private education should be abolished.
- All people have roughly the same level of intelligence.
- The learner's job is to absorb the knowledge teachers give them.
- Corporal punishment is always wrong.

▶ MEET THE EXPERT
Watch an interview with Rob Gueterbock, a Montessori teacher, about the Montessori method of education.
Turn to page 152 for video activities.

Let's go to the cafe that/where
Gia is my friend who
Last night I read the book.

* Which one (no adjective)
* Long subject
* Complex structure/sentence

6.3 SHOULD UNIVERSITY BE FREE?

READING

1 Work with a partner to discuss the following.
1. Is university free in your country?
2. Do you know any countries in which university is free for everyone?
3. Do you know any countries where students have to take out big loans to pay for their education?

2a Read the article quickly and find three reasons why the writer thinks that university should be free for everyone.

2b Read the article again and match the summary sentences below to the paragraphs 1–5.

5 a Some poor people will not go to university if costs are high.
3 b University should be free because it is good for society as a whole.
1 c David Keller is in favour of a rise in university fees.
4 d University should be free because of economic reasons.
2 e University should be free because it promotes greater equality.

3 Challenging opinions Work in pairs. Find the four opinions in the article that you find the most interesting. Then think of four counter-arguments to those opinions.

4 In small groups, discuss the following.
1. Is it worth going to university if fees are high?
2. What percentage of the population should go to university?
3. Do you think university should be free for everyone?

THE UNIVERSITY NEWS — *Student newspaper of the year*

EDITORIAL AND OPINION

HOME | NEWS | OPINION | SPORT | TRAVEL | **FEATURES** | BLOGS

Free University Education
By Jessica Brook

1 A few weeks ago, David Keller, who is rich enough to pay for all his children to go to private school, wrote a column in News Focus supporting a further increase in university fees. His attitude, which was very unsympathetic to students, made me angry. It has motivated me to explain why I feel strongly that university should be free for everyone.

2 There are a number of reasons for my opinion. First, greater equality. Free university education enables everyone to have the opportunity to study. If there are tuition fees, students have to take out big loans to finance their studies. They will take years to pay back the money. When they graduate, instead of working for their future, they will be working to pay back their past. Young people from poor backgrounds are less able to get into debt, but students whose parents are rich can pay off their loans more easily. Tuition fees, therefore, are very unfair. Free university education will be a step towards a more equal society.

3 Second, the benefits for society. Young people who graduate benefit society as a whole. They use their knowledge and skills to help other people. For example, a qualified doctor helps to treat other people. People with degrees can become teachers and share their knowledge with others. When the number of people who get a university education rises, the number of people who benefit from their education also rises. Surely it is right that society, which needs highly qualified people, should pay for those students' education.

4 Third, the economic argument. Higher education produces a more educated and qualified workforce. Countries with high rates of university education have higher levels of innovation and growth. They attract foreign investors and create new businesses which lead to more jobs for their citizens. Because people who go to university will earn more, they will pay more tax. As a result, there will be more money for essential social services such as health, education and welfare.

5 People like David Keller do not live in the real world. They do not understand one simple fact. Many poorer young people, who don't have rich parents to rely on, will be put off by the high cost of studying at university even if loans are available. Their talent will be lost to our country. Free university education is a right, not a privilege. It would bring enormous benefits to our society.

30 APRIL — DELIVERED EVERY FRIDAY TO YOUR INBOX

SHOULD UNIVERSITY BE FREE? 6.3

GRAMMAR
NON-DEFINING RELATIVE CLAUSES

5a Look at these examples from the article of a non-defining relative clause and a defining relative clause.

His attitude, which was very unsympathetic to students, made me angry.
People who go to university will earn more.

Which relative clause:
a gives extra information about the person, thing or idea in the main clause? N
b gives essential information that completes the meaning of the sentence? D

5b Look at the highlighted examples of non-defining relative clauses in the article and choose the correct answers in the rules for this type of relative clause.

Non-defining relative clauses:
1 *have* / do not have commas before them, and after them if necessary.
2 do / *do not* use that.

> **GRAMMAR TIP**
>
> Non-defining relative clauses can come in the middle or at the end of the sentence:
> *Barbara, who spent three years at university in Cambridge, is going back to live there.*
> *Barbara is going back to live in Cambridge, where she spent three years at university.*

➡ Language reference and extra practice pages 136–137

6 Read the sentences and put commas where necessary.
1 Oxford University , which was number four in world university rankings last year , has fallen to number eight.
2 John F Kennedy went to Harvard University which is the oldest institution of higher education in the United States.
3 Jean-Jacques Rousseau who was born in 1712 set out his views on education in his book *Emile*.
4 The Kumon method for teaching Maths was developed by Toru Kumon who graduated from Osaka University.
5 Oxford's Bodleian library which is one of the oldest libraries in Europe was originally founded in 1320.
6 Heidelberg University which was founded in 1386 has its own student prison.

7 Join the following pairs of sentences to make one sentence containing a non-defining relative clause. Use *whose*, *which*, *who* and *where*. Use commas appropriately.

1 American universities are now facing a lot of competition. They have attracted the world's best students for over 50 years.
   American universities, which have attracted the world's best students for over 50 years, are now facing a lot of competition.
2 Last month I went back to the Sorbonne. I had studied history there.
3 There are over 39,000 students at the University of Manchester. It's the biggest university in the UK.
4 Aristotle wrote books on many subjects. He studied under Plato.
5 Hilary studied politics at Harvard. She has just been offered a professorship there.

8 Write sentences that are true for you using these prompts. Include extra information using non-defining relative clauses.

My home town
Manchester, which has the largest university population in the UK, is in the north west of the country.

My home town   My university
My school   My mother

LISTENING AND SPEAKING

9 6.3 Listen to four people talking about university. Which speaker(s):
1 thinks going to university was a waste of time?
2 thinks their degree is a big advantage?
3 did not work hard?
4 doesn't think or is unsure that their degree helped them get a job?

10a Work in groups of four. You are going to read some information about the educational system of a country. Make notes.

Student A: Turn to page 156.   Student C: Turn to page 160.
Student B: Turn to page 159.   Student D: Turn to page 162.

10b Tell your group about the educational system you have read about. Compare the different systems with the system in your country. Which system is most like yours? Which would you most like to study/have studied in?

6.4 SCENARIO
TROUBLE AT LAKESIDE

SITUATION

1 Read the situation below and the extract from the Lakeside College prospectus. Work with a partner to discuss the following.

1. If you were planning to go to university, which of Lakeside College's facilities would particularly interest you?
2. What sort of things do students at university often complain about?

Lakeside College is located in Switzerland. It is a private university with a board of managers led by the Principal, Marie Laforêt. There are four student representatives on the board and four staff representatives. During the last three years, serious problems have arisen. The number of students at Lakeside College has fallen from over 5,000 to 2,600, while complaints from students have greatly increased.

LAKESIDE College

Our college has an informal, friendly atmosphere, and enjoys excellent facilities, including:

- a spacious campus
- a peaceful atmosphere for studying
- well-equipped lecture rooms
- a hall of residence
- a well-stocked library
- state-of-the-art computer laboratories
- excellent sports facilities.

We have an outstanding teaching staff and tutorial system. Students meet lecturers each week and have lively discussions about the subject they are studying.

2 A student representative sends an email to Marie Laforêt mentioning a number of problems that the managers need to deal with. Read the extract about two of the problems. Then work with a partner to discuss this question.

Which do you think is the more serious problem? Why?

To	enquiry@Lakeside.College.ed

In the university prospectus, it states that the university has 'a well-stocked library' and 'a peaceful atmosphere for studying'. Neither of these statements is true.

A lot of us are unhappy about the library. There are not enough books in many subjects, and essential books and journals are often not on the shelf where they are meant to be. Furthermore, the internet connection is very slow and this puts students off doing research in the library. There are also not enough sockets available for the students to recharge their devices. The reading rooms also are not up to standard. The tables are too small, and there are not enough lights in some areas.

There is another serious problem I'd like to draw your attention to. It's about noise in the evening. It seems that some students have a party every week in their rooms. The noise they make is preventing other students from studying properly, and I get the impression the noise level is increasing week by week. It's not true, therefore, to say that there is a 'peaceful atmosphere for studying' in our college.

6.4 TROUBLE AT LAKESIDE

KEY LANGUAGE
DISCUSSING OPTIONS

3a 🔊 6.4 Listen to a meeting between two student representatives and Marie Laforêt. Complete Marie's notes about the problem of noisy parties in the halls of residence. Use one or two words in each gap.

- Problem 2: ¹ _late-night_ parties, make a lot of noise, really ² _annoy_ people
- Solutions?
  (Marie) – ban parties in rooms or only ³ _allow_ parties after exams
  (Pablo) – let each floor of the hall have one party ⁴ _per semester_
  (May Cheng) – students can book a room in the ⁵ _main building_
- ⁶ _May_ 's solution is best. Discuss at next ⁷ _management_ meeting.
  committee

3b Listen again. Number the expressions in the order you hear them.

- 3 a … the good thing is that it's fair to everyone, but the bad thing is, it wouldn't be very popular.
- 6 b Yes, good idea. That's the best solution.
- 1 c There are several ways to deal with this.
- 7 d The best way is to discuss the matters at our Management Committee meeting.
- 8 e Why don't you send me notes on all the problems …?
- 2 f Let's look at our options.
- 4 g Supposing we let each floor of the hall have one party per semester.
- 5 h How about letting the students book a room in the main building …?

↑ Language activities
Suggestion – responding
c d e f g h a b

TASK
PROBLEM-SOLVING

4a Work in small groups. You are members of the Management Committee. Read the problems below and choose four to discuss.

4b As a group, discuss each problem you have chosen and try to come up with a solution.

4c Present your solutions to the rest of the class.

5 As a class, decide on the best solution for each problem.

Copy & paste onto handout

Problems

1 Library (see Exercise 2)

2 Noisy parties (see Exercise 3a)

3 Boring lecturers Lecturers read their lectures. They do not use visual aids or provide good reading lists. Tutorials are not useful. Lecturers talk most of the time and do not encourage students to participate and ask questions.

4 Attendance at classes and lectures is poor. Students miss early morning lectures. Many students fail their degree because of poor attendance.

5 Facilities The swimming pool, tennis courts and gym are not well maintained. The swimming pool is often unsupervised. New, more modern gym equipment is needed urgently.

6 Bullying A new student, Camilla, has complained that a senior member of staff is bullying her. He makes fun of her in tutorials and is not interested in her opinions. She is unhappy and wants to leave the college. In the past, other students have complained of the lecturer's attitude and behaviour.

7 Cheating and plagiarism This has increased in recent years. Students pass information to each other in examinations and buy essays on the internet. Lecturers say that some students copy material directly from the internet without giving references.

6.5 STUDY AND WRITING SKILLS

THE REACH OF DISTANCE LEARNING

Shekema Silveri is the chair of the English Department at Mt. Zion High School in Jonesboro, USA.

People who are against distance learning give several reasons for opposing it: lack of face-to-face contact between student and teacher; problems with technology resources (i.e. equipment and broadband internet) for low-income and rural students; insufficient teacher training.

In my experience, however, these problems can be solved by better teacher preparation and by gaining the essential technology skills before starting the actual coursework. I have found distance learning to be very valuable to the classes that I teach. In fact, ==I'm proud to say that my classroom is almost completely paperless.==

My students use lectures from the OER Commons (a free internet resource) to support our curriculum. For example, by using Dr Paul Fry's introduction to theory of literature course, we can bring the knowledge of Yale University to our study programme. ==Best of all, it's absolutely free.==

We use Skype for our writers' conferences and Global Speakers Series, which brings guest speakers from around the world into our classroom space. Even our literature study groups are done online now by using Collaborize Classroom and Google Docs for group projects. Our course blog, 'In Session: Sentiments from Silveri's Class', is an important space for writing and research, and it allows me to introduce videos, presentations and other documents.

My students can complete most of their coursework outside of class. The classroom time is reserved for further writing, discussion and debate. Our blog also has a ClustrMap. This shows us that students from all over the world are visiting our course blog and using our classroom from the comfort of their own homes.

==Now, imagine if distance learning is used in every classroom.== The knowledge and growth potential are vast.

STUDY SKILLS
READING STRATEGIES

1 There are two common techniques you can use when getting information from a text: *skimming* and *scanning*. Read the definitions, then answer the questions.

Skimming
You use skimming to get a general idea of a text. For example, you look through a text quickly to find out what the topic is and its main idea.

Scanning
You use scanning to find key words or specific points in a text. In most cases, you know what you are looking for, so you're focusing on finding a particular answer.

Which technique would you use to find:
1 the general opinion of a hotel from several online guest reviews?
2 a writer's opinion in a report on the future of distance learning?
3 a version of a popular song on YouTube by a singer you like?
4 an article in a magazine which was interesting and worth reading?
5 the score of your favourite team in a list of football results?
6 the cheapest price of a book from a range of prices in an online bookstore?

2 Predicting Before you read a text, it is helpful to use your knowledge to anticipate what the text is about. This is called predicting. It will improve your reading ability because you can check your predictions during your reading. Work with a partner to discuss the following.
1 What do you know about distance learning?
2 Are you for or against this method of learning?
3 What do you want to learn about the topic from the text?

3a Skimming Skim the text and answer the questions.
1 What is the main idea of the text?
2 Do you think that the text is interesting?

3b Scanning Now scan the text and find the following.
1 the two ways the writer uses to solve the problems mentioned in paragraph 1
2 where her students obtain lectures for additional reading
3 how she uses the real classroom space

3c Inferring When you read a text, you can form an opinion about the writer's meaning or attitude. For example, you infer why the writer wrote the text (the writer's purpose) or you may wish to infer the writer's attitude to what he or she is writing about. In small groups, discuss the following.
1 What do you think is the writer's purpose?
2 What is the writer's opinion about distance learning?
3 What can you infer from the ==highlighted== sentences?

STUDY AND WRITING SKILLS   6.5

4 Work with a partner to discuss the following.
1. What is your opinion of the methods the writer uses to teach her students?
2. Which do you prefer: traditional classroom learning or the distance learning approach of the writer?
3. Do your think distance learning will become more common than classroom learning in the future? Explain your answer.
4. Discuss the advantages and disadvantages of distance learning.

WRITING SKILLS
A FORMAL LETTER

5a Quickly read the letter from the Head of a Students' Union in a university. Then answer the questions.
1. What is the letter about?
2. Where will the event take place?

Mr Richard Kim
CEO, Education Unlimited
Kungsbruhn 85
Uppgang G8
11122 Stockholm
3200 Sweden

Head, Students' Union
University of Helensbrough
Scotland

Telephone: +44 (0) 206 548
Email: studentunion@helbro.ac.uk
21st August

Dear Mr Kim,

As head of the Students' Union at Helensbrough University, I would like to invite you to take part in a panel discussion on 'Digital Learning Resources' which will be held in the Students' Union building on 12 September from 2 p.m.– 4 p.m.

We would appreciate it greatly if you could join the panel as a guest speaker. A visiting lecturer at our university, Steffan Nielson, gave us your name. He suggested you would be an ideal person to have on our panel. You are an expert on the topic of digital learning, and we know that you are an adviser to colleges and universities all over the world on how to use digital resources. Your knowledge and insights would be immensely valuable for the undergraduates and graduates attending the discussion.

There will be three other experts on the panel in addition to a student representative. Each of you will make a short presentation of your ideas (5–10 minutes), after which there will be questions from the audience.

Following the event, we would like to take you for dinner to a local restaurant or, if you prefer, we could have dinner with you at your hotel.

We hope that you will agree to be a guest speaker and look forward to receiving your reply. If you need any further information, please do not hesitate to contact me.

Yours sincerely,

H Bloomfield

Helen Bloomfield: Head of Students' Union

5b Read the letter again and choose the correct answer to each question.
1. What is the title of the discussion?
   a Digital Resources
   b Digital Facilities
   c Digital Learning Resources
2. How did Helen Bloomfield hear about Mr Kim?
   a She saw his name in a journal.
   b Someone recommended him.
   c A student knew him well.
3. What does Mr Kim do when he travels abroad?
   a gives talks on the internet
   b makes presentations to schools
   c advises colleges and universities
4. How many people will be on the panel if Mr Kim accepts the invitation?
   a 3
   b 4
   c 5
5. What will Mr Kim do after the panel discussion?
   a answer questions
   b go to the airport
   c have dinner

6 Letter conventions Are these statements true or false? Correct the false statements.
1. A formal letter should always have a date.
2. You put the address of the person you are writing to directly under your address.
3. You should begin a formal letter with *Dear* + first name + surname.
4. If you begin your letter with *Dear* + name, you can finish the letter with *Yours sincerely* or *Kind regards*.
5. You should end a formal letter by signing it and typing your name and position under your signature.
6. In formal letters, you should use idiomatic phrases and short forms such as *I'm, we're, isn't, aren't*.

7a Make a list of things that Richard Kim might want to ask Helen Bloomfield. What additional information might he need, for example, travel information, accommodation arrangements, etc.?

7b As Mr Kim, write a reply to Helen Bloomfield.

8 Work with a partner and compare your letters. Did you ask the same questions? Comment on each other's letter organisation, language and style. Consider these questions.
- Do the paragraphs have a logical order?
- Is the language grammatically correct?
- Is the vocabulary appropriate and well chosen?
- Is the style of the letter appropriate for the context and person who receives the letter?

7 Design

7.1 DESIGN IS EVERYWHERE

IN THIS UNIT

GRAMMAR
- modals (necessity and obligation)
- modals (present deduction)

VOCABULARY
- word building
- design adjectives
- materials, shapes and textures
- abstract nouns

SCENARIO
- describing qualities
- evaluating designs

STUDY SKILLS
- proofreading

WRITING SKILLS
- a product report

Design occupies a unique space between art and science. Terence Conran, 1931–, British designer

READING

1 Think about objects in your home. Which do you think are particularly well designed? Why?

2a Look at these extracts from an introduction to a design book. In which extract does the writer mention these things?

a incorrect ideas about design
b the essential element in good design
c what design is
d the restrictions on designers
e what designers do

2b Read the extracts again and correct the statements below.
1 Designers are the same as scientists and engineers.
2 Magazines rarely make mistakes when talking about design.
3 Design is all about appearance.
4 The secret of good design is to be new and different.
5 Designers, like artists, have a lot of freedom.

2c Reacting to the text Which idea in the text is the most interesting? Why?

What is design?

1 THE WORD 'DESIGN' means different things to different people. One definition given by designer Richard Seymour is 'making things better for people'.

2 Scientists can invent technologies, manufacturers can make products, engineers can make them work, and salespeople can sell them. However, only designers can combine all these. Designers turn an idea into something that is desirable, commercially successful and adds value to people's lives.

3 Good design begins with the needs of the user. A good design fulfils a user's need. A design doesn't have to be new, different or impressive to be successful in the market place, but it must fulfil a need. However, it is also true that design methods often lead to innovative products and services.

4 Many people have misconceptions about design. Magazines often use the word 'design' when they mean style or fashion. For example, when they show a toaster or bottle opener which is well designed, the result is that people think that design is only about how things look. Design is also about how things work. In reality, the way a product looks is something which happens at the end of a product development process.

5 Designers, unlike artists, can't simply follow their creative feelings. They work in a commercial environment, which means there are many points to consider. Designers have to ask themselves questions such as: 'Is the product really wanted?', 'How is it different from everything else on the market?', 'Does it fulfil a need?', 'Will it cost too much to manufacture?' and 'Is it safe?'.

7.1 DESIGN IS EVERYWHERE

VOCABULARY
WORD BUILDING, DESIGN ADJECTIVES

3a Work with a partner to complete the word families in the table below. Check your answers in the text.

3b Look at the suffixes (endings) of the words in the table. What type of word ends in:
1 -ic? adj
2 -er? pers
3 -ion? n
4 -ing? n
5 -or? n

verb	noun (person)	noun (thing, concept)	adjective
design	er		ing
	ist	'science	scientific
	erer	manu'facturing	
pro'duce	producer	product / produce	pro'ductive
engineer	er	engineering	
ua	er	use	usable
develop	de'veloper		developing
innovate	'innovator	innovation	
invent	inventor	in'vention	inventive
		art	artistic

PRONUNCIATION

4 [7.1] **Word stress** Look at the words in the table and mark the stress. Some have been done as examples to help you. Listen and check, then repeat the words.

5a Complete these questions using words from the table. Sometimes more than one answer is possible.
1 Can you name an _____? What did he/she invent?
2 Are there any factories in your town/city? What do they _____?
3 What are the three _____ you could not live without?
4 What do you think is the best _____ of the 21st century?
5 Is the _____ of a product important to you? Why?/Why not?
6 What products do you think _____ will develop in the next ten years?

5b Work with a partner and ask and answer the questions above.

5c Write some questions of your own to ask other students using words from the table in Exercise 3.

6a The following adjectives are often used to describe designs. Work with a partner to check that you understand them all.

elegant functional futuristic handmade
innovative mass-produced retro simple
streamlined stylish traditional up-to-date

6b Find words in Exercise 6a that refer to the following.
1 the past (2 words) retro traditional
2 methods of manufacture (2 words) handmade mass-produced
3 designs which are new and different (2 words) innovative futuristic

6c Find words in Exercise 6a that mean the following.
1 attractive and fashionable stylish
2 modern up to date
3 with a smooth shape streamlined
4 attractive and graceful elegant
5 not complicated simple
6 useful functional

SPEAKING AND WRITING

7a Think about the following items. In small groups, discuss what qualities you look for in them. Look back at the vocabulary in Exercise 6a to help you.

phone   car   shoes   handbag   watch

use a photo if you like!

7b Look at the photos below. Say which design of car and phone you prefer and why.

8 Write a short paragraph describing your favourite design, either on this page or of an object you own.

7.2 DESIGN THROUGH THE AGES

READING AND VOCABULARY
MATERIALS, SHAPES AND TEXTURES

1a Designers need to think about the following when designing new products: material, shape, texture. Look at the words in the box and put them into the correct category.

steel	smooth	curved	leather	rough	angular
aluminium		canvas	wooden	polished	square
plastic	soft	circular	paper	straw	hard

1b Look at the three chairs in the photos. How would you describe each one?

1c Which do you prefer? Why? (Think about comfort, style, practicality, etc.)

2 You are going to read about design during three different decades of the 20th century: the 1930s, the 1960s and the 1990s. Before you read, discuss the following in small groups.
1 Look at the photos of the chairs. Which of the three periods does each chair come from?
2 Look at the ideas in the box below which influenced design at the different times. Discuss in which period you think they are mentioned and why.

advances in communication	recycling
young consumers	short-lived products
streamlining (smooth in shape)	
ergonomic design (designs adapted to human needs)	

3a Work in groups of three. Read your text quickly, then share your information with your group. Compare the information with your ideas from Exercise 2.

Student A: Read the text above.
Student B: Read the text on page 160.
Student C: Read the text on page 163.

3b Read your text again and complete the chart for your text. Then in your groups, summarise the key facts about your text so that the others in your group can complete the chart.

	1930s	1960s	1990s
Ideas	streamlining		
Designers			
Products			
Materials			

4a *Justifying opinions* Work on your own.
Which design period was for you:
• the most exciting?
• the most useful?
• the most interesting?

Make notes on the reasons for your choices.

4b Work in groups and present and justify your choices.

DESIGN THROUGH THE AGES 7.2

1960–1969

THIS WAS a period of optimism and self-belief. At this time humans travelled faster than sound and walked on the Moon. During the period, the power of advertising, particularly on television, created mass consumerism, with a huge increase in the buying and selling of new types of products. Manufacturers began to recognise the buying power of teenagers and started to develop products aimed at the youth market. These new young consumers wanted change and variety. It was a time of short-lived products and the idea of a 'throwaway' society. New materials, new shapes, and new colours appeared in all areas of design.

There were many unusual furniture designs. The Danish designer Verner Panton produced his bright red plastic chair, for example, and Eero Aarnio created his extraordinary Ball Chair.

The ideas of this period, also known as the 'space age', also influenced fashion. Designers created clothes in strange and futuristic materials. Courreges' 'silver foil' suits and Pierre Cardin's silver and plastic dress designs were examples of this.

VOCABULARY
ABSTRACT NOUNS

5a Find the noun forms of the verbs below in the texts.
1 advertise
2 consume
3 industrialise
4 recycle
5 communicate
6 streamline

5b Complete the questions below with the nouns from Exercise 5a.
1 Is there enough _____ of harmful products like batteries?
2 Do _____ and curved shapes make products look more stylish?
3 Is _____ the best way to get people to buy products?
4 Is _____ leading to people becoming more selfish?
5 Has _____ damaged the Earth so much that it cannot recover?
6 Does better _____ technology lead to better lives?

5c Work with a partner and ask and answer the questions above.

LISTENING

6 7.2 Listen to two designers talking about ideas for a new product and answer the questions.
1 What product do they discuss?
2 Who will use the product?
3 What materials do they mention?
4 When do they want to launch the product?

GRAMMAR
MODALS (NECESSITY AND OBLIGATION)

7 Underline the modal verbs in these sentences. Then use the verbs to complete the statements below.
1 We need to reach as many people as possible.
2 We can't use steel.
3 We should make it in just three colours.
4 It must be cheap if we want to be competitive.
5 It doesn't have to be very different.
6 The rules say it has to be strong enough to support a heavy person.
7 We don't need to rush.
8 We really mustn't miss this opportunity.
9 We shouldn't launch it until we're really ready.
10 I can do some designs before we meet again.

To talk about:
a things that are important and necessary to do we use _____, _____ and _____.
b things that are not essential (i.e. where you have a choice) we use _____ and _____.
c rules and regulations we often use _____ and _____.
d when it is necessary and important *not* to do something we use _____ and _____.
e something that is advisable we use _____.
f something that is not advisable we use _____.

→ Language reference and extra practice, pages 138–139

8 Choose the correct modal verb.
1 This material *doesn't have to / mustn't* be used as it harms people's health.
2 In some countries you *don't need to / can't* show certain images in your designs.
3 There's a problem with the design, but it *doesn't have to / shouldn't* take us much time to resolve. We *have to / should* finish it today!
4 We *shouldn't / have to* change the shape of the model so that it meets government regulations.
5 We *don't need to / must* hire that designer. She's the best in the business.
6 It's not breaking any regulations, but I think we *should / have to* change the design.

SPEAKING

9 Work in groups. You are going to design a product.
1 Choose one of these products: a chair, a table, a kettle, a toothbrush, a coffee machine.
2 Decide which group of consumers you are aiming at, e.g. older people, young adults, children, etc.
3 Discuss your ideas and sketch a design. Think about shape, colour, materials, size, appearance, rules and regulations. Try to use modal verbs.

▶ MEET THE EXPERT

Watch an interview with Freyja Sewell, a furniture and product designer, about her designs.
Turn to page 152 for video activities.

7.3 ALESSI'S INNOVATIONS

READING

1 Look at the photos. What are they? Would you like to own any of these Alessi designer products? Why?/Why not?

2a Read the article about Alessi quickly and find the following.
1 the name of one great artist
2 the names of three members of the Alessi family
3 the names of three Alessi products
4 the names of three designers that have worked for Alessi

2b *Identifying main ideas* Read the article again and match the headings to the paragraphs.
a The way forward
b The importance of design
c How designs are developed
d Famous designers
e International expansion

2c Find words in the text which mean the following.
1 someone or something that is not successful (para 1)
2 to change (para 2)
3 the use of new ideas or methods (para 2)
4 introducing new methods for the first time (para 3)
5 a great idea about what you should do (para 3)
6 something famous that is admired by many (para 4)

ALESSI'S *inventions*

1 ____
Italians only keep beautiful and useful things in their homes, an Italian friend once told me. Perhaps that's why most of them love Alessi, the famous Italian design company. Alessi rates design very highly, even placing it above profitability. The president, Alberto, does not worry about his failures, according to an article in Fast Company. He holds his meetings with designers in the Alessi private museum, which contains material from all of Alessi's products including some flops, to remind him about the importance of taking risks. Alberto believes that the most original design concepts come from the borderline between what is possible and what is not.

2 ____
The company was founded in 1921 by Giovanni Alessi, Alberto's grandfather. Giovanni's son, Carlo, began Alessi's tradition of design. It was Alberto, however, who transformed the company into a world-wide success by employing freelance designers, increasing exports, and enhancing its reputation for beautiful, useful products and innovation. Alessi's core business is metal working and the company continues to use metal, e.g. stainless steel, primarily. However, Alessi has also introduced the use of other materials such as plastic, which is easier to mould and a cheaper material to produce, to incorporate the idea of fun into design.

3 ____
When Alberto began working at Alessi at twenty-four, one of his first projects was 'Alessi d'Après'. He commissioned Salvador Dalí and other artists to design a piece of art to be mass-produced and available for the general public. The pioneering project was very difficult so after a while his father, Carlo, stopped production, but not before Dalí created an object for the company. Apparently nobody knows what the product's purpose was, but commissioning these artists shows Alberto Alessi's inspiration, and indicates why Alberto places such importance on learning from every project, even if unsuccessful. As a result, the company uses a formula to decide whether designs should be developed which emphasises whether they have a practical function, whether they please the senses, and if they fit with current trends and confer status on the owner. It is also important that the product can be sold at a reasonable price.

4 ____
Richard Sapper, Aldo Rossi and Philippe Starck are just some of the great designers that have worked for Alessi. The company has created many icons, such as Starck's 'Juicy Salif' citrus squeezer, the 'Anna G.' corkscrew and the 'Mami' stockpot, which was designed by Stefano Giovannoni.

5 ____
Alessi is no longer only a manufacturer of kitchen and tableware products. Its range has included watches, cordless telephones, bulbs and lights, glasses and even cars. Alessi recently paired with Fiat to design the Fiat Panda Alessi, which features internet access and has a picture of the Alessi man on its wheels! This world-wide Italian company can be expected to continue its tradition of promoting the very best design whilst forever reinventing itself.

ALESSI'S INNOVATIONS 7.3

LISTENING

3a 🔊 7.3 Listen to three pairs of students at a museum of design. In which order do they talk about the things below?

3b Listen again. Are these sentences true, false or not given?
1 The first design is by da Vinci. T (sign) *flys* *before*
2 This design is over 500 years old. NG
3 Da Vinci's most famous painting is the Mona Lisa. NG
4 Pablo and Irina are looking at a corkscrew. T *must be*
5 The corkscrew was designed in the early 1980s. F *1994*
6 The third object is the designer's best-selling design. NG
7 George would like to buy one of these. F *bestseller*

GRAMMAR
MODALS (PRESENT DEDUCTION)

4a Look at Audio script 7.3 on page 170 and underline the modal verbs *must*, *can't*, *might* and *could*. Look at the words around them.

4b Match each modal verb with one of these meanings.
1 It can't be true. **c**   a I think this is possible.
2 It might/could be true. **a**   b I'm certain that this is true.
3 It must be true. **b**   c I'm certain that this is not true.

4c Look at the modal verbs in Exercise 4b. What is the opposite of *must be* when we are talking about deduction?

➡ Language reference and extra practice pages 138–139

5 Rewrite the sentences below using *must*, *can't*, *could* or *might*.
1 I'm sure this design is by Armani.
   This design must be by Armani.
2 Alessi is definitely one of the most influential design companies of all time. **must be**
3 I'm sure this painting is not by da Vinci. **can't**
4 Maybe this painting is by Picasso, but I'm not sure. **could**
5 Not many people are attending the exhibition. I'm sure they aren't promoting it very well. **can't**
6 This product looks dangerous to me. **must**
7 People are not sure if it is a Starck design. **could**
8 I'm sure that designer is working very hard. I've seen a lot of her designs. **must**

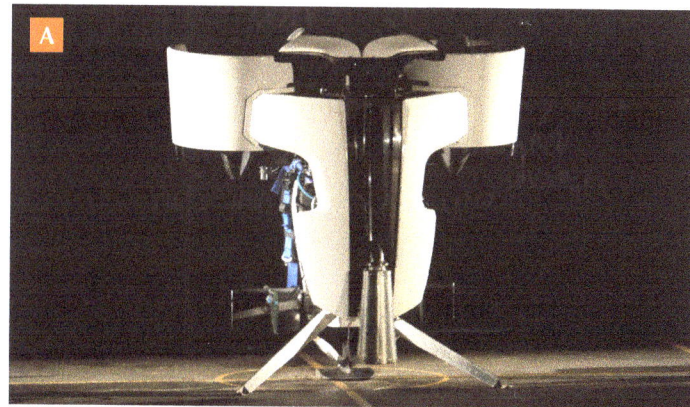

6 Work with a partner to discuss what you think the designs above are. Try to use these words and phrases.

must   might   could   can't   I'm sure/certain …
maybe/perhaps …   It's possible that …
It's not possible that …

SPEAKING

7 If you had the skills, what would you like to design/re-design?

71

7.4 SCENARIO
MARTELLI DESIGN COMPETITION

SITUATION

1 The advert below appeared in the design magazine *Trendsetter*. Read the advert and answer the questions.

1. Who can enter the competition?
2. How can a competitor get an entry form?
3. What is the purpose of the competition?

Francisco Martelli
Design competition

The competition is open to young designers who are still studying or who have graduated during the last five years. Entry forms will shortly be sent to design schools, university departments and design studios all over the world.

The competition is open to any designer who has produced a prototype of their design. The aim of the competition is to recognise and reward outstanding product designs.

Total prize money is $20,000.

FOR FURTHER INFORMATION,
PLEASE VISIT
www.martellispritze.com/international

KEY LANGUAGE
DESCRIBING QUALITIES

2a 7.4 Listen to one of the judges commenting on a design which won first prize last year. The product is a travel jacket. Answer the questions.
1. What kind of person would buy it?
2. What special features does the jacket have?
3. What reasons does the judge give for suggesting the jacket should win first prize?

2b Listen again and complete the sentences.
1. As you can see, it _____ very modern and stylish.
2. It's _____ _____ young people. It will _____ _____ people who are on the move.
3. It has several special _____.
4. One of the jacket's best _____, I'd say, is that the zips have a lifetime guarantee.
5. The jacket has two _____ features.
6. It's _____ _____ a new material which is very strong, _____ and heat resistant.
7. Another strong _____ is the _____ on the sleeve.
8. The jacket's durable, _____, easy to use and, above all, _____.

2c Work in pairs. Think of an article of clothing you own, or would like to own, for example a coat or jacket. Describe it to your partner, using some of the language from Exercise 2b.

TASK
EVALUATING DESIGNS

3a Work in groups of four. You are judges for this year's competition and will choose the winning design. Choose one product each from the text on page 73. Read the description and take notes on the key points.

3b Describe your product to the other judges in your group. You may add extra information you wish to cover all the catagories. Complete the evaluation form for the other three products as you listen to the other judges. Marks are out of ten. Do not evaluate your own product.

	Design ____	Design ____	Design ____
stylish			
innovative			
functional			
easy to use			
durable			
value for money			
TOTAL			

3c Add up the marks of the three judges for each product and find the winner.

7.4 MARTELLI DESIGN COMPETITION

A wheelchair

A user-friendly wheelchair with several innovative features. It has only five main components: two side wheels, a seat, a seat back, a foot rest and four lights. Because of this, it's lightweight and easy to maintain, take apart, assemble and transport. It allows users to quickly access a car or plane. It's ergonomic and easy to push. A unique feature is that it is very visible at night because of its powerful lights and coating of luminous paint. Its frame is made of carbon fibre, and can be adapted to each person's size and weight.

Suggested price: $899

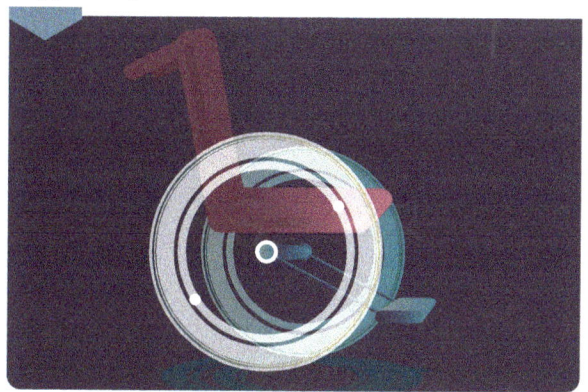

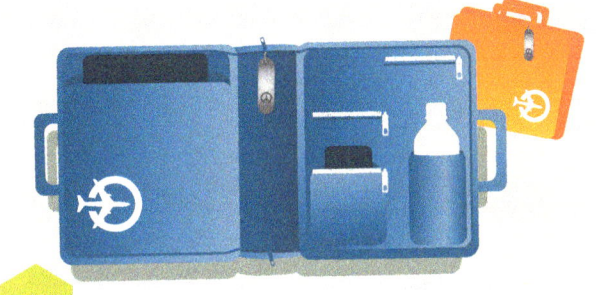

A carry-on airline bag

A stylish, elegant carry-on bag for men and women. It is ideal for use on budget airlines because passengers are usually allowed only one piece of luggage. It will appeal to fashion-conscious travellers because its silver identity tag and logo have a unique design. The bag is small and compact, measuring only 35cm x 30cm x 16cm, but it can hold many items without looking bulky. It has three small pockets with zips and one large compartment. There is also a special pocket for a water bottle. It comes in five colours.

Qualities: Well constructed, durable, versatile, with a place for everything. Ideal for short flights when you carry a lot of technological items such as smart phones, laptops and tablets.

Suggested price: $140

A sports watch

Taptap is a sports watch for athletes. It aims to provide information which will help athletes to improve their performance, but it also acts as a standard, everyday watch. It has several innovative features. It has advanced tap screen technology, so it is very easy to use. The athlete simply taps the screen to activate the various functions of the watch, such as the stop watch and display of running times. It has a unique alarm system which will appeal to long-distance runners. The alarm tells the runner when he or she needs to have more water or food. The watch has a long-lasting battery which lasts at least three years. It is water resistant up to 120 metres, so it will also appeal to people who enjoy water sports. Taptap looks sporty and fashionable. Its face and case is silver, and it has a wide, rubber strap, available in several colours.

Suggested price: $199

A study area (desk and bed unit)

This unit is perfect for students living in small rooms, preparing for examinations.

It consists of a desk and eight drawers for storing things. The desk is exceptionally sturdy.

Above the desk is a bed. An innovative feature is that the height of the bed can be adjusted quickly and easily to the height of the room.

A solid wood staircase with wide steps leads up to the bed. There is a shelf at the headboard for holding books and a light. The ergonomic chair is specially designed for students who sit for long periods of time. It won a design award recently at an international exhibition of furniture in Geneva.

Qualities: The study unit is innovative, functional and space saving.

Suggested price: $1,200

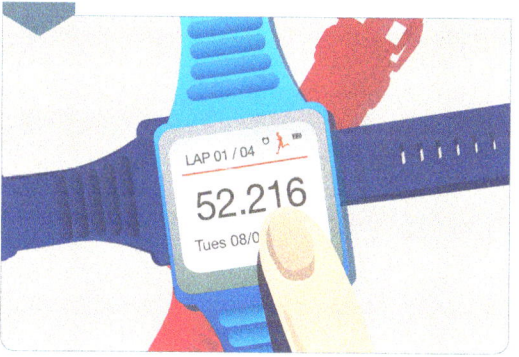

7.5 STUDY AND WRITING SKILLS

STUDY SKILLS
PROOFREADING

1 Work in pairs or small groups to discuss these questions.
1 When you write a formal document, e.g. a formal email, essay or report, do you prefer to use pen and paper first or to write directly onto a screen? Explain your answer.
2 Do you ever edit your own work or other people's work?
3 Which of the tools do you use in your work or studies?
   a an online dictionary   c a grammar check
   b a spell check   d a word count
4 What other digital tools do you use?

2a It is important to make sure your writing is accurate and your meaning clear. You are going to listen to a lecturer giving some tips on checking written work. Work with a partner. What points do you think she will mention?

2b 7.5 Listen to the conversation. Note down the points the lecturer mentions. Are they the same as the points you discussed in Exercise 2a?

2c Listen again and answer the questions.
1 What examples does the lecturer give of the following mistakes?
   a spelling   b irregular verbs   c prepositions
2 Complete the final piece of advice she gives.
   'Is my meaning _____?' 'Will someone _____ my work _____ what I'm trying to say?'

3 What are the main problems you have when you write in English? What mistakes do you often make?

4 Proofreading Eastern University plans to buy a hundred bicycles for students to hire during the university year. Read the report on two bicycles, written by the university's Purchasing Officer, Debora Carr. There are some errors in it. Find the following errors in the report.
   a four incorrect spellings
   b two missing capital letters
   c one missing full stop
   d two incorrect apostrophes
   e one example of incorrect word order
   f a phrase that is repeated unnecessarily
   g one incorrect tense
   h two incorrect prepositions

Report on two hybrid bicycles: Trekker 101 and Groundbreaker

Introduction
At the request of Jeremy Schooler, vice President of eastern University, this report
5 compares two hybrid bicycles and recommends one of the models to be purchased by the university

Price
10 There is a significant price difference between the two bicycles. Trekker 101 costs €460. It is much cheeper than Groundbreaker which costs €540.

Size
15 The bicycles are similar on length but not in weigh. Trekker 101 weighs just 14.1 kg whereas Groundbreaker weighs 16.4 kg.

Rider Position
20 On both bicycles, the rider is positioned right at the back so that so that he or she is centred over the rear wheel. Both
25 bicycles are suitable to riders up to 175 cm tall. For someone over that height, Groundbreaker is more suitable.

The seat
30 The Groundbreaker seat is more comfortable and can be adjusted easily. To adjust the Trekker 101 seat, you need a special tool.

TREKKER 101

Performance:
35 a *Riding along*
Trekker 101 is lighter. It is, therefore, much faster on flat ground, but is it not good on bumpy surfaces. Groundbreaker is slower but gives a
40 much smoother ride on rough surfaces.

b *Cornering*
Both bicyles corner well and feel stable, even in slippery conditions. Groundbreakers' stability is good when
45 cornering but it is slower because of its extra weight.

c *Climbing*
Both bicycles are performing well when climbing. Trekker 101 can accellerate
50 faster on the steep sections of a hill. Groundbreaker is better if the rider has to climb several hills in a short time.

GROUNDBREAKER

Gears
The highest and lowest gears of both
55 bicycles are the same. Nevertheless, Groundbreaker has a big advantage. It's gear change is much faster and smoother.

Conclusion and Recommendation
The university should purchase the
60 Groundbreaker model. It is built for strength and durability, which are important qualities for hire bicycles. It performs much better on rough surfaces. This is important because many of our
65 students will want to ride the bicycles in the forest and mountain areas.

Signed: Ms Debora Carr, Purchasing Office
Date: 16 September …

STUDY AND WRITING SKILLS 7.5

5 Read the report and answer the questions.
1 Which bicycle:
   a is cheaper?
   b is lighter?
   c is faster?
   d will probably last longer?
   e has a more flexible seat?
   f has a better gear change?
2 What similar features do both bicycles have?
3 Why does the writer of the report prefer the Groundbreaker?

WRITING SKILLS
A PRODUCT REPORT

6a Linkers Look at the words in italics in each sentence below. Which word/phrase is used to show: a contrast, additional information, a result?
1 Trekker 101 is lighter. *Therefore*, it is much faster on flat ground.
2 Groundbreaker's gear change is faster. *Moreover*, it is much smoother.
3 Groundbreaker is heavier. *On the other hand*, it is stronger and more durable.

6b Work with a partner. Decide whether the words in the box introduce a result, a contrast or additional information. Try to add one more word/phrase to each group.

| also | although | as a result | consequently |
| furthermore | however | in addition | whereas |

7 Link the pairs of sentences using an appropriate word/phrase from Exercise 6.
1 Groundbreaker's seat can be adjusted easily. You need a special tool to adjust Trekker 101's seat.
2 Both bicycles climb well. Trekker 101 can accelerate faster.
3 Trekker 101 is cheaper than Groundbreaker. It is much lighter.
4 Both bicycles are suitable for riding in town. They are ideal for riding on mountain tracks.
5 Groundbreaker is a heavier bicycle. It is slower when going round tight corners.
6 Trekker 101 is suitable for medium-sized riders. Groundbreaker is much better for tall people.

8 The head of a large airline has asked you to write a report on two top-of-the-range headphones, recommending one of them for use in the airline's First Class cabins. Write the report, using the notes on the right.

New › Edit   My notes

KristalClear Headphones
Price: US$ 180
Weight: 170g
Design: Attractive and stylish. 5-star rating (outstanding) from Sound and Vision magazine.
Over-the-ear headphones. Comfortable, easily adjustable, thin headband, might wear out quickly.
Colours: Black, metallic silver and red
Sound: Bass tones not very powerful. High-end tones excellent. Best for classical or light pop music.
Noise: Sound doesn't leak out and annoy people. Blocks out most outside noise.
Durability: Well made. Cable maybe a bit weak.
Special feature(s): A unique sound system greatly reduces outside noise. Headband flexible and easily adjustable.
Overall impression: Great style and sound quality, affordable price.

Sonar Headphones 3001
Price: US$ 265
Weight: 185g
Design: Attractive and stylish. 3-star rating from Sound and Vision magazine.
On-the-ear headphones. Comfortable – headphones cover the whole ear. Rather heavy and bulky (take up a lot of space). Headband – flexible plastic wrapped in soft leather. Strong cable.
Colours: Black, white and grey
Sound: Powerful and deep bass tones. Good high-end sounds. Lots of energy and power. Headphones best for electronic, hard rock or urban music.
Noise: Keeps away some outside noise. Not a strong feature of the headphones.
Durability: Well built, strong construction. Made to last.
Special feature(s): Control system on the cable. Users can turn the sound up and down.
Sponge pads on the headphones covered in soft leather. Very comfortable.
Overall impression: Well constructed, excellent bass and high-end sounds. Not cheap. Good sound quality + durability.

8 Business
8.1 IN BUSINESS

IN THIS UNIT

GRAMMAR
- past continuous
- past perfect simple

VOCABULARY
- business terms and roles
- collocations (2)

SCENARIO
- the language of negotiation
- negotiating

STUDY SKILLS
- recognising formal and informal language

WRITING SKILLS
- formal and informal correspondence

Eat and drink with your relatives; do business with strangers. Greek proverb

VOCABULARY AND READING
BUSINESS TERMS AND ROLES

1 Work with a partner to discuss these questions.

1. Can you name a successful business from your country?
2. Can you name a business from another country which is successful in your country?
3. Why do you think these businesses are so successful?

2a Complete the statements with the words in the box.

| community | competitors | customer | law |
| loss | prices | profit | staff | taxes | wages |

To succeed in business you should:

1. value your _____.
2. focus only on making a big _____.
3. pay employees low _____.
4. charge high _____.
5. never break the _____.
6. avoid paying _____ to the government.
7. believe the _____ is always right.
8. invest in the local _____.
9. put your _____ out of business.
10. be prepared to make a _____ for at least the first year.

2b Work with a partner to discuss the statements.

The secret of my success

The retailer
'Well, the customer is not god, but it is a good thing to believe they are always right. When you sell luxury products you need to charge high prices if you want to be taken seriously. But remember, high prices don't always mean making big profits. Shops and retail can be difficult to get right.'

The entrepreneur
'Well, you have to prepare carefully. Do your market research, then set up your business. And be prepared to make a loss during the first year. That's the most difficult time. Get it right, and it's the best thing in the world. I work alone, but I get a lot of help from my family.'

The partner
'My first business failed. I went into business with my best friend, but it just didn't work. My new partner is simply a financial investor. I run the business on a day-to-day basis. But you need good people around you. I value my staff and the company is doing well because we are a strong team.'

76

IN BUSINESS 8.1

3 Match the people in the box with their role.

customer   entrepreneur   manufacturer   partner
retailer   supplier   wholesaler

1 sells directly to the public
2 makes goods
3 starts new businesses
4 is one of the owners of a business
5 buys large quantities of goods from producers and sells them to shops and businesses
6 buys directly from a shop or a company
7 provides goods/parts to shops and businesses

4a Read a page from a website on starting a new business. Whose advice do you think is the best for your situation? Which of the business areas would you prefer to work in?

4b Read the webpage again and underline examples of the vocabulary from Exercises 2a and 3.

5 Work in groups to discuss the following.
1 Which are your favourite retailers?
2 Name three large manufacturers.
3 What services can a wholesaler offer a retailer?
4 Give an example of good/bad customer service you have experienced.
5 What problems can a business have with its suppliers?
6 Can you name a famous entrepreneur?
7 If you started a business, who would your partner be? Why?

LISTENING

6a Allan Smith appears regularly on the radio giving advice on starting a business. What advice do you think he might give?

6b **8.1** Listen to the first part of an interview with him and answer the questions.
1 In his first tip, Allan mentions four areas of business. What are they? *finance, tax, selling, marketing*
2 Which of the following does Allan mention in his second tip? *marketing – must make a profit*
   • advertising   • promotion
   ✓ price   ✓ competitors
   ✓ costs   • tax
3 What does Allan think the 'key to success' might be? *marketing – different way to different pzpl*

6c **8.2** Listen to the second part of the interview and complete the summary.
Firstly, some failed because the market had ¹ *moved on*, and the business was left behind. The second reason was over-dependence on one ² *main customer*. Other reasons are poor ³ *planning*, cash flow problems, bad debts and not dealing with ⁴ *tax* properly.

6d **8.3** Listen to the third part of the interview. Are these statements true, false or not given?
1 Business plans are very important. *T*
2 Business plans help to improve sales. *NG*
3 You should keep your business plans in your head. *F*
4 At the beginning, you may make mistakes when you forecast. *T*

7 **Summarising** In your opinion, what are the key pieces of advice which Allan gives? Summarise these as Dos and Don'ts.

SPEAKING

8 **8.4** Listen to two people talking about an idea for a business in their home town. Answer the questions.
1 What type of business is it? What's its name? *car washing*
2 What advantages of the business are mentioned? *low cost equipment*
3 Do you think it is a good idea? Why?/Why not? *supermarket lot   car klean discount*

9 You have ten minutes to plan a business idea to start in your home town. Work with a partner and choose an idea from below or think of your own.

a garden care service   selling second-hand items
a mobile hairdressing service   selling fresh flowers

Think about the name and location of the business, the goods or services you will offer and your target market.

The manufacturer
'I run a successful manufacturing business with three factories, thanks to careful management and not taking risks. Thinking about the future is the key. It's important to put money back into the business, but make sure you leave enough to pay your taxes and wages! We also try to invest in the local community, to put something back. We sponsor the local football team.

 ▶ MEET THE EXPERT

Watch an interview with Teresa Le about the Vietnamese food business she set up in London.
Turn to page 153 for video activities.

8.2 BUSINESS DILEMMAS

READING

1 Work with a partner to discuss these ethical dilemmas.
1 Your best friend gives you an expensive birthday present. You do not like it. What do you do?
2 Your friend's husband has lost his job – you've seen him at the job centre. His wife doesn't know this. Would you tell her?

2a Read the three texts quickly and match them with the following ethical problems.
a You have information that could damage the company you work for.
b A company that gave you an expensive present is trying to become a supplier for your company.
c You have a colleague who is not honest.

1

You work in the clothing department of a store

Your friend, Julia, works in the same department. She is a good friend who supported you when the two of you didn't get a good bonus at the end of last year. There was a lot of shoplifting in the clothing department at that time: *people were stealing expensive items like designer shirts and silk ties.* Your boss said that you weren't paying enough attention to your work and didn't deserve a good bonus.

Yesterday, you were having a drink with Julia after work in a local café and you noticed that Julia had two new men's shirts in her bag. 'Wow! They look expensive,' you commented. Julia laughed. 'You don't think I paid for them, do you? I take a few things from time to time to make up for our rotten bonuses.'

3

You are Chief Executive of a car manufacturer.

You visited an overseas supplier some time ago, and when you left, he gave you an expensive watch as a present. On returning, you were planning to tell your colleagues about the present, but forgot.

Last week, you were sitting in your office when another present from the same supplier arrived. It was a magnificent antique clock! At the time, you were considering three competing offers to supply radios for a new range of cars. Your generous supplier had made one of the offers. His firm's radios were more expensive than those of another supplier, while the quality of the products was similar. You have never done business before with the supplier of the cheaper radios.

2

You are an environmental manager for a chemical firm.

All last year, the company was looking for ways of reducing costs because it was making a loss. It decided, therefore, to cut back on investment in technology.

As a result, the company did not spend money on buying some expensive new equipment which reduces a special toxin in waste water. At present, scientists don't know exactly how poisonous this toxin is, and your waste is within legal limits. However, the polluted waste from the factory flows into a nearby lake and river. It seems to be affecting fish and wildlife, and a local scientist has warned that people should not eat fish caught in the river.

If you tell the press or the local authorities about the waste water, the firm will have to buy the expensive equipment. The company could go bankrupt and everyone, including yourself, would lose their jobs.

BUSINESS DILEMMAS 8.2

2b Read the texts again. Are these statements true or false?

Text 1
1 Your manager complained that you (Julia's friend) were not paying enough attention to him. F
2 Julia said she stole things because she did not get a decent bonus. T

Text 2
3 The company was acting illegally. F
4 The expensive equipment could stop the company going bankrupt. F

Text 3
5 You did not tell your colleagues about the expensive watch. T
6 You were given an expensive watch, an antique clock and some radios as gifts. F

3 What do the following words highlighted in the text refer to?

1 them   5 he
2 it   6 It
3 It   7 those
4 their

SPEAKING

4a Reacting to the topic In groups, discuss these questions.

1 What would you do in the situations described in the texts if you were:
   a Julia's friend?
   b the environmental manager?
   c the Chief Executive?
2 What punishment, if any, do you think Julia should receive?
3 Is there a difference between a gift and a bribe?

4b Work with a partner. Talk about a time when you or a person/company that you know had to make a difficult ethical decision.

GRAMMAR
PAST CONTINUOUS

x state verbs
be, know, like, believe

5 Look at the examples of the past continuous in *italics* in the texts and match them with their uses. Look at the context in the text to help you.

a for a longer background action in the past when a shorter action interrupts it or happens during it
b for repeated actions in the past that take place over a period of time
c to emphasise the duration or continuity of a past action

➔ Language reference and extra practice pages 140–141

6 Match the beginnings of the sentences with the endings. Then write out the sentences in full with the verbs in the correct form (past continuous or past simple).

1 c I (meet) my old boss   met + c
2 d IBM (offer) me a job   offered + d
3 e The company (have) financial problems were having + e
4 b I (work) at my computer   was working + b
5 f She (find) the missing file   found + f
6 a We (talk) about our future strategy in a meeting were talking + a

a when the Chief Executive suddenly (announce) her resignation. announced
b when the power cut (happen). happened
c while I (travel) to Warsaw for a conference. was travelling
d while I (study) at Harvard. was studying
e when a fantastic new contract (be) agreed. was
f while she (look for) some other documents. was looking for

PRONUNCIATION   + G1 if necessary

7a 8.5 **Weak forms** Listen to the following sentences. Circle the weak forms (/wəz/ and /wə/) and underline the strong forms (/wɒz/ and /wɜː/) of *was* and *were*.

1 We were having a meeting when the fire alarm went off.
2 When the phone rang, I was talking to a customer.
3 'Was he working for you then?' 'No, he wasn't.'
4 'Were they planning to buy another shop?' 'Well, they said they were.'

7b Listen again and repeat the sentences.

8a Work on your own. Choose one of the events and make notes to answer the questions below.

- an accident at home or work
- a big event in your school's/company's recent history
- an important world or national event
- a big family event (e.g. the birth of a child)

Where were you when this happened?
Who were you with?
What were you doing?
What did you do next?

8b Work in groups and share your stories.

When I first heard about the earthquake, I was having lunch with a friend.

WRITING

9 Write a short paragraph describing the event you discussed in Exercise 8.

8.3 BUSINESS ICONS

READING

1 In groups, discuss these questions.
1 What famous brands do you know for cosmetics, soft drinks, sports clothing and technology?
2 What do you know about the people who started these brands?

2 Work with a partner to read about some business icons. Try to answer as many of the questions below as you can. Share your answers with your partner.

Student A: Read texts 1 and 2 on this page.
Student B: Turn to page 160 and read texts 3 and 4.

1 What area of business was each person in?
2 What was each person most famous for?
3 Who started out:
   a as a bus conductor?
   b as a lawyer?
   c as a scientist?
   d working in a hardware store?
4 Who:
   a used words from two languages to come up with the name for their company?
   b thought that you did not need to succeed at university in order to succeed in business?
5 Which two people:
   a were very good sales people?
   b liked sports?
   c had a connection with Austria?
   d wrote a book?
   e came from a poor family background?
6 Which person:
   a didn't have a business partner?
   b was born first?
   c lived the longest?
   d had the most children?

3 Identifying similarities and differences
Work in small groups to discuss these questions.
1 What are the similarities and differences between the childhoods and education of the four people?
2 How did their childhood experiences help in their success?
3 Do you think a difficult childhood helps people become successful in business?
4 Do you think it is more difficult for women to succeed in business than men? Why?/Why not?

---

1 Estee Lauder

OBITUARIES

1 The founder of the giant US cosmetics firm died on 24 April at the age of ninety-six. She was born Josephine Esther Mentzer in New York in 1906 to Hungarian and Czech parents and had eight siblings. Her childhood was hard and the family struggled with money. Most of the nine children helped in the family hardware store. This early experience gave her an understanding of business and what makes a successful retailer. As she grew up, Estee became interested in her uncle's business, New Way Laboratories, which sold beauty products. She graduated from Newtown high school and after this focused on his business, helping to sell the products – first to her friends and then to beauty shops.

2 She founded the Estee Lauder company with the Austrian-born Joseph Lauter in 1935, who she had married in 1930. The company only sold four products at this time. Her lucky break came in 1949 when she got an order from the famous Saks Fifth Avenue department store in New York.

3 However, it was in 1953, with the launch of the 'Youth Dew' perfume that the company's fortunes were really transformed. By the mid 1960s, she had launched the Aramis range for men, followed by Clinique in 1968. It has become one of the world's best-selling skincare brands.

4 Today the company also owns a number of famous brands, including Jo Malone, Aveda, MAC and Bobbi Brown, while the Estee Lauder brand is known in 120 countries.

5 She married the same man twice (in 1930 and 1942) and is survived by her two sons, Leonard and Ronald.

Estee Lauder (Josephine Esther Mentzer), born 1 July 1906; died 24 April 2004.

---

2 Akio Morita

OBITUARIES

1 Akio Morita, co-founder of the Sony corporation, died on 3 October in Tokyo. He created one of the first truly global companies. His strategy was so successful that Sony was recently voted the number one brand by American consumers, ahead of Coca-Cola and General Electric.

2 Morita had a comfortable childhood. He was the eldest son of a wealthy family from Nagoya. He trained as a physicist. Before he celebrated his twenty-sixth birthday he had founded his own company with a partner, Masaru Ibuka.

3 In 1949 the company developed recording tape and in 1950 sold the first tape recorder in Japan. In 1957 it produced a pocket-sized radio and a year later renamed itself Sony. For the new name Mr Morita combined the latin word for sound, sonus, with the English expression 'sonny boy' to give an impression of a company full of energy and youth. In 1960 it produced the first transistor television in the world.

4 He moved with his family to the USA in 1963. This helped him to understand Americans, their market and customs. Many people believe this was the key reason for his global success.

5 Sony launched the Walkman in 1979 after Morita had noticed young people's love of music.

6 Morita was a workaholic, but he was also a playaholic. He loved art and music, and was a sports fanatic.

7 He also wrote a book in the 1960s called *Never Mind School Records*, which argued that academic achievements are not important for success in business.

8 He is survived by his wife Yoshiko, two sons and a daughter.

Akio Morita, born 26 January 1921; died 3 October 1999

BUSINESS ICONS 8.3

VOCABULARY
COLLOCATIONS (2)

4a The texts contain some business collocations, e.g. set up/found a company.

Match the verbs in the box with the words and phrases below to make more collocations.

| run | set up | do | make | reduce | go | recruit | launch |

1 **make** a business plan, _____ money / a profit
2 **go** into partnership, _____ out of business
3 **set up** an overseas branch, _____ a company
4 **launch** a new product range, _____ an advertising campaign
5 **do** some market research, _____ the first year accounts
6 **run** the business badly, _____ a factory
7 **recruit** a new manager, _____ talented employees
8 **reduce** production costs, _____ the number of staff

4b Put the collocations from Exercise 4a into a logical order in the life of a company. Discuss your ideas with a partner.

before	start	during	end
make a business plan			go out of business

GRAMMAR
PAST PERFECT SIMPLE

5a Look at these two sentences from the text about Akio Morita and underline the verbs.

Before he celebrated his twenty-sixth birthday he <u>had founded</u> his own company ... .

Sony launched the Walkman in 1979 <u>after Morita had noticed</u> young people's love of music.

5b Answer the following questions and complete the rule.

1 Which verb in each sentence is in the past simple? (The other verb is in the past perfect simple.)
2 Which action happened first in each sentence?
3 Which action happened second?
4 Do we use the past perfect simple for the action that happened first or the action that happened second?

We form the past perfect simple with **had** + (not) + the past participle.

5c Find the two sentences in the texts that start as below. Which tense do we often use to talk about events that happened by a certain time?

1 By the mid 1960s, ... (text 1, para 3)
2 By the end of his life, ... (text 3, para 4)

→ Language reference and extra practice pages 140–141

6 Complete the text with the past simple or past perfect of the verbs in brackets.

By the time he [1] **was** (be) 20, Steve Jobs [2] **had created** (create) the personal computer and started Apple. By the age of twenty-five, his fortune [3] **had risen** (rise) to $100 million. Jobs [4] **left** (leave) Apple in 1985 and [5] **became** (become) CEO of Pixar. When he [6] **rejoined** (rejoin) in 1996, Apple [7] **had lost** (lose) its place in the market. However, by 1998, Jobs [8] **had brought** (bring) Apple from making a loss to making a profit with the iMac. Later, he [9] **developed** (develop) iTunes, the iPod, the iPhone and the iPad. He has been described as the 'Father of the Digital Revolution'. He [10] **died** (die) on 5 October 2011.

7a What had the following people done by the ages/dates mentioned? Match the sentences 1–9 with the phrases a–i.

1 By his 26th birthday, Akio Morita ... **d**
2 By the time of his death, Chaleo Yoovidhya ... **i**
3 By the mid-1960s, Estee Lauder ... **a**
4 By 1990, Mark McCormack ... **g**
5 By the age of six, Mozart ... **f**
6 By the age of twenty-two, Usain Bolt ... **c**
7 By the age of five, Leonardo DiCaprio ... **h**
8 By the age of twenty-two, Lionel Messi ... **b**
9 By the age of twenty-seven, Amy Johnson ... **e**

a launch the Aramis range
b win the FIFA player of the year
c break the 100m and 200m world records
d found his/her own company
e fly to Australia
f compose his/her first piece of music
g become the most powerful person in sport
h appear on TV
i become one of Asia's richest men

7b Check your answers with a partner by making sentences with the past perfect.

'What had Akio Morita done by his twenty-sixth birthday?'
'He had founded his own company.'

SPEAKING

8 Discuss these questions.

1 Who are the business icons in your country?
2 Why are they successful?
3 Who is the most successful person you know?
4 Why are they successful?

8.4 SCENARIO
SUNGLASSES AFTER DARK

SITUATION

1 Work with a partner to discuss the following.
1. How often do you negotiate in your everyday life?
2. Who do you need to negotiate with? What about? For example, you may negotiate with a friend or partner about what film to see at the cinema, where to eat or what time to meet. When was the last time? What was the result?

2 Work with a partner. Which of these tips do you think are most important for a successful negotiation? Try to agree on four.
- Tell the other person exactly what you want.
- Listen carefully.
- Don't change your plan when you negotiate.
- Have a clear aim.
- Ask a lot of questions.
- Try to get a win–win result.
- Keep calm. Do not show any emotion.
- Give a lot of reasons for what you want.

3 Read about Domino s.p.r.l. Why is the market for sunglasses growing?

Domino s.p.r.l., an Italian wholesaler, wants to import sunglasses from a manufacturer in the United States or Asia. They will supply retailers all over Europe. Although the peak season for sunglasses is in the summer months, market research suggests that more and more people are wearing sunglasses all year round – even in the evening as fashion accessories!

4a 8.6 Listen to Vanessa from Domino s.p.r.l. speaking to a potential manufacturer in San Francisco, USA. Is the discussion successful?

4b Listen again and answer the questions.
1. How many pairs of sunglasses did Vanessa want?
2. What were the problems concerning the delivery date and the payment?

8.4 SUNGLASSES AFTER DARK

KEY LANGUAGE
THE LANGUAGE OF NEGOTIATION

5a Listen again and complete the extracts.
1 BOB: How many would you like to _____?
2 VANESSA: We're thinking of _____ quite a large order.
3 BOB: I'm _____ that would be a bit difficult, Vanessa.
4 VANESSA: What about if we _____ earlier? _____ you be able to deliver in August?
5 BOB: Let me check if I _____ you, do you mean payment on delivery?
6 VANESSA: How do you _____ about that?
7 VANESSA: I'll think it over and maybe get back to you.
   BOB: That sounds _____. Well … I hope to hear from you soon.

5b Match the sentences with similar ones from Exercise 5a.
a Let's see if I've got this right.
b We're considering buying a large quantity.
c What sort of quantity do you have in mind?
d That seems OK.
e If we pay more quickly, can you get the goods to us earlier?
f What do you think of the offer?
g I'm sorry. That could be a problem.

TASK
NEGOTIATING

6a After the failure of the earlier negotiation, a meeting is now arranged between Domino s.p.r.l and Sunspex, another manufacturer based in San Diego, USA. In small groups, look at the negotiation details then discuss the questions.

Group A (Domino representatives): Turn to page 157 and read the information carefully.
Group B (Sunspex salespeople): Turn to page 159 and read the information carefully.

1 What are your most important needs in the negotiation?
2 Are some of your points less important? Can you offer them to the other side to get what you want?
3 What do you think will be important for the other side?

6b Work in pairs of one Domino representative and one Sunspex salesperson. Negotiate and try to get a good deal for your company.

7 Work in your groups from Exercise 6a to discuss these questions.
1 Were you happy with the result?
2 Do you think the deal was good for both sides?
3 Did you have a strategy? Do you think the other side had one?
4 How did the other side react to your ideas? Were they flexible?
5 If you did the negotiation again, what would you do differently?

83

8.5 STUDY AND WRITING SKILLS

STUDY SKILLS
RECOGNISING FORMAL AND INFORMAL LANGUAGE

1a Look at the extracts from different pieces of correspondence. Match them with the types below.

report	email	note	minutes	SMS message
1	3	2	5	6

1b Is each piece of correspondence formal or informal? Why?

2a **Recognising register** Which of the following are features of formal/informal writing?

- F 1 use of contractions, e.g. *I'm*
- I 2 no contractions, e.g. *I am*
- F 3 passive constructions, e.g. *It is designed*
- I 4 phrasal verbs, e.g. *call back*
- F 5 longer words instead of shorter, more common ones, e.g. *assistance* (not *help*), *information* (not *facts*), *reserve* (not *book*), *receive* (not *get*)
- I 6 direct questions, e.g. *Can you …?*
- I 7 missing out words, e.g. subject pronouns
- I 8 use of imperatives, e.g. *tell me* (like an order)
- I 9 abbreviations, e.g. *thx* (= *thanks*)

2b Find examples of the features in the extracts.

what texts do/will you write?
1 – N – f?

1
Conclusion
Although there are cost benefits of using Achieve, it is clear that Team Spirit is a much more professional organisation and therefore the best option to help improve staff morale.

Recommendations
It is recommended that Team Spirit are contacted as soon as possible and informed of our requirements.
If possible a staff teambuilding weekend should be arranged for March/April.

2
Jane,
Mr Forster called. I'll get back to him tomorrow about the details of his visit. Can you find out what stuff he needs for his presentation? Time tbc. Also wants some help with booking a hotel. Let me know what info you get asap.
Thanks,
Dan

3 **Beginning and ending correspondence** Look again at the emails in extracts 3 and 4 below. Underline the phrases used to begin and end them.

WRITING SKILLS
FORMAL AND INFORMAL CORRESPONDENCE

4 Put the procedure into a logical order for writing emails. (Tip: the answer should spell a word.)

Type …	(type a draft)
Who …	is the email to? (the reader(s) and your relationship with them)
Send …	(add any attachments and send)
Edit …	(edit and check)
Register …	(is the email formal/neutral/informal?)
Information …	(brainstorm the content/functions, and think of the information you need to include)

WRITES

3
Dear Mr McLennan,

Further to your invitation of 15 March, I am notifying you that I will unfortunately be unable to attend the conference on Friday, due to a prior engagement. However, I would be very grateful if you could send me a copy of the post-conference report.

Yours sincerely,
Elena D'Angelo

4
Hi Carlos,

Great news: got the contract! Let me know if you want to work with us on this one. I'll be in touch in the next couple of days to firm up our needs.

Best wishes,
Nils

5
page 1 of 5

Agenda Item	Discussion	Action
Marketing Plan	The budget for this was approved. Martin Schwarz will prepare in detail for next meeting.	MS to prepare detailed budget by 21 Feb.

6
ETA 14.30 pls send taxi cu l8r.

STUDY AND WRITING SKILLS 8.5

	Formal	Neutral	Informal
First contact	I am writing to enquire … / I am writing to inform you …	I am writing to ask/tell you …	I'd like to find out / let you know about …
Referring to previous contact	With reference to your letter of …	Thank you for your letter of …	1_____
Giving good news	I am delighted to inform you …	2_____	Great news!
Giving bad news	3_____	Unfortunately, …	Sorry, but …
Making an offer	If you wish, I would be happy to …	Would you like me to …	Shall I …
Making a request	4_____	Could you possibly …	Please can you …
Refusing an invitation	I am unable to attend due to …	I will not be able to come because …	5_____
Apologising	I would like to apologise for …	I am sorry about/for …	Sorry about/for…
Closing remarks	If you have any further questions, please do not hesitate to contact me.	6_____	Call/Mail me if you need more help.
Attachments	7_____	I am attaching …	Here is …
Referring to the future	I look forward to hearing from you in the near future.	Looking forward to meeting you.	8_____

5 Look at the phrases below and add them to the table of useful expressions above.

5 I can't make it as …
3 I regret to inform you …
6 If I can help in any way, please contact me again.
4 I would be grateful if you could …
2 I have some good news (about …)
1 Got your message on …
7 Please find attached …
8 Speak to you / See you soon.

6a Using the table, change the parts in bold in the first email from formal to neutral register. Make any other changes necessary.

6b Using the table, change the parts in bold in the second email from informal to formal register. Make any other changes necessary. *Write emails to each other*

7 Write an email for the following situations. Use the W.R.I.T.E.S. procedure from Exercise 4.

1 Marco, a colleague from an overseas branch of your company wrote to you last week. You promised to send some documents to him, but forgot. He has just written again to remind you.
2 A customer, Mrs Daley, phoned you and asked you to send her your latest catalogue.
3 Jenny, a friend who works in the same department, wants to go for a drink tonight after work. You are unable to go as you are going to the cinema, but you could go on Friday.

1

Dear Customer

I am writing to advise you of a new development at *Shoes 4U*. **I am delighted to inform you that** in future you will be able to order online. We aim to provide our customers with the best possible service. In order to do this, **I would be grateful if you could** take a few minutes to register your details on the website; after, you will be able to start using the new service right away.

If you have any further questions, please do not hesitate to contact me.

I look forward to hearing from you soon.

Yours sincerely,

2

Dear Louise,

Got your email on Friday. Thank you for the invitation. **Sorry, but I can't make it** as we have a teambuilding seminar that weekend. **Please let Mark know** about the new products.

Please feel free to call/mail me again if you need any more help.

Speak to you soon.

Denise

Homework: email teacher

9 Engineering

9.1 FROM ENGINES TO ENGINEERS

IN THIS UNIT

GRAMMAR
- the passive
- articles

VOCABULARY
- collocations (3)
- hazards and global threats

SCENARIO
- discussing options, making decisions
- assessing a project

STUDY SKILLS
- participating in a group discussion

WRITING SKILLS
- describing a process

A scientist can discover a new star but he cannot make one. He would have to ask an engineer to do it for him. G. L. Clegg

READING

1 What do engineers do? Do you know any? What different types are there?

2a *Identifying genre* Look at the text. Where do you think it comes from? Who is it aimed at?

2b Choose the most suitable heading for each paragraph.
- a Engineers' contribution to society 2
- b Origin and definition of *engineer* 3
- c Women in engineering 1
- d Engineering and science 4
- e Types of engineer 5

2c Match these inventions with the types of engineering mentioned in the text.
1. roads — civil
2. aircraft — aero
3. a washing machine — mech
4. microchips — comp
5. a heart pacemaker — biomed

roads – civil engineering

A Man's World?

When you hear the word engineer, do you think of someone who is a) male? b) boring? or c) dirty? Or all three? Well, time to think again.

1 Engineering has often been seen as a male profession. For example, only nine percent of US engineers are women, while in the UK it is just over eight percent. However, there is no reason for this: engineers are simply talented people who make our everyday lives easier. In fact research shows that women make the best problem solvers.

2 Engineers find solutions to problems that are important to society. They control and prevent pollution, develop new medicines, create advanced technologies and help explore new worlds. They make the world a cleaner, safer, healthier place by inventing, building and improving everything from microchips to household appliances, from skyscrapers to spacecraft.

3 Interestingly, the word 'engineer' does not come from the word 'engine'. In fact it comes from the Latin word 'ingeniosus' meaning skilled. An engineer is really a clever, practical problem solver. Although the fields of engineering and science are connected, there are also differences.

4 While a scientist will ask why a problem occurs or happens, an engineer will want to know how to solve the problem. As one writer once said: scientists build in order to learn, whereas engineers learn in order to build.

FROM ENGINES TO ENGINEERS 9.1

LISTENING

paraphrase
tense, order

3a 9.1 Lindsey Barone is one of the few women engineers in a high position. Listen to the interview. What type of engineering has she worked in?

3b Listen again and correct the statements.
1. She started her career in a car manufacturing company. *test lab*
2. She worked on military aircraft before her present job. ~~army~~ *commercial*
3. She works closely with a lot of other women. *men*
4. She likes engineering because it's well paid. *fun, exciting, challenging*

4 Work with a partner to discuss the following.
1. What did you find most interesting about the interview with Lindsey Barone?
2. Would you like to have her job? Why?/Why not?
3. Why do you think there are fewer female engineers than male engineers?
4. Should there be more women in engineering? Why?/Why not?

5 There are all sorts of opportunities in a variety of engineering fields such as aeronautical, biomedical, civil, mechanical and computer engineering. Engineers work alone or in teams, and in locations such as offices, factories, research labs, outdoors and even outer space! How many of the modern world's greatest engineering achievements will you use today? A car, a computer, a telephone? Think about it.

Now is the time for women to engineer the future. Break the stereotype. Build a career. Sign up today!

VOCABULARY
COLLOCATIONS (3)

5a Match the verbs with the most appropriate words and phrases.
1. test ~~g~~ e   a safety tests
2. build g   b a breakthrough
3. solve c   c a problem
4. make b   d a deadline
5. do a   e a theory
6. do f   f some research
7. meet d   g a model/prototype
8. find h   h a solution

5b Listen to the interview again and check your answers. What other combinations of the words in Exercise 5a can you think of?

5c Complete the sentences with the correct form of the collocations in Exercise 5a. The first letter of the noun is given.
1. Following the accident, engineers had to *do* a lot of s*afety tests* before the machine could be used again.
2. After a long period of failure, they *made* an important b*reakthrough*.
3. They *found* an imaginative s*olution* to the problem after working with models in the test lab.
4. One part of the engineering process is to *build* a smaller working m*odel* before moving on to a full-size or production version.
5. It can take a long time to fully *test* a complicated t*heory* before putting it into practice.
6. The whole team had to *do* a lot of careful r*esearch* into the causes of the problem.
7. In the end we were able to *solve* the most serious p*roblem*.
8. On many engineering projects there is great pressure to *meet* strict d*eadlines*.

5d Look back at the reading text and find three different combinations of *problem* and *solve*.

SPEAKING

6 Work in small groups. Look at the list of some great engineering achievements and do the following. *Comparatives, superlatives, opinion*
1. Add one more achievement to each category.
2. Decide which is the greatest engineering achievement in each category.
3. Give reasons for your choices.
Choose a president. Vote most persuasive.

around the house	entertainment
the fridge, the microwave oven, the vacuum cleaner	radio, television, the internet
getting around	**construction**
the train, the plane, the car	the pyramids, the Eiffel Tower, the Panama Canal
medicine/health	
contact lenses, the thermometer, laser surgery	

WRITING

7 Write a short paragraph about what you think is the greatest engineering achievement. Think about these questions: Why do you think it is the greatest achievement? How has it improved people's lives? What would people's lives be like without it?

87

9.2 SURVIVAL ENGINEERING

VOCABULARY
HAZARDS AND GLOBAL THREATS

1a Match the words in the box with their meanings.

asteroid   meteor   meteorite   extinction
collide   deflect   probe   hazardous

1 a small piece of rock or metal that is burning up in the Earth's atmosphere
2 a piece of rock or metal that has come from space and landed on Earth
3 a very large piece of rock that is moving through space
4 a spacecraft without people, sent into space to gather information
5 dangerous
6 make something move in a different direction
7 crash violently into something
8 when animals or plants stop existing

1b Complete the text using some of the words from Exercise 1a.

A massive ¹_____ might ²collide with the Earth in the year 2040 causing mass ³extinction. Scientists have been discussing how to ⁴deflect potentially ⁵hazardous asteroids to prevent them hitting the Earth. One possibility is to send a ⁶probe to land on the asteroid and monitor its progress.

READING

2 Read the title of the article. How much do you know about the threat of asteroids? Work in small groups and share your information.

3a Read the article quickly and put the topics below into the order they appear in the text.

- [2] 2005 YU55
- [1] Yucatan Peninsula
- [4] Methods to avoid collisions with asteroids
- [3] 99942 Apophis

3b Read the article again and make notes about the four topics.

3c Now work in pairs. Take it in turns to tell your partner about each of the topics without looking at the text.

4 Identifying facts Read the article again and find two known facts and two things that are speculation.

5 Can you think of any other ways of preventing asteroids hitting the Earth?

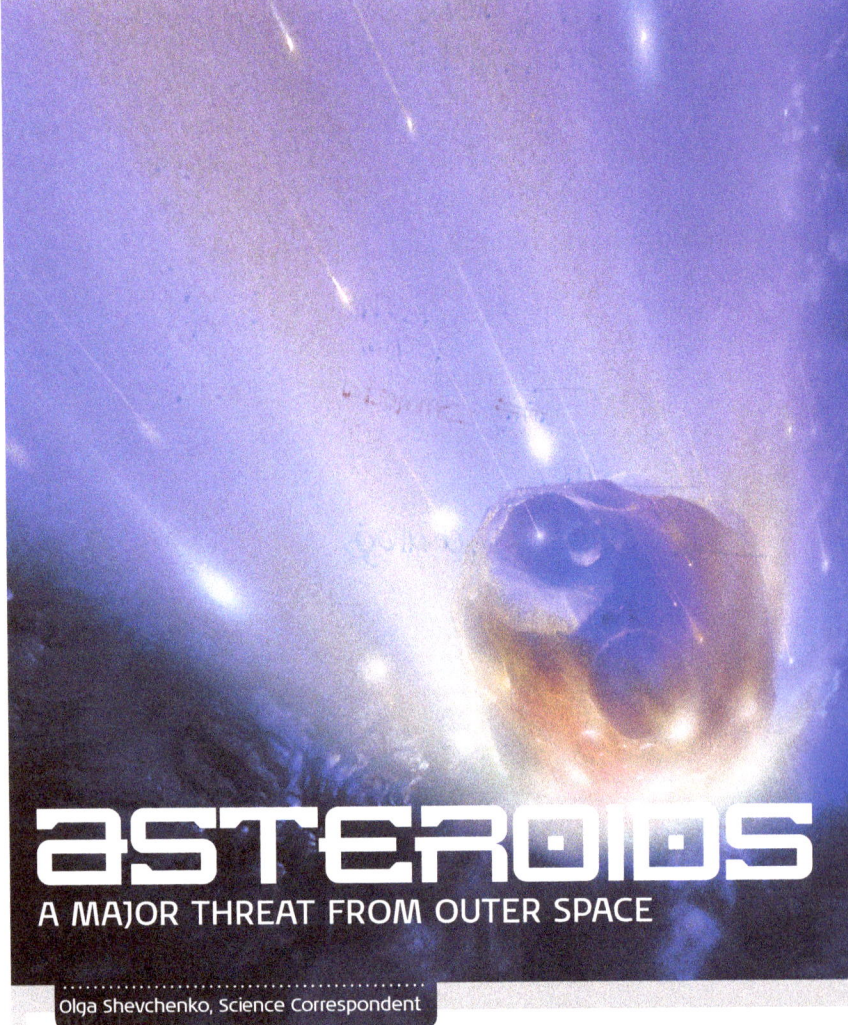

asteroids
A MAJOR THREAT FROM OUTER SPACE

Olga Shevchenko, Science Correspondent

Most scientists agree that the threat of a large asteroid or meteor hitting the Earth is real, although they cannot predict when such an event will occur. However, a recent event in Russia reminded everyone of the danger of meteors and asteroids. In the Urals region, on 15 February, a meteor flashed across the sky and broke up over the city of Chelyabinsk. The huge explosion followed by shock waves smashed windows, destroyed roofs and injured around 1,200 people. The meteor weighed 10 tonnes and was travelling at an estimated speed of 50,000–60,000 km/h before it disintegrated. According to residents, it was a terrifying experience.

The Earth has been struck many times in the past by large objects. A meteorite, estimated to be about twelve kilometres in diameter, collided with the Earth in the region of the Yucatan Peninsula (now Mexico) 65 million years ago. Many scientists and historians believe that the extinction of the dinosaurs and other animals was a result of this collision.

Just recently, an asteroid as big as an aircraft carrier passed within the Moon's orbit. It was the largest object to approach the Earth in more than thirty years. The rock, 2005 YU55, as its name suggests, was first seen in December 2005 and came within 325,000 kilometres of the Earth. NASA, the US space agency, tracked the asteroid as it approached, using high-powered instruments and its massive radio telescope in Puerto Rico.

The space agency classified the asteroid as 'potentially hazardous' but there was no danger of it colliding with the Earth. However, if the asteroid had crashed into the Earth, it could have caused a huge earthquake. If it had fallen into the ocean, it could have produced a 20-metre tsunami. Scientists worldwide are concerned

SURVIVAL ENGINEERING

9.2

GRAMMAR
THE PASSIVE

6a The passive is often used for the following reasons.
1 When the person doing the action is not important, not known or is obvious.
2 When we want to start a sentence with information that is known or has been mentioned before.
3 When we want to include the person who does the action, we introduce them with the preposition *by*. **end**

Look at the highlighted phrases in the article, and match them to the statements above.

GRAMMAR TIP

We form the passive with a form of *be* followed by the past participle of the main verb:
The Earth **has been** struck .. **by an asteroid.**

6b Look at the article and find all the other examples of the passive and underline them. Then match all the examples of the passive with these tenses.
a the present simple passive
b the past simple passive
c the present perfect passive
d the passive in the future
e the passive with a modal verb

➡ Language reference and extra practice pages 142–143

7 **huh? Too difficult!** Complete the text using either the passive or the active form of the verbs in brackets.
30 million people ¹ **were killed** (kill) by the global flu epidemic of 1918. In recent years, people ² _____ (shock) by the arrival of 'new' infectious diseases. These ³ _____ (call) superbugs. Many superbugs ⁴ _____ (live) harmlessly on or in the body and only ⁵ _____ (cause) problems when people become sick with other illnesses. These bugs are particularly dangerous to people who ⁶ _____ (weaken) by surgery, childbirth or old age. The bugs also ⁷ _____ (cause) problems for babies. Scientists say vaccines capable of beating deadly superbugs like MRSA ⁸ **will** / (find) within ten years. However, some people think that with the rise of genetic engineering, the world ⁹ _____ (wipe out) by a GM superbug.
will / could

8a Work with a partner to do a passives quiz. Make passive sentences using the table on page 157. Write as many sentences as you can in ten minutes.

8b Compare your sentences with another pair.
What have you got for number 1?
The ballpoint pen was invented by …

8c Now close all your books. In your groups of four, how many passive sentences can you remember from the quiz? The team with the most correct sentences wins.

SPEAKING

9 In groups, look at the following global threats. Choose the three most serious. Then discuss and rank them 1–3 (1 = most serious).

overpopulation   asteroids   drought   famine   carthquakes   tsunamis
hurricanes   superbugs   alien invasion   genetic engineering   volcanoes

about the threat from asteroids striking the Earth. They agree that action should **e** be taken to prevent an asteroid or comet colliding with our planet.

Russia's top space researchers are particularly worried about asteroids. They plan to send a probe to an asteroid which could be a threat to the Earth in the near future. They want to deflect 99942 Apophis, an asteroid that will fly close to the Earth two decades from now. This asteroid is about 300 metres wide The threat from Apophis is considered by **a** Russian scientists to be the most serious now facing our planet.

These scientists believe there is still time to change the path of the asteroid before it approaches the Earth.

Several methods have been proposed by **c** engineers to avoid collisions with asteroids. One idea is that a spacecraft could land on the asteroid. It would then use electric motors to change the path of the asteroid. Other methods include hitting it with missiles or using a satellite to change its direction. Further research will be carried out in the future. **d**

The threat of Apophis has focused people's minds on protecting our planet against asteroids and other objects from outer space. Recently, Rusty Schweickart, a former Apollo astronaut, called for action to defend the planet. He wrote in the *New York Times*, 'By preventing dangerous asteroid strikes, we can save millions of people, or even our entire species.'

9.3 SUPERSTRUCTURES

SPEAKING

1 Work with a partner to discuss the following.
1. What is the largest man-made structure you have ever been in or on? How did you feel?
2. How would you feel if you were:
   a. at the top of a very tall building?
   b. in a tunnel deep in the ground?
   c. in a building at the bottom of the sea?

GRAMMAR
ARTICLES

2 Read the text quickly. Tell a partner what you found most interesting.

3 Look at the highlighted words in the text and find examples for each of these rules:

We use a/an …
1. when we mention something (a singular noun) for the first time. *a train*

We use *the* …
2. when we refer to something that has been mentioned before. *the train*
3. with the names of some countries. *UK*
4. with the names of geographical features, e.g. seas, oceans, rivers. *Atlantic, the Gulf Stream*
5. with superlatives. *most expensive, largest*
6. when there is only one of something. *the world*
7. when we know which thing the speaker refers to. *the anchors*

We don't use an article …
8. with plural countable nouns. *decades, giant anchors*
9. with the names of towns and cities, and most countries. *NY*

→ Language reference and extra practice pages 142–143

4 Complete the text with *the*, *a* or *an*, or leave the space blank if no article is needed.

Hakan, who is ¹ _an_ engineer from Turkey, studied Civil Engineering at ² _—_ Istanbul Technical University. He is originally from ³ _—_ Ankara, which is ⁴ _the_ capital of ⁵ _—_ Turkey and ⁶ _the_ country's second largest city after ⁷ _—_ Istanbul. He is ⁸ _an_ expert in hydraulic engineering. He is currently working in ⁹ _—_ China on one of ¹⁰ _—_ China's biggest projects: the South to North Water Transfer Project. The plan is to transfer huge volumes of water from ¹¹ _the_ wet and rainy south of ¹² _the_ country to ¹³ _the_ dry plains of ¹⁴ _the_ north. Over ¹⁵ _the_ next 40 years, ¹⁶ _—_ China will build huge canals over ¹⁷ _the_ country. Before that, Hakan worked on the Sutong Bridge in China, which is ¹⁸ _the_ longest spanning bridge with cables in ¹⁹ _the_ world.

PRONUNCIATION

5a 9.2 **Weak forms** Listen to five sentences and write them down. Then underline the weak forms.

5b Practise saying the sentences.

TRANSATLANTIC TUNNEL

Engineers have proposed cutting journey times from New York in the United States to London in the United Kingdom to 54 minutes, travelling on a magnetically-raised train. The idea is that the train will travel through a tunnel floating in the Atlantic Ocean. The tunnel will be 45 metres below the surface of the sea and it will be nearly 5,000 kilometres long. The train will travel at speeds of well over 1,000 km/h, many times faster than today's fastest trains.

Giant anchors will be sunk into the bottom of the sea, in some places up to 8 kilometres deep. 54,000 tunnel sections will be transported by a special ship and will then be lowered into place. The tunnel sections will then be attached to the anchors. The tunnel will have to stand up to some of the Atlantic's strongest currents, including part of the Gulf Stream. The tunnel will probably cost $12 trillion and need one billion tonnes of steel. It will take decades to build. If it is built, it will be the largest and the most expensive engineering project in the history of the world.

SUPERSTRUCTURES 9.3

SAHARA SOLAR FARM

It is hoped that a huge solar and windfarm project in the Sahara desert, including countries in North Africa and Arabia, may provide 15% of Europe's electricity by 2050 and help solve climate change problems. Huge farms of solar panels in the Sahara will provide clean electricity. As sunlight is more intense there, the solar panels in North Africa will generate up to three times the electricity compared with panels in Europe.

The ambitious scheme led by Germany to build a €45 bn supergrid will start in Morocco, probably near the desert city of Ouarzazate. The Moroccan solar farm will cover 12 square kilometres. Tunisia and Algeria will probably be the next countries as they are close to Europe. Libya, Egypt, Turkey, Syria and Saudi Arabia may join the network from 2020.

The panels have metal cradles made in Egypt and glass troughs made in Germany. Scientists have wondered how the troughs will perform in very bad weather. However, there is usually only one sandstorm a year. The main challenge will be keeping the panels clean due to the dusty conditions. They need to be cleaned daily which takes up a lot of local water.

THE BELO MONTE DAM

The Brazilian government is planning to build the Belo Monte Dam on the Xingu river in the Amazon. The hydro-electric dam will be the third largest in the world behind the Three Gorges Dam in China and the Itaipu Dam which is jointly owned by Brazil and Paraguay. The Belo Monte dam will be 90 metres high, 3,545 metres long and will cost around US$ 18.5 bn.

It is estimated that the dam will produce 11,000 megawatts of electricity, which would help Brazil depend less on fossil fuels like oil. The government also wants to help the country's economy with large scale projects like this one, and others like new road systems.

However, the effects of the dam may not all be positive and the project has been heavily criticised by environmentalists. The dam will destroy vast areas of land, flooding 500 square kilometres along the Xingu and forcing more than 16,000 people to find new homes. Campaigners are particularly worried about the future of local tribes in the area, whose lives totally depend on the forest and river.

READING

6a Scan the three texts and note down all the countries mentioned. Why is each country mentioned?

6b Read the three texts again and complete as much of the table as you can.

	Tunnel	Solar farm	Dam
height			
cost			
length			
area covered			

6c Read the texts again and answer the questions.
1. How long will it take to get from New York to London?
2. What can travel at many times the speed of today's fastest train?
3. What is the depth the anchors will be sunk under the bottom of the sea?
4. What are the advantages of the Sahara solar panels?
5. Why will the solar panels in North Africa generate more electricity than panels in Europe?
6. Where is the proposed Belo Monte dam?
7. Why does the government want to build the dam?

7 Identifying problems Work in pairs to discuss the following.
1. What problems do the three texts mention?
2. Which problem do you think will be
   a   most serious
   b   most difficult to solve?
3. Can you think of other problems that might arise in the three projects?

SPEAKING

8a You are going to hold a debate on the following motion.

Spending billions on superstructures cannot be justified when people are starving.

Divide into two groups, one for and one against the motion.
Group A (for the motion): Turn to page 157 and prepare your arguments.
Group B (against the motion): Turn to page 163 and prepare your arguments.

8b When you have prepared your arguments, debate the motion as a class.

9.4 SCENARIO
THE MEGA PROJECT

SITUATION

1 Read the situation below. In your opinion, what big construction projects might impress foreign visitors?

A country in South-East Asia has an expanding tourist industry. However, it would like to attract more business travellers to use its conference facilities. To achieve this objective, the government plans to have a big project which will be exciting, good for its citizens and create worldwide interest. The Minister of the Environment, Susan Lau, has come up with an interesting idea.

2a 9.3 Listen to an extract from a television news programme. Discuss these questions.
1 What is Susan Lau's new idea?
2 Why will the project probably appeal to foreigners?

2b Listen again and complete the information.
The Mega Project
Type of project: _____
Height: _____
Width: _____
Number of people living in the city: _____
Number of people working in the city: _____
Facilities in the city: _____
Future action by the minister: _____

3a Work in pairs. Read the facts about the country below and divide them into these two categories.
a Situations that the new city will improve
b Problems that the new city will face

- The capital city is overpopulated and polluted. There is a serious housing problem in the city.
- The weather is hot throughout the year. Temperatures often reach 45°C.
- Strong winds and even hurricanes occur at times in the country. The area is also at risk from earthquakes.
- Traffic moves slowly, so commuters spend a long time travelling to work.
- There are many poor and homeless people in the area, and the crime rate is high.
- The unemployment rate is high, especially in the construction industry.
- Many businesses have closed down recently in the area chosen for the vertical city.
- People in the north of the country want to create an independent state. There are often violent anti-government demonstrations in the area.

9.4 THE MEGA PROJECT

3b In your pairs, discuss this question.
What do you think will be the main advantages and disadvantages of building the new city?

4 [9.4] Listen to two city planners talking about the benefits of the project. Note down the benefits they mention. Compare them with the ones you discussed in Exercise 3b.

KEY LANGUAGE
DISCUSSING OPTIONS, MAKING DECISIONS

5 [9.5] Listen to a conversation between three city planners about a name for the vertical city and complete it.

A: What ^{1}_____ _____ it Mega City? It's easy to remember.
B: Mmm, it's a possible solution, I suppose, but there are ^{2}_____ _____. How about Hope City? It's a really good name because it'll provide a lot of housing for poor people. Give them hope for the future.
C: Yeah, Hope City. It ^{3}_____ _____ to me, I must say. But what other names can we think of?
A: Well, one ^{4}_____ would be to call it Tower City. That's exactly what it would be – a towering city, one of the highest in the world.
B: I don't know, I'm not too keen on that name. We have one other option, you know. If we ^{5}_____ _____ Paradise City, I think most people ^{6}_____ _____ that name. It suggests the city would be a wonderful place to live and work in. That's what we all want, don't we?
C: Mmm, ^{7}_____ _____, I really like the name.
A: Me too. OK, we all seem to like it. Are we ^{8}_____ _____ then? Have we ^{9}_____ _____ _____? It'll be Paradise City.
B/C: Yeah. Agreed.
A: OK then. I'll ^{10}_____ the name to the minister. We're all ^{11}_____ . It's the best name.

6 Work in pairs to discuss the following.

1 Which of the four names is your favourite? Why?
2 What is the best name for a shuttle service from the airport to the new city?

TASK
ASSESSING A PROJECT

7a You are studying engineering at the capital city's biggest university. Susan Lau has sent your department a list of questions about the new project for discussion. In small groups, look at the questions below and choose five which interest you. Discuss the questions and make decisions.

1 Which material should be mainly used to build the new city? Glass? Concrete? Steel? Other?
2 What should be the general shape of the city? One tower? Several towers?
3 Who should the new city be for? Poor people? Rich and poor people? Anyone who can afford to live there?
4 What style would be suitable for the apartments? Classical? Modern? Futuristic? Other?
5 What kind of restaurants or other food outlets should there be?
6 How can the planners make the city safe for people living and working there?
7 Should the new city have closed circuit television? Everywhere? In special areas?
8 What kind of transport should there be inside the building? Lifts? A monorail? Minibuses? Bicycles? Other?
9 How can the builders protect the city against fire, hurricanes and very hot weather?
10 What other things do the planners need to think about?

7b In your groups, tell another group which questions you chose and what your decisions were. Give reasons.

7c As a class, decide whether the Mega Project is good for the country. Is it feasible?

9.5 STUDY AND WRITING SKILLS

STUDY SKILLS
PARTICIPATING IN A GROUP DISCUSSION

1 In pairs or small groups, discuss these questions.
1. What kind of group discussions do you attend at work or in your studies?
2. Do you enjoy taking part in group discussions? Why?/Why not?
3. How do you rate your performance in this activity? Excellent? Good? Average? Poor?
4. What problems, if any, do you have when taking part in a group discussion?
5. Think of a person who is good at group discussions. What abilities and skills do they have?

2a ▶ 9 Four students from a Faculty of Engineering are taking part in a group discussion at their university's Engineers Club. The topic for discussion is: 'Engineers are wasting their time doing management studies.' Watch the video and match the photos and the names of the students: Sheeba, Jake, Davide and Valerie.

A Jake   B Valerie   C Sheeba   D Davide

2b Do the students agree with the statement? Put a tick (✓) against the name if the student agrees and a cross (✗) if they disagree.

Sheeba ✗   Jake ✗   Davide ✓   Valerie ✓

2c Which person's opinion do you agree with most? Why?

3a Watch the discussion again. Tick (✓) the expressions below that you hear.

Turn taking
☐ I'd like to make a comment.
☑ Can I come in here, please?

Clarifying
☑ Let me explain my point of view.

Interrupting politely
☑ Can I make a quick point, please?

Keeping your turn
☑ Hang on, let me finish what I want to say.

Bringing other speakers in
☑ I think you agree with me, don't you, Valerie?

Asking questions
☐ Can I ask a question, please? What do Sheeba and Jake think?
☑ I'd like to ask Sheeba and Jake a question, if I may.

3b Now look at Video script 9 on page 172. Underline other expressions and add them to the categories in Exercise 3a.

4a Body language Watch the discussion again. Which student makes each of the gestures below? What does each one mean? Match 1–4 with a–d.
1 **b** shaking the head slightly from side to side
2 **c** putting forward a hand with the palm forwards
3 **a** moving the arm forward and raising the hand to shoulder height
4 **d** making open hand gestures in front of the body in time with important words

a indicating that he/she wants to speak
b indicating disagreement
c stopping someone else interrupting
d emphasising key points while explaining something

4b Which of the gestures would not be acceptable in your country? What gestures would normally be used in your country for the above actions?

5a 9.6 Listen to a college lecturer from the UK giving advice about how to participate effectively in a group discussion. Take notes under the headings Do and Don't. IWB

5b Think of some more tips and add them to your lists from Exercise 6a.

6 Work in groups of three or four. Choose one of the controversial statements below. Prepare some arguments for or against the statement. Then have a group discussion. Use some of the phrases from Exercise 3 in your discussion.

- Nuclear power is too risky. It should be banned in all countries.
- Cloning (copying an animal or plant) is immoral and dangerous.
- Few people will buy books in twenty years' time.
- Space exploration is a waste of time and money.
- The dangers of global warming have been exaggerated.

STUDY AND WRITING SKILLS 9.5

How aircraft are made

Aircraft production is a huge and costly business. Most aircraft are made by companies who can produce them in large quantities and who can invest time in planning as well as production. Planning alone can take up to 12 years for a large aircraft and production can also be a very long process. The production stages are as follows.

First, the construction company produces designs for the aircraft. These designs are used for the initial simulations. Then a model of the aircraft is put in a wind tunnel. The way the air moves around the model is studied by engineers and scientists, as well as how the model acts in the tunnel. This gives them a good idea of how a real, life-sized aircraft of the same design will fly. Smaller parts of the aircraft are also tested in wind tunnels.

Next a prototype of the aircraft is made, and after that a limited number of aircraft are produced to test on the ground. Representatives from a government aviation agency often make the first flight. Flight tests continue until all the requirements are met. Finally, the government agency authorises the construction company to begin production of the aircraft. A certificate is issued and the aircraft is sold all over the world.

WRITING SKILLS
DESCRIBING A PROCESS

7 Read the description of how aircraft are made and answer the questions.
1 Why are the following used to produce an aircraft?
 a a model   b wind tunnels   c flight tests
2 What document must a construction company get before it can sell its aircraft? *certificate*

8 Using the passive In English, we prefer to start a sentence with information that is already known, not new. We sometimes use the passive to put known information at the beginning of a sentence. For example:

Aircraft production is a huge and costly business.
↓
Most aircraft are made …

We are unlikely to write:

Aircraft production is a huge and costly business. Companies make **most aircraft** …

Find two more examples of this in the text.

9 There are several stages in the production and launch of a new motorbike. Look at the notes below and put them in the correct order. Think about how the passive is sometimes used at the beginning of a sentence. The first and last have been numbered.

- [8] Show the new motorbike at trade exhibitions all over the world.
- [1] Plan the new motorbike and produce the first designs. (Design team)
- [6] Contact journalists and invite them to test drive the new motorbike.
- [4] Changes are made to the prototype and the design is modified. (R&D department)
- [2] Build the first prototype, with the help of engineers. (R&D department)
- [3] The prototype is tested on special roads. Check if there are any problems and if any changes are necessary.
- [5] Do further tests, then make more modifications and changes to the engine.
- [7] Results of the test drive are recorded and the journalists prepare articles about the new bike.
- [9] Mass-produce the new motorbike. Launch an international marketing campaign.

10 Write an article on the stages in the production and launch of a new motorbike, for inclusion in some school course materials on engineering processes. Use the notes above and the linkers in the box to structure your article.

first of all   next   after that   then   finally

10 Trends

10.1 IT'S THE NEW THING

IN THIS UNIT

GRAMMAR
- expressions of quantity
- infinitives and -ing forms

VOCABULARY
- phrasal verbs (3)
- fashion

SCENARIO
- raising and responding to issues
- participating in a meeting

STUDY SKILLS
- recording and learning vocabulary

WRITING SKILLS
- describing a trend

Don't follow trends, start trends. Frank Capra, 1897–1991, US film-maker

SPEAKING

1a Look at the list of trends below. Work with a partner to discuss these questions.

1. Which are current trends in your country?
2. Which are trends in other countries?
3. Which are old-fashioned trends which you think could return?

- Recycling and looking after the environment
- Being concerned about diet and health
- Having cosmetic surgery
- Retiring at 70 years old
- Reality TV shows
- Not using cash even for small purchase
- Sunbathing
- Getting married later in life
- American-style coffee shops, e.g. Starbucks
- Wearing sportswear/training shoes (when not playing sport)
- Beauty competitions

1b Think about possible future trends in the following areas. Then discuss your ideas in small groups. Which do you think are the most likely?

- Personal appearance
- Family life
- Work
- Education
- Leisure time

READING

2a Skim the text. What is the main purpose of the text?

1. to entertain an audience of scientists
2. to persuade people to buy a book
3. to inform a general audience about a common term

2b Read the text again and match the ideas below to the correct paragraph.

a. Trends are like illnesses.
b. Change happens quickly, not a little at a time.
c. Trends can become global more easily than before.
d. Certain types of people are important in developing trends.
e. The idea of tipping points comes from science.
f. Gladwell made people more aware of the idea of tipping points.

3 Reflecting on the topic In small groups, discuss these questions.

1. What do you think of Gladwell's ideas?
2. How influenced are you by other people?
3. What was the last trend you followed?
4. Which trendsetters do you admire?

96

10.1 IT'S THE NEW THING

Become an expert on ...

TIPPING POINTS

1 It can be a problem these days keeping up with the number of overnight YouTube sensations and viral marketing campaigns on the internet. It is also difficult to explain how these suddenly become popular. We tend to think that change happens gradually and steadily over time. However, often this is not the case, especially with new trends which seem to catch on very quickly.

2 A term heard a lot in this context is 'tipping point', but what does it mean? The tipping point is a term which originally came from physics, although it has been used in many fields of study, from economics to ecology. The idea describes the time in any process when very rapid change happens. In sociology the term was first used by Morton Grodzins when he was studying movements of people into and out of neighbourhoods in America.

3 Although used by scholars and academics for years, it became more widely known as a popular term relating to trends because of Canadian author Malcolm Gladwell. He wrote a best-selling book called *The tipping point or how little things can make a big difference*. In the book Gladwell compares changes in behaviour and new trends to the way outbreaks of disease develop. He shows how they suddenly take over and are everywhere, and then later slow down in popularity and finally die out. Sometimes, for example in fashion, they reappear years or even decades later. Gladwell claims in his book that, just like epidemics, trends move rapidly through a population as people buy into them, although not all academics agree with his theory.

4 Gladwell also talked about the importance of word of mouth in helping people to pick up on new ideas and trends. He identified three types of people who are influential in the development of trends: Connectors (who have a wide range of contacts), Mavens (who are experts with a lot of knowledge to share) and Salesmen (who have influence and people want to copy).

5 These days social networking allows people to find out about trends which are global, whereas before they were only local or national. What do you think the next global trend will be? Where and when will it start?

NEXT WEEK: chaos theory

VOCABULARY
PHRASAL VERBS (3)

4a Look at the phrasal verbs highlighted in the text and match them with their meanings below.
1 discover
2 gain control of something/someone
3 maintain the same level as
4 become less fast/rapid
5 notice something which is not easy to notice
6 become fashionable or popular
7 disappear completely
8 believe in and be influenced by

4b Replace the words in italics in the questions below with the correct form of a phrasal verb from Exercise 4a.
1 What was the most recent trend to *become popular* with young children?
2 Do you try to *have the same lifestyle and possessions* as your friends and neighbours?
3 Why do you think trends *become less rapid*?
4 Which trends that have *disappeared* will have a revival, do you think?
5 How do you personally *discover* which trends are becoming popular?
6 Which trends seem to have *become dominant* on the internet recently?
7 Which newspapers and magazines are the first to *notice* new trends in your country?
8 Which recent trend are you not going to *be influenced by*? Why not?

5 In small groups, ask and answer the questions in Exercise 4b.

WRITING

6 Write a paragraph about a recent trend in your country.

▶ **MEET THE EXPERT**

Watch an interview with Cate Trotter, a trend consultant, about how understanding trends can help businesses. Turn to page 153 for video activities.

10.2 TRENDS IN FASHION

READING AND SPEAKING

1 You are going to read an article about cultural influences on fashion trends. Work in groups and predict what cultural trends the article might mention.

which ones. Not in order of text

2 Scan the article quickly and find the following.
1 a French luxury fashion house
2 a cartoon personality
3 a modern artist
4 a TV programme
5 a street movement
6 a major influence on fashion trends
7 a visual art
8 a star in the fashion industry
9 a fashion blogger

3a Read the text again and make notes on the main points in each paragraph.

3b Work with a partner and compare your notes.

4a Identifying examples Look at the text and find seven different phrases used to introduce an example (paragraphs 2–5).

4b Look at the sentences below and think of an example for each one. Add your idea to the sentence using a phrase from Exercise 4a.
1 A number of sports stars have become very rich due to endorsing major brands.
2 The leading countries in fashion design are hoping for a revival in the fashion industry this year.

(5) Work in pairs to discuss these questions.
1 What trends influence what you wear?
2 What do clothes tell you about someone's personality?
3 If you could own one fashionable item, what would it be?
4 Have you ever bought something just because it was fashionable?
5 Does the fashion industry exist mainly to persuade people to spend money on things they do not really need?

VOCABULARY
FASHION

6a Match the words and phrases in the box with their meanings.

| fashion victim (5) | fashionable (1) | fashion conscious (4) | fashion statement (8) |
| unfashionable (2) | designer fashion (3) | high street fashion (6) | fashion show (7) |

1 popular or thought to be good at a particular time
2 not modern or popular
3 expensive, fashionable clothes made by a famous designer
4 interested in the latest fashions and in wearing fashionable clothes
5 someone who always wears very fashionable clothes, even if the clothes sometimes make them look silly
6 the type of clothes that are affordable for the average person but keep up with fashion trends
7 a show for the public where models wear new styles of clothes
8 clothes that you wear to attract attention and show people the type of person you are

Fall/Winter 2012-2013 ready-to-wear collection

6b Work in pairs and take it in turns to ask and answer these questions.
1 What colours are fashionable at the moment?
2 What is your favourite high street fashion shop?
3 Who is the most fashionable person you know? Explain why they are fashionable.
4 Have you ever tried to make a fashion statement? What did you wear?
5 What is the most unfashionable outfit you have ever worn?

LISTENING

7 Do you think it is exciting/glamorous to work in the fashion industry? Why?/Why not? Would you like to work in the fashion industry? Why?/Why not?

8 10.1 Listen to a conversation between the manager of the fashion department of a major upmarket store and a new salesperson, Chloe. Tick (✓) the pieces of advice which the manager gives Chloe.
1 Don't talk to the other trainees.
2 Find out about other departments in the store. ✓
3 Always wear the store uniform.
4 Give customers a lot of attention. ✓ *Chloe*
5 Pressurise them to buy something.

CULTURAL INFLUENCES ON FASHION TRENDS

1 Everyone working in the fashion industry needs to be aware of social and cultural movements because these have a strong influence on fashion trends. If designers, retailers and fashion buyers can predict future trends, they are likely to be successful in their work. There are three main influences on fashion trends. They can be classified as high culture, pop culture and subculture.

2 Fashion designers are often influenced by 'high culture', especially the visual arts of painting, sculpture and photography. For instance, a summer collection of Jill Sanders showed the influence of Pablo Picasso's ceramics and the dresses of designer Mary Katrantzou have been inspired by the crash car sculptures of the contemporary artist John Chamberlain.

3 Popular culture (pop culture) is greatly influenced by celebrities. Famous athletes, film stars, television personalities and musicians are trendsetters. For example, stylish television shows such as Mad Men have had a big influence on the way people dress because everybody wants to look like the actors and actresses. Celebrities are role models for many people, so fashion companies try to persuade them to use their products, and Hollywood stars are increasingly appearing in fashion advertising. A good example of this trend is the film star Leonardo DiCaprio, who has appeared in adverts for Tag Heuer watches.

4 The third influence on fashion trends is subculture. This includes street movements like graffiti, hip hop and other groups outside the mainstream. For instance, the surf and skateboard culture has had a lasting influence on how young people dress, particularly on their sports and street wear.

5 Fashion designers need to observe street culture, keep up with the visual arts and be aware of pop culture. A perfect example of these influences is Marc Jacobs, a star of the fashion world. He designs three major clothing labels and has worked as Creative Director of the French luxury design house, Louis Vuitton. According to one fashion expert, he 'is the master of merging the creative with the commercial'. He can produce a handbag range for Vuitton or T-shirts for his Marc line. His clothes sell because 'people are proud to wear anything he has designed'.

6 Jacobs understands contemporary culture and is inspired by culture at all levels. His house in Paris is full of artworks by Andy Warhol, Ed Ruscha and other modern artists. One of his 29 tattoos shows the cartoon character Spongebob Squarepants. He has worked with Richard Prince, a contemporary artist, on a range of accessories for Louis Vuitton, and named one of his £1,000 handbags after a fashion blogger named BryanBoy. These examples show how he is influenced by high culture and street culture. Jacobs' fashions exemplify, perhaps more than any other designer, the three main influences on fashion trends.

GRAMMAR
EXPRESSIONS OF QUANTITY

9a Look at the sentences from the conversation and try to predict which expressions of quantity should go in the gaps in the sentences. Then listen to the conversation again and check your answers.

1 We've got _____ time before my next meeting.
2 I've talked to _____ the trainees and served _____ customers.
3 Not really, just _____ customers who were a bit difficult.
4 First of all, _____ trainees think they don't need to know …
5 We have _____ rules about uniforms.
6 I used to do all the trips on my own with _____ help but last year I took _____ of the assistants …
7 … we've got _____ ideas and we'll get _____ information from the organisers soon.
8 … give customers _____ time to make up their minds …
9 Give them _____ attention and _____ advice …
10 We have _____ sales assistants to do the job properly.

9b Complete the table using the phrases from Exercise 9a, according to which kind of noun they are used with. Some can be used with both.

| used with countable nouns | a lot of |
| used with uncountable nouns | a little |

→ Language reference and extra practice pages 144–145

10 Underline the correct quantifiers in the sentences below. In some sentences both are correct.

1 We met *a little / a few* Italian designers when we were in Milan.
2 They gave us *some / a couple of* advice on how to improve our service.
3 There will be *plenty of / a lot of* journalists at the fashion show.
4 We'll have to do *a lot of / many* work when we get back from the show.
5 We are looking at *a couple of / a few* new designs for the spring collection.

11 Make sentences about the people below. Try to use as many of the expressions of quantity as possible.

| A few
Some
Enough
Many | | people in my country/town/family … |
| Plenty
A couple
A lot
None | of | the students in my class …
my friends/colleagues … |

A lot of my friends are interested in fashion.

10.3 DEATH OF THE MUSIC INDUSTRY?

SPEAKING AND READING

1 Work with a partner to discuss the following.
1 Where do you get your music from?
2 Do you pay for your music? Why?/Why not?
3 Do you prefer to get singles or albums?
4 Do you know of any trends in the music industry?

2 10.2 Listen to six people talking about their music habits. How do they get their music and why do they like that form of music?

3a Scan the article quickly and decide which of the three people think we should pay for our music.

3b Read the article again. Which person says/implies the following: the downloader (D), the music industry executive (M) or the artist (A)?
1 Overall music sales are falling. A
2 Overall music sales are up this year. M
3 We should download music for free and then pay for what we like. D
4 How important streaming is for teenagers. A
5 Why sales results have improved this year. M
6 Who had the best album in the previous year. M
7 How a music group made money. D

3c Answer these questions about the article.
1 Why were overall music sales down from 2004 till recently?
2 How are CD sales doing compared to digital sales?
3 Why have sales results improved recently?
4 How did the Arctic Monkeys become famous?
5 How are teenagers' music habits changing?
6 Which country rewards musicians fairly?

4a Reacting to the text Look at the following statements. Indicate how strongly you agree or disagree with each statement (1 = agree strongly, 5 = disagree strongly).
1 People should pay for their music.
2 People should pay for books and films.
3 It is impossible to stop people from downloading for free.
4 When authors and singers die, we should not have to pay for their books and songs.

4b Work with a partner to discuss the statements.

Should we pay for our music?

The downloader

I've supported musicians by spending hundreds of dollars on concert tickets and T-shirts. However, I've only paid for ten CDs in my life. I like listening to singles rather than to albums. I go on YouTube and Pandora and I also download songs for free.

Record companies and some artists expect the public to continue paying for music. They want us to believe that if we stop buying music the way they have decided to sell it then the music industry will die. They are wrong. They should allow us to download music for free and then we can start to pay for what we like. The Arctic Monkeys got famous this way and made money. And anyway, they can't do anything to stop people downloading music for free, so they might as well join the 21st century and start supporting creativity.

The music industry executive

It is important to look at the figures. For many years we have read reports on the music industry saying that overall music sales are down due to piracy and illegal downloading. However, this year, for the first time since 2004, overall sales are up. Album sales are up 1.4% to 330.57 million units from 326.15 million the previous year. Adele had the best-selling album, moving 58.2 million copies in the US alone. CD sales fell by 6%, whereas digital downloads rose 20% to 103.1 million.

So, the so-called 'death of the music industry' has not happened. This year's improved results are due to more marketing, the public paying for digital music and the power of social media.

However, it is clear that if people continue downloading music illegally, then the music industry and artists in certain countries will not be able to keep on working. Therefore people should continue to pay for their music.

100

DEATH OF THE MUSIC INDUSTRY? — 10.3

PRONUNCIATION

5a 🔊 10.3 **Numbers** Say the following figures and phrases. Then listen and repeat.

1.4%   58.2 million   20%   103.1 million   21st century
$38.49   64%   2,118,200   4 out of 5   80%

5b Work with a partner. Ask each other what the figures refer to.
What does 1.4 percent refer to?
Album sales rose by 1.4 percent from last year's figures.

GRAMMAR
INFINITIVES AND *-ING* FORMS

6a Look at the highlighted phrases in the text and choose the correct answer in the rules below. In one case both alternatives are possible.
a *expect* is followed by an object + ~~the *-ing form*~~ / infinitive with *to*.
b *decide* is followed by the ~~*-ing form*~~ / infinitive with *to*.
c *continue* is followed by the *-ing form* / infinitive with *to*. ✓
d *suggest* is followed by the *-ing form* / ~~infinitive with to~~.

The artist

Most artists enjoy playing music, but if we do not pay people to record their music, the music industry may collapse, especially since music sales are decreasing. Why would anyone work for free?
The ways teenagers like to listen to their music are changing. 64% of US teenagers mainly listen to music on YouTube. The co-writer of the song 'Heaven is a Place on Earth' only received $38.49 for the 2,118,200 streams the song had on YouTube in one quarter. I suggest looking at fairer ways to reward artists and songwriters. I want us to follow the example of the Swedish people. In Sweden, 4 out of 5 Spotify users pay for the service. For one Swedish independent record label, Hybris, 80% of their income now comes from Spotify.
It is not up to governments or companies to make us choose to behave morally. We have to do that ourselves and pay musicians what they deserve.

6b Complete the table with the verbs in the box. You may want to look at a dictionary. The verbs in bold are all in the article.

expect	**decide**	**continue**	**suggest**	advise
allow	begin	deny	hate	hope	**like**	love
manage	promise	refuse	**start**	teach

Verbs followed by (object +) infinitive with *to*	Verbs followed by *-ing*	Verbs followed by both forms
expect	suggest	continue

GRAMMAR TIP
When we use a verb after a preposition, the verb is always in the *-ing* form.
… keep on working.
Verbs for future intentions tend to take the infinitive, e.g. *try to, hope to, intend to*.

➡ Language reference and extra practice pages 144–145

7 Which two verbs in each sentence below are correct?
1 She _____ downloading her music.
   a enjoyed   b started   c hoped
2 He _____ listening to rock music.
   a decided   b continued   c enjoyed
3 We _____ to go to the concert.
   a promise   b enjoy   c want
4 They _____ getting a new sound system.
   a talked about   b succeeded in   c wanted
5 She _____ going to the cinema.
   a suggested   b decided   c hated
6 He _____ playing music.
   a gave up   b started   c taught
7 She _____ to buy some tickets.
   a hoped   b suggested   c tried

8 Work with a partner and take it in turns to ask and answer these questions.
1 Do you enjoy singing?
2 Do you prefer listening to pop music or watching television?
3 What did you avoid doing last year?
4 What did you finish doing last year?
5 Which teacher encouraged you to work the hardest?
6 Can you remember a time when somebody advised you not to do something?
7 Can you remember a time when somebody persuaded you to do something?

10.4 SCENARIO
BELLEVIEW

SITUATION

1 Read the situation below. Which problem or trend is most serious, do you think?

Twenty five years ago, Belleview, a town on the east coast of England, was well known for its quiet charm and peaceful atmosphere. Many people, tired of life in the capital city, came to Belleview to enjoy its sunny climate and healthy, relaxing lifestyle.

How times have changed! Belleview's population has risen from 60,000 to over 100,000 in the last ten years. More than half the residents are under 30 years old, and Belleview has become a noisy, exciting city. It has two new universities, many more schools and colleges, over 100 language schools for overseas students and a large international population. Business conditions are excellent: new cafés, bars, restaurants and night clubs appear each month.

But the change in Belleview's character has brought problems: dirty beaches, not enough low-cost accommodation, expensive parking, bad behaviour by young people at weekends, increased crime, air pollution. A recent proposal to develop part of the beach has also upset many people.

KEY LANGUAGE
RAISING AND RESPONDING TO ISSUES

2a 10.4 Listen to the Mayor of Belleview, Michael Harvey, answering questions from callers on a radio phone-in programme called 'Speak Your Mind'. Its presenter is Claire Maxwell. Answer the questions.

1 What are the three problems that the callers mention in the phone-in?
2 What action will the mayor take to deal with each problem?

10.4 BELLEVIEW

2b Listen again. Complete the phrases.
1. I want to talk about the parking problem. I'm very _____ about it.
2. Mmm, I _____ how you feel, Brenda.
3. It's a _____ and we're _____ various ways of dealing with it.
4. Thanks very much for your _____.
5. It's _____ the noise and awful behaviour of young people on Friday and Saturday nights.
6. What are you _____ _____ _____ about it, Mr Harvey?
7. We're very _____ about this problem.
8. We're taking it _____ and thinking about various _____ to deal with it.
9. I want _____ _____ _____ you about pollution.
10. I'm _____ _____ you're thinking of leaving our city _____ _____ your health.

3a 10.5 Listen to two residents of Belleview talking about two issues they want to raise at Thursday's meeting. Take notes on the issues.

3b Work with a partner. Take it in turns to summarise one issue each.

TASK
PARTICIPATING IN A MEETING

4a The Mayor of Belleview has arranged a meeting in the town hall so that people can raise issues that concern them. Work in groups of four or five. Choose a role and read your role card.

Mayor: Turn to page 157.
Environment officer: Turn to page 163.
Resident 1: Turn to page155.
Resident 2: Turn to page 161.
Student: Turn to page 159.

4b Now hold the meeting. The mayor leads the discussion.
1. Discuss each problem and possible solutions.
2. Suggest which three problems should have priority. The Council will deal with these problems before the other ones.
   - parking
   - young people's behaviour at weekends
   - increased crime
   - pollution
   - dirty beaches
   - proposed development at Sandy Cove
   - student accommodation

4c Compare your decisions with the other groups.

10.5 STUDY AND WRITING SKILLS

STUDY SKILLS
RECORDING AND LEARNING VOCABULARY

1 Work with a partner to discuss these questions.
1. Do you find it easier to learn vocabulary or grammar?
2. How successful do you think you are as a vocabulary learner?
3. Which statement is most true for you?
   a. I find it easy to learn and remember new vocabulary.
   b. I find it easy to learn new vocabulary at the time, but difficult to remember.
   c. I find learning and remembering vocabulary difficult.

2 How do you record and learn vocabulary? What techniques or strategies do you have?

Exercises 3, 4 and 5 introduce some different techniques for vocabulary learning.

3 Look at the techniques below for recording new vocabulary. Which do you do? Write 1 for *always*, 2 for *sometimes* and 3 for *never*. Compare your answers with a partner.
1. write a translation of the word/phrase in your own language _____
2. write an explanation of the word/phrase in English _____
3. record the pronunciation, including stress _____
4. write the part of speech (verb, noun, etc.) _____
5. write synonyms/antonyms (words with the same/opposite meaning) _____
6. write other words in the same family (e.g. *trend* – noun, *trendy* – adj, *a trendsetter* – noun, person) _____
7. record collocations (words often used together, e.g. *upward trend*, *fashion conscious*) _____
8. record grammatical patterns (e.g. verb patterns, prepositions, etc.) _____

It is a good idea to organise your vocabulary in a variety of ways. This will help you to see patterns and make connections. Do Exercises 4a–4c to see the different methods. Which methods do you find useful?

4a Topic headings Match the verbs in the first box with the nouns in the second box and then put them under the most appropriate heading.

Business	Engineering	Trends
	build a prototype	

| build | do | follow | launch | go out | value | go |
| solve | start | | | | | |

| into partnership | of fashion | staff | a prototype |
| a product | a problem | fashion | a trend | safety tests |

4b Diagrams Add some words to the word web.

4c Pictures/symbols Match the chart types with the pictures below.

(line) graph   table   bar chart   flow chart   pie chart

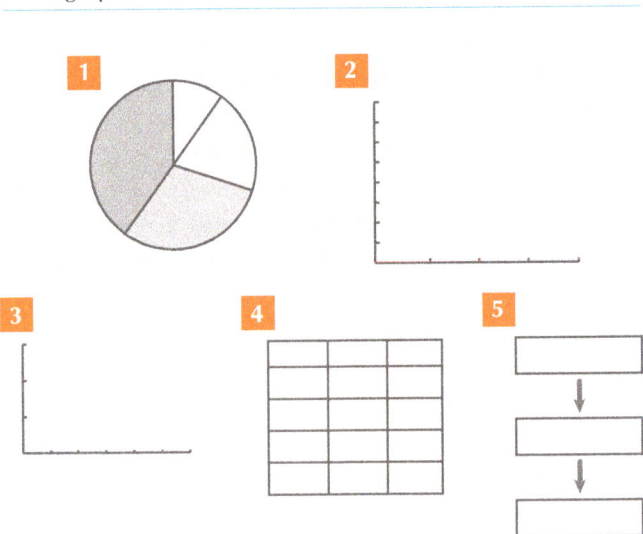

5a 10.6 Learning vocabulary Listen to six students talking about how they learn vocabulary. Write the number of the speaker by the technique he/she describes.
a. putting vocabulary into categories _____
b. displaying new words on a wall _____
c. filling gaps in sentences _____
d. hearing and saying words several times _____
e. learning groups of words with the same origin _____
f. remembering a key word, i.e. something that reminds you of the word _____

6 Which of the techniques above are most useful for you?

STUDY AND WRITING SKILLS 10.5

WRITING SKILLS
DESCRIBING A TREND

7a Complete the table with the words and phrases in the box. Use a dictionary to check whether each word or phrase is a noun, a verb, or both.

| increase | drop | decline | level off | rise | fall | peak |
| grow | go up | decrease | stabilise | remain stable |

7b Describe each of the graphs below, using an adjective from the box and a noun from Exercise 7a. Use a dictionary to help you decide which words collocate. There may be more than one possibility.

| dramatic | significant | steady | sharp | slow |
| gradual | slight | sudden |

1 _slow fall_ 3 _____ 5 _____

2 _____ 4 _____ 6 _____

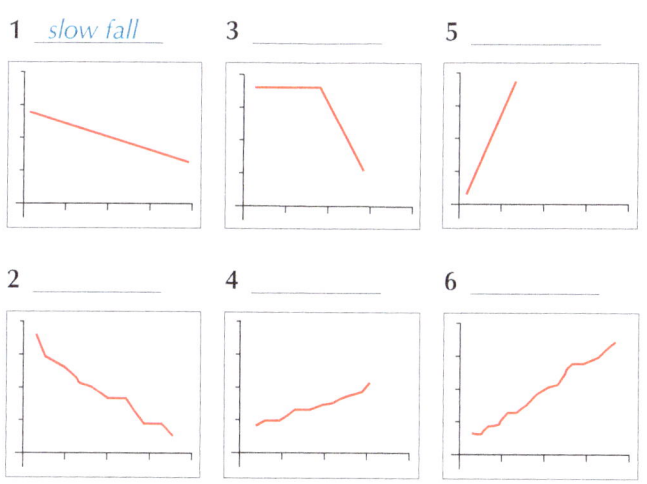

8 Read the extract from a report on spending on recorded music in different formats between 1973 and 2009 on the right. Match each paragraph with its purpose.
a gives the main trend
b gives the conclusion
c gives more detail and any surprising or opposite trends
d gives the source of the information and what it shows

9 What do you think will happen in the future to music sales?

10 Avoiding repetition Read the report again and replace the words in bold with the words and phrases in the box.

conducted	findings	finds	largest decrease
a marked fall	relatively stable	small
sudden decrease	survey	twice as much as

11 Which verb tenses are used in the report to indicate changes? Find some examples.

What does the future hold?

¹ This chart shows the **results** of a study **carried out** for the Recording Industry Association of America into spending per person on recorded music in the USA. The **study** compares spending from 1973 to 2009 across several different formats of music: 8-track, vinyl, cassettes, CD, video and digital.

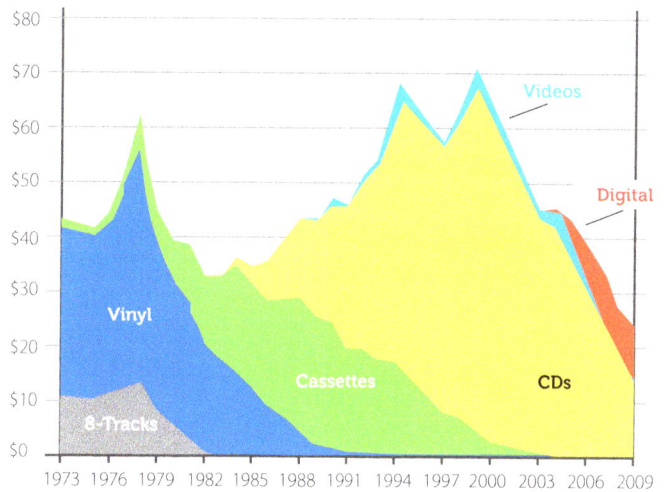

² Overall, the survey **shows** that after reaching a peak in 1999 spending on music has been falling. Spending on music per capita is nearly three times less than it was in 1999. Since 2003 CD, video and digital have all shown a **sharp drop** in revenue.

³ Between 1973 and 1975 there was a **slight** decrease in sales of 8-track, vinyl and cassettes. However, from 1975 to 1979 all the formats showed a **fairly constant** rise, although with the arrival of CDs in the early 1980s revenue fell. From the mid 1980s CD spending continued growing while that of vinyl and cassettes went down. (Sales of the 8-track format were completely finished by 1982.) Interestingly, the value of the US music industry in 1973 was almost **double** that of 2009.

⁴ In summary, music spending in the US has shown **significant decline** since 2000, and 2004 to 2009 are the worst five years since 1979. It could be that we are now seeing the **greatest fall** in music spending since the industry began.

12 Look at the chart below showing trends in US recorded music single sales and the recent digital formats. Write a description of the changes the chart shows. Use the description above as a model and the words and phrases from Exercise 7.

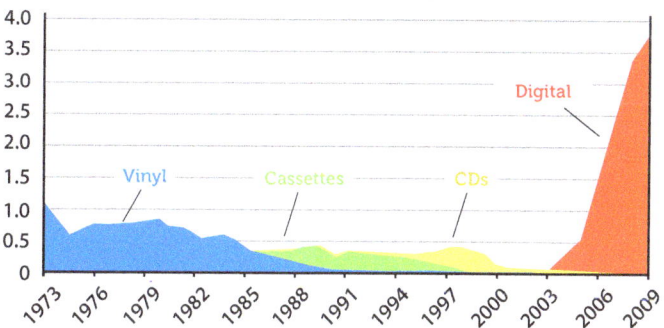

105

11 Arts and media
11.1 TYPES OF MEDIA

IN THIS UNIT

GRAMMAR
- reported speech
- reported questions

VOCABULARY
- describing books and films
- media genres
- words connected with the arts

SCENARIO
- comparing and contrasting
- choosing a film to produce

STUDY SKILLS
- delivering a presentation

WRITING SKILLS
- a short formal report

In the future everyone will be famous for 15 minutes. Andy Warhol, 1928–1987, US artist and film-maker

[handwritten: Not enough vocab review. Bit dull!]

READING AND LISTENING

1a In groups, look at the different types of media in the box. Do you use them? How often? Where?

| radio | newspapers | magazines | films | TV |
| books | internet | computer games | ebooks | apps |

1b Which of the types of media from Exercise 1a do you prefer for the following?
- finding out about news
- education
- entertainment
- research

2a Read the three reviews on this page. Match each one with one of the types of media in Exercise 1a. Which words or phrases helped you to decide?

2b *Inferring the writer's opinion* Which of the following star ratings do you think the critic gave at the end of each review? Which words or expressions helped you make your choice?

0 TERRIBLE * POOR ** AVERAGE *** GOOD
**** VERY GOOD ***** EXCELLENT

3a  11.1 Listen to three more reviews and match each one with one of the types of media in Exercise 1a.
[handwritten above: radio book film]

3b Listen again and give each review a star rating.

*[handwritten notes:
4 monday hilarious recommend en (real)
5 sorry no real plot, noise had read cowboy wolf had read recent huge disappointment
6 old film classic horror edge of seat]*

WATCH

1 NEW SERIES ...
In this breathtaking <u>documentary</u> series, Professor Brian Cox takes us to the most extreme locations to explain some of the natural wonders of the solar system. The groundbreaking new filming techniques film the Sun, the magnificent rings of Saturn and Olympus Mon on Mars, the tallest mountain in the solar system.

2 <u>NASA engineers</u> have created an out-of-this-world <u>application</u> for tablets and smartphones that will keep you up-to-date and better informed about NASA missions, space science and new discoveries. You can stream live NASA TV or view the stunning Pictures of the Day. If I could only choose one application for my tablet, this would be the one.

3 'I was disappointed with Roller Coaster World'
I have to say I was disappointed with *Roller Coaster World*. The <u>graphic</u>s are just about adequate but the instruction menus were impossible to follow. Nothing exciting happens after you have created the roller coaster. I would think long and hard before buying this one.

TYPES OF MEDIA

11.1

7 The Hunger Games is the first book of the Hunger Games trilogy, the international best-selling series for young adults by Suzanne Collins. The first few pages of the ¹ _novel_ got me completely hooked. It's entertaining and very disturbing. I enjoyed reading every ² _chapter_. The dramatic life-or-death ³ _plot_ is very gripping. Collins has presented us with a great story full of heroism, fighting and love.

8 THE ARTIST is a silent French ⁴ _rom com_ in black and white. The ⁵ _location_ is Hollywood and it is set in 1929, when ⁶ _audiences_ flocked to films with sound rather than silent films. The ⁷ _lead_ is Jean Dujardin and the ⁸ _cast_ includes Berenice Bejo as Peppy Miller and Uggie as Jack (the dog). It is the first French winner of the Academy Awards' Best Picture.

9 Radio week

It's a laugh is an outstanding new radio ⁹ _series_, on every Monday evening. My favourite sketch of this week's show is 'Shop Trek', a hilarious sketch based on shopping in the future.

FILM REVIEW

10 Another classic horror film of the 1950s has been re-released this week. Hitchcock's Psycho, with its brooding dark _atmosphere_ in the house on the hill and the breathtaking shower scene in the motel, is the perfect example of 'edge-of-your-seat suspense'.

VOCABULARY
DESCRIBING BOOKS AND FILMS; MEDIA GENRES

4a Complete reviews 7–10 with the words in the box.

atmosphere   plot   series   romantic comedy   location
chapter   novel   lead actor   audiences   cast

4b Find adjectives in the seven reviews that mean the following.
1 keeps your attention and interest _edge of your seat_
2 extremely beautiful _breathtaking stunning_
3 using new ideas and methods _groundbreaking_
4 excellent, very good _outstanding_
5 very funny _hilarious_
6 important and typical of its type _classic_
7 incredible and exciting _breathtaking dramatic_
8 good enough, but not very good _adequate_

5a Look at the words in the box and add them to the word web.

soap   R&B   crime   documentary   thriller   quiz show
horror   current affairs programme   reggae   reality
drama series   rap   hip hop   animation   rom com
autobiography   science fiction   opera   garage

5b Can you think of any other examples to add to the headings?

SPEAKING

6a Choose two of your favourite TV series, books, films or computer games. Think about these questions and take notes.

- What genre or type is it (horror, science fiction, etc.)?
- Where and when is it set?
- What is the basic plot?
- Who are the main characters?
- What adjectives would you use to describe it?
- Why is it your favourite?

6b In groups, take it in turns to tell each other about one of your favourites. Listen to the other speakers, ask them questions and give your opinions, e.g. Did you know about it? Does it sound interesting? Would you like to watch/read/play it?

6c As a group, decide which was the best description. Then that person retells their summary to the whole class.

WRITING

7 You have bought one of the following online: a film, DVD, computer game, novel. Write your own review and give it a star rating. Use the reviews to help you write your review.

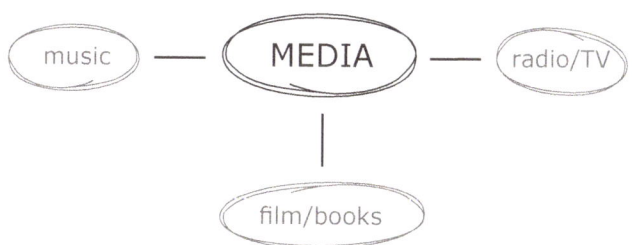

11.2 MEDIA RECLUSES IN THE ARTS

READING

1 You are going to read about a famous recluse. What do you think a recluse is? Guess, then read the introduction of the article below to check your answer.

A recluse is someone who:
a likes media attention.
b avoids media attention.
c comes back after a period away from media attention.

2a In groups of three, each read about one recluse and answer the questions.

Student A: Read the article below.
Student B: Read the article on page 162.
Student C: Read the article on page 161.

1 How is the person's character described in the article?
2 What is their most famous piece of work?
3 How was their relationship with the media?
4 What did they do later in life?
5 Is there anything surprising in the article?

2b Tell your group about your article. Use the questions in Exercise 2a to help you.

2c Discuss in groups. Which person/people:

1 was/were worried about personal safety?
2 moved to the countryside?
3 pretended to be someone else?
4 won an award?
5 had their work connected to a famous crime?
6 returned to his place of birth?
7 moved to another country?
8 was/were offered a lot of money for any new work?
9 didn't like travelling by air?
10 had a book written about them by one of their children?

VOCABULARY
WORDS CONNECTED WITH THE ARTS

3 Find words or phrases in the texts that mean the following.

1 a very successful book (article 1, para 5)
2 a great work of art (article 1, para 6; article 2, para 1; article 3, para 1)
3 a book about someone's life (article 1, para 7)
4 very successful songs or pieces of music (article 2, para 1)
5 a very well-known person (article 2, para 2)
6 payments made to a writer of a book, song, etc. (article 2, para 2)
7 a very long book or film (article 3, para 2)
8 a very successful film (article 3, para 3)
9 people whose job it is to give their opinions of books, films, etc. (article 3, para 3)

J.D. Salinger (1919–2010)

Out of sight, out of mind?

¹ In today's multi-media age, it seems no artist with something to sell can afford not to do interviews and chat shows to publicise their latest product. People's interest in celebrity means we often know more about the artists than their work. Below, our reporter Wendy Finch profiles three recluses from the world of the arts who decided not to play the media game. Why are we fascinated by the artists themselves when really their work should speak for them?

² The American writer J.D. Salinger was known as a recluse. He did not give an interview after 1974, nor publish any new work after 1965. Salinger's complete published works consist of one novel and 13 short stories, all written in the period 1948–59.

³ In 1997, a rumour started that Salinger was going to release the first book version of his last published story. Fans became very excited. However, because of the publicity, Salinger changed his mind.

MEDIA RECLUSES IN THE ARTS 11.2

SPEAKING

4 Justifying opinions In groups, discuss these questions.
1 Which of the three profiles did you think was the most interesting? Why?
2 Which books, songs and films do you think are masterpieces?
3 Do you think celebrities have the right to a private life? Why?/Why not?

GRAMMAR
REPORTED SPEECH

5a Look at this example of how J.D. Salinger's words are reported. What two changes are there between the two sentences?

'I like to write but I write for myself.' → He told a reporter that *he liked to write but that he wrote for himself.*

4 Strangely for a future writer, when he was at college one of his professors insisted he was the worst English student in the history of the college. Before writing his famous book, he had only published a few short stories in magazines.

5 Salinger established his reputation with a single novel, *The Catcher in the Rye* (1951), an immediate bestseller which still sells 250,000 copies per year. It is also famously the book Mark Chapman was obsessed with, and calmly reading, when he was arrested for the murder of John Lennon in New York in 1980. The main character, Holden Caulfield, is a sensitive, rebellious teenager experiencing the growing pains of highschool and college students.

6 Salinger did not do much to help publicise his masterpiece and asked that his photograph should not be used in connection with it. The public attention which followed the success of the book caused him to move from New York to the far away hills of Cornish, New Hampshire. From the late 1960s he tried to escape publicity. In 1974 he told a reporter that he liked to write but that he wrote for himself and his own pleasure.

7 Later, he tried to stop publication of a biography which included letters he had written to other authors and friends. In 2000 his daughter published a biography. In it she claimed her father was not a recluse. She said he travelled often and had friends all over the world. She added that he enjoyed being with people and was friendly except where publicity and celebrity were concerned.

8 Salinger refused to sell the movie rights to any of his stories to Hollywood and did not allow films of any of his works.

5b Find other examples of reported speech from the profiles of J.D. Salinger, Syd Barrett and Stanley Kubrick that match these direct quotes. Write them down.
1 J.D. Salinger: 'I like to write but I write for myself.'
He told a reporter that he liked to write but that he wrote for himself.
2 A professor: 'You are the worst English student in the history of the college.'
3 Salinger's daughter: 'He also enjoys being with people.'
4 Syd Barrett: 'I walk a lot.'
5 A bald, fat man: 'Syd can't talk.'
6 Syd Barrett: 'Please leave.'
7 Stanley Kubrick: 'I travel to London four or five times a year.'

6a Look at the examples of reported speech that you have written and answer the questions.
1 What do you notice about verbs in reported speech?
2 Which verbs are used to report the statements in Exercise 5b (e.g. *told*)? Write them down.
3 Look at the structures following the reporting verbs. When do we use the infinitive with *to* instead of a *that*-clause?
4 Look at the verbs *say* and *tell*. Which one needs a personal object (*him, her, them*, etc.)?

6b In reported speech we usually change the tense of the speech we are reporting (e.g. present perfect → past perfect, present continuous → past continuous).

How do we change the present simple and *can* when we report them? Look again at the examples in Exercise 5b.

GRAMMAR TIP

In reported speech, we often also make changes to pronouns, e.g. *I* → *he/she, our* → *their*, and to adverbs, e.g. *today* → *then/that day, yesterday* → *the day before*.

↪ Language reference and extra practice pages 146–147

7 Change these sentences to reported speech. Use the phrases in brackets to help you.
1 We expect our new release to be a big hit. (*The band said …*)
The band said that they expected their new release to be a big hit.
2 I am writing a new article today. (*He said he …*)
3 I have just finished writing a new book for my publisher. (*She said …*)
4 Val refused to speak to the reporters yesterday. (*He said Val …*)
5 We'll finish the recording tomorrow. (*They said …*)

8 Think about the last interview you saw on TV with a famous person (e.g. a musician, actor, film-maker, writer, politician, sportsperson). Tell your partner as much as you can remember about what was said.

109

11.3 THE LIFE OF A FOREIGN CORRESPONDENT

LISTENING

1 You are going to listen to a journalist, Richard, talking about an interview he attended for a job as a foreign correspondent. Discuss these questions.
1 What does a foreign correspondent do?
2 What questions do you think the interviewer will ask the journalist?

2a 11.2 Listen to the conversation. Tick (✓) the questions that Richard was asked in his interview.
1 Why do you want to be a foreign correspondent?
2 What parts of the world are you interested in?
3 Have you travelled a lot?
4 Do you speak any foreign languages?
5 Where did you go to university?
6 Have you taken any further qualifications?
7 What articles have you written?
8 What qualities does a journalist need to be a foreign correspondent?
9 When can you start work?
10 Are you physically fit?

2b Listen to the conversation again and cross out the incorrect option.
1 Richard has worked
  a for a local newspaper
  b for a national newspaper
  c in TV
2 He is interested in
  a Australia
  b Argentina and Brazil
  c Arab countries
3 He speaks
  a English and Arabic
  b Japanese and Korean
  c Spanish and Portuguese
4 He has
  a qualifications in IT and new digital technologies
  b a Masters in Media
  c a Diploma in Communications
5 For exercise he
  a goes to the gym
  b goes jogging
  c does karate

3 Would you like to be a foreign correspondent? Why?/Why not?

GRAMMAR
REPORTED QUESTIONS

4a In the conversation, Richard told Nura about the interview. Look at the questions you ticked in Exercise 2a. Find the reported versions of these questions in Audio script 11.2 on page 174.

Why do you want to be a foreign correspondent?
She asked me why I wanted to be a foreign correspondent.

4b Choose the correct answer in each rule.
1 We use *if* or *whether* to report *yes/no questions* / *wh- questions*.
2 When questions are reported, the word order *changes* / *doesn't change* from the order of the original direct question.
3 The reported question has the same word order as a *statement* / *question*.
4 The verb in the reported question *often* / *never* changes tense from the tense in the direct question.

→ Language reference and extra practice pages 146–147

5 You are a foreign correspondent. You were interviewed about your job by some university students. Write their questions below in reported speech. Start with 'They asked me …'
1 Are you able to write notes quickly?
2 What time do you usually start work?
3 Do you enjoy working as a reporter?
4 What do you do when people don't answer your questions?
5 How much time do you spend travelling abroad?
6 Do you ever feel afraid in a crisis?
7 What problems do you have when you are reporting?

THE LIFE OF A FOREIGN CORRESPONDENT

ME AND MY CAREER:
Rageh Omar

Foreign correspondent, TV news presenter and writer. Has worked for the BBC, Al Jazeera and ITV News.

Currently: Special correspondent and presenter for ITV News.

1 _____

I first became interested in my teens. I'm originally from Somalia and lots of my family have travelled far and wide, throughout Africa, the Middle East and Europe.

I saw journalism as a really good way of getting out into the world and, as someone who was born in Somalia, educated in the west and is a Muslim, I feel at home in several different cultures.

2 _____

I wangled my way into a month's traineeship at the *Voice* newspaper in Brixton but my first real job in journalism was as a stringer* for the BBC in Ethiopia. I really didn't want to go back into education, so I went out to Ethiopia in May 1991 with £800 in my pocket in the hope of getting some work. BBC Africa said they'd take occasional pieces from me. I came back a year later and was offered a job with the *World Service*.

3 _____

It's hard to single out one in particular but one moment that was really touching was when we were covering Kosovo along with thousands of other journalists. We were in a village on the border with the Former Yugoslav Republic of Macedonia, doing a story about a hospital. All the soldiers had left and we were interviewing one of the main surgeons.

After we had switched off the camera, he said that it felt as though we had been with him every night. He had been hiding in a basement there because there was no way of getting into Kosovo and every night he would translate our reports to all the others present. It brought home to me how much responsibility we had.

4 _____

As a stringer I was paid by the piece. I got £45 for each dispatch and £60 for a live radio interview. Each month the BBC would send me out my little cheque with details of how many dispatches I'd done. Obviously, it depended on how much news there was around at the time but it was quite tough to survive for that first year, even in Ethiopia.

5 _____

Don't be daunted and don't be shy in any sense. If there's a programme or an organisation you really like, call them, ask to come in and see them. You'd be amazed how often you get a positive response.

You need that nerve but also remember it's about integrity and storytelling. You must be able to listen as well as talk and convey the story as accurately as possible.

* A *stringer* is a person who regularly sends stories to a news organisation but who is not employed by them.

READING

6 Why do you think people choose to be foreign correspondents? What qualities do you think you need to be a foreign correspondent?

7a Identifying topics Read the extracts from an interview with Rageh Omar, a foreign correspondent. Fill the gaps with these questions.

a   What was your best experience?
b   What advice do you have for those starting out?
c   What was your first salary?
d   What was your first job?
e   How did you become interested in journalism?

7b In which section (1–5) can you find this information?

a   what qualities a foreign correspondent needs to have
b   where Rageh Omar was trained
c   why he decided to be a journalist
d   where he was born
e   when he first went to Ethiopia
f   how he was paid
g   an experience that showed him that journalism was an important job

8 Find words and phrases in the interview that mean the following.

1   got something by clever, and maybe dishonest, methods (section 2)
2   a short period when someone learns about a job (section 2)
3   to choose one thing from many others (section 3)
4   made me realise (section 3)
5   discouraged, worried (section 5)
6   the quality of being honest and having high moral standards (section 5)

SPEAKING AND WRITING

9 Work with a partner. One of you witnessed an important news event. Decide together what the event was (e.g. the effect of an earthquake or hurricane on a city).

Student A: You are a reporter. Write five questions about what Student B saw. Then interview him/her.

Student B: You are an eyewitness. Make a few notes about what you saw. Then answer A's questions.

After the interview, write a short summary of it. Use reported speech.

Anna said she had felt very frightened. I asked her what had happened and she said she had felt the building shaking and …

11.4 SCENARIO
THE SILVER SCREEN

SITUATION

1 Read the situation below. What sort of film would be good to invest in, do you think?

Gemini Television is a large independent broadcaster. They have had success in television with mini-series and situation comedies. Recently the company has decided to move into film-making in order to both raise its profile and to increase profits. They have received some film proposals or 'pitches' from directors working in different countries. They are considering investing in one of the projects, which they will sell around the world.

2a 11.3 Listen to two executives from Gemini Television talking about the move into film-making. Do they agree on the direction they want to follow?

2b Listen again. Tick (✓) the things the executives mention.

1. the genre of the film
2. originality of the idea
3. actors
4. experience of the director
5. locations used
6. how easy it will be to sell around the world
7. the surprise element
8. the cost

KEY LANGUAGE
COMPARING AND CONTRASTING

3a Listen again and complete the sentences and phrases.

1 AMY: ... it's very ___ ___ the kind of things we've done in the past.
2 BOB: It's the ___ ___ TV really, just everything's bigger.
3 AMY: ... which is ___ ___ ___ the sort of stuff we usually make.
4 BOB: ... something ___ ___ ___ what we've been doing recently.
5 AMY: ... unhappy housewives. ___ ___ ___ , I don't think the genre is that important really.
6 BOB: Actually, I think the director is ___ ___ ___ the location.
7 AMY: ... different places. On ___ ___ ___ , it'll have more international appeal, ...
8 AMY: ... and find we have something ___ ___ ___ than our usual TV series.

3b Read the film descriptions and compare them to films which you know. Try and use some of the key language above.

Film 1 sounds quite similar to ...

11.4 THE SILVER SCREEN

1 Title: Hands up for Happiness

Genre: romantic comedy
Plot: Two pairs of identical twins, one Italian and one Russian, meet and start relationships. They have problems telling the difference between each twin. Will they end up with the right person?
Cast: unknown actors as need to be real twins
Special features: very romantic locations, e.g. Venice, St Petersburg. Also will be popular in many countries and promotes international relations.
Budget: $20–30 million max.
Audience: 20–35-year-olds

2 Title: Alien Dawn

Genre: science fiction
Plot: Story takes place 500 years in the future. The Earth is attacked by aliens. A small group survive the attack and try to save the planet. Will they succeed before the aliens breed?
Cast: to be decided (by the director)
Special features: stunning special effects, exciting visually
Budget: $40–60 million max.
Audience: 15 upwards

3 Title: Exit Strategy

Genre: thriller
Plot: A woman picks up the wrong bag at an airport and is mistaken for a foreign agent who has secret documents. She is chased around the world by criminals, government agents and the real owner of the bag.
Cast: major Hollywood star as lead actress
Special features: many locations around the world, lots of twists and turns in the story, strong possibility for a sequel, and for turning the lead character into a female James Bond
Budget: at least $80–100 million
Audience: 15 upwards

4 Title: Midnight Sun

Genre: action/adventure
Plot: A story of family honour, revenge, great love and of good versus evil. A young Japanese man brought up in the USA returns to the country of his birth. He discovers the dark secret of the family, and the reason he was brought up in the USA. His search for the truth leads him to the Philippines and to the beautiful princess Satsuki.
Cast: young, unknown actors
Special features: superbly choreographed fight scenes
Budget: $45–65 million max.
Audience: worldwide, but probably over 18 due to violence

TASK
CHOOSING A FILM TO PRODUCE

4 You are executives at Gemini Television. It is your job to decide which film Gemini should make. Read the four film descriptions again. Use the evaluation form below to score each film out of 10 in the different categories. (10 = excellent, 1 = very poor). Note down reasons for your score.

	Hands up …	Alien Dawn	Exit Strategy	Midnight Sun
Genre				
Plot				
Locations				
Cast/actors				
Special features				
Potential for success				
TOTAL				

5 Work in groups of four. Discuss the advantages and disadvantages of each film and decide in your groups which film you want to produce.

6a Join with another group and report on your discussion and decision.

6b Try and agree on a final decision as a class.

11.5 STUDY AND WRITING SKILLS

STUDY SKILLS
DELIVERING A PRESENTATION

1a ▶ 11.1 You are going to see extracts from two presentations about a music and dance festival. Work with a partner. Watch the first presentation, then discuss these questions.
1 What is the main topic of the speaker in each extract?
2 What is your general impression of the speaker's delivery of the talk?

1b Watch the presentation again. Match each statement to the correct extract, 1, 2 or 3.
a He speaks too quietly so the audience can't hear what he says.
b He reads directly from his notes without looking at the audience.
c He does not begin by giving a plan of his talk.
d He forgets what the next topic is.
e He puts too much on his slide.
f He turns his back on his audience.
g He cannot find the right place in his notes.
h He touches his hair and tie, showing that he is very nervous.

1c What other mistakes do you think he made?

2a ▶ 11.2 You are now going to see a different way to present. Watch the introduction. Number the following in the order you hear them.
a I've divided my talk into three parts.
b Next, I'll talk about our sponsors.
c Finally, I'll discuss our plans for advertising the event.
d I'm going to tell you about our plans for the festival.
e I'll start by telling you about the kind of performers we want to attract.
f Thank you for coming to my talk.

2b ▶ 11.3 Look at the statements below. Then watch the whole talk. Which six statements does the speaker demonstrate?
The speaker:
1 has good eye contact with the audience.
2 explains clearly the organisation of the talk.
3 starts his talk with a joke.
4 asks a question to the audience.
5 speaks very loudly at all times during the talk.
6 changes the pace of his speech and varies his intonation.
7 uses slides clearly and effectively.
8 regularly looks at a transcript of his talk.
9 signals that he will introduce a new point.
10 is happy to answer questions at any time during the talk.

3 Expressions for a presentation Match the expressions to their functions. Work in pairs and practise saying each expression.
Expressions
1 I'm going to tell you about our plans for the festival.
2 Right, moving on now.
3 OK, let me sum up.
4 Are there any questions you'd like to ask me?
5 I've divided my talk into three parts.
6 Good morning, everyone. Thanks for coming to my talk.
7 Can you give me a show of hands, please?
8 I'm confident the festival will be a fantastic success.

Functions
a showing enthusiasm
b signalling that the speaker will introduce a new point
c interacting with the audience
d starting the talk
e ending the talk
f stating the purpose of the talk
g explaining how the talk is organised
h restating the key points of the talk

4a Work with a partner. You are both going to give the same presentation. Look at the situation and notes below and prepare what you are going to say.

You are an organiser of a street festival (a festival with people who perform their acts in the street to passers-by) in the area where you live.

Location: in the city centre – main square
History of the festival: Has been held for the last ten years. Always very successful. People of all ages attend. Children love the festival.
Dates: 15–20 April
Times: 11 a.m.–6 p.m.
Performers: singers, dancers, jugglers, puppeteers, comedians, etc., local acts and from abroad. Interest from all over the world.
Special event: performance by a famous US singer
Advertising: newspaper ads, radio spots, leaflets, posters
Advantages to sponsors: low charges for all types of advertising, e.g. posters, banners, etc. Thousands of people will see the adverts.
Other information? Other special events? Food? Security?

STUDY AND WRITING SKILLS 11.5

4b Take it in turns to deliver your presentation. The listener should take notes using the evaluation questions below. After the talk, give feedback to each other on the presentation and performance.

PRESENTATION EVALUATION

Rating: 1–5
(1 = needs improving, 3 = good, 5 = excellent)

Eye contact with audience? ____

Stated the purpose of the talk / how it was organised? ____

Spoke clearly (not too loud or soft)? ____

Spoke at a good pace (not too fast or slow)? ____

Body language (confident, relaxed, no sign of nerves)? ____

Slides or visual aids? ____

Total score ____ /30

---

5 Prepare a short talk (five minutes) about a festival or event you have been to / regularly go to. Work in small groups and deliver your talk to the rest of your group. Answer any questions they may have.

WRITING SKILLS
A SHORT FORMAL REPORT

6a Read the report by an organiser of a street festival. Choose the most suitable heading for each paragraph.

a Conclusion
b Audiences
c Performers
d Recommendations
e Refreshments
f Introduction

6b Work with a partner to discuss the following.
1 What were the good points about the festival?
2 How can the organisers improve next year's festival?

7 Making generalisations There are several examples of making generalisations in this report. When you generalise, you say that something is true about most people or things. Look at two examples of words/phrases used to generalise from the report.

Overall, the festival was highly successful …
Most of the performers were excellent …

Work with a partner to find other examples of generalising in sections 2–6 of the report.

8 Imagine that the festival you talked about in Exercise 4 has now taken place. Write a report on the festival, with recommendations for improving it next year. Use 'generalising language' where appropriate.

Report on Street Festival
(April 15–20)

1 _____

Overall, the festival was highly successful, attracting over 50,000 people. The weather was good, although it rained heavily on the first day. Most of the performers were excellent and well received by the public.

2 _____

People attending were mainly families. However, there were people of all ages, and a large number from the various ethnic groups in our community. The acts appealing to children were particularly popular.

3 _____

The majority were singers and dancers, but there was a wide variety of acts from over 20 countries. Almost all of the performers started and finished their acts on time. Perhaps the highlight of the festival was the music and dance routines of a group from Ethiopia.

4 _____

There were many outlets offering hot and cold food. On the whole, people were satisfied with the quality of the food and service. However, some people complained that the queues were too long at the more popular outlets and said that there needed to be a greater variety of ethnic foods.

5 _____

The festival gave great pleasure to a large number of people and it brought together the different cultural communities within our city. In general, the sponsors were very pleased with the organisation of the festival. Most of them wanted to participate in next year's festival.

6 _____

- Ways of reducing crowds at the most popular events should be considered.
- More signs need to be provided and a wider variety of food offered.
- Programmes showing daily events should be sold to spectators.
- Special access for mothers with young children could be arranged.
- It is vital to hire more security staff.
- We must start to advertise the event much earlier.

12 Crime

12.1 REAL CRIMES?

IN THIS UNIT

GRAMMAR
- third conditional
- modals (past deduction)

VOCABULARY
- crime
- collocations (4)

SCENARIO
- reaching a decision
- discussing court cases

STUDY SKILLS
- summarising

WRITING SKILLS
- a cause and effect essay

Behind every great fortune there is a crime. Honore De Balzac, 1799–1850, French novelist

SPEAKING

1a Work in groups. Look at the following activities. In your opinion, is each one:

a   quite a serious crime?
b   a crime, but not a serious one?
c   not a crime at all?

- writing graffiti
- making personal phone calls from work
- taking small items from hotel bedrooms when you are a guest
- saying nothing when you get too much change in a supermarket
- parking in a space for disabled drivers
- driving at 20km/h more than the speed limit on a motorway
- finding a wallet/purse containing money and not taking it to the police
- buying an essay on the internet
- making your CV/resume better by not including information or putting incorrect information
- not giving all the facts when making an insurance claim

1b Think of one more activity for a), b) and c) in Exercise 1a. Then discuss your ideas in groups.

REAL CRIMES?

12.1

READING AND VOCABULARY
CRIME

2a Look at the title of the article and read the first line. What does the first line tell you about the title?

2b Read the newspaper reports and answer the questions.
1. Which story/stories involve taking/trying to take money?
2. Which story/stories involve taking possessions?
3. Which story/stories involve automobiles?
4. Which story/stories involve damaging property?

3 Which is your favourite story from the text?

4 *Inferring emotions* How do you think the people highlighted in **bold** in the text felt? Choose from the adjectives below or use others you can think of. Explain your choices to a partner.

worried   angry   surprised   amused
frightened   confused

5 Complete the word web with words from the text. (The first letter of each word is given.)

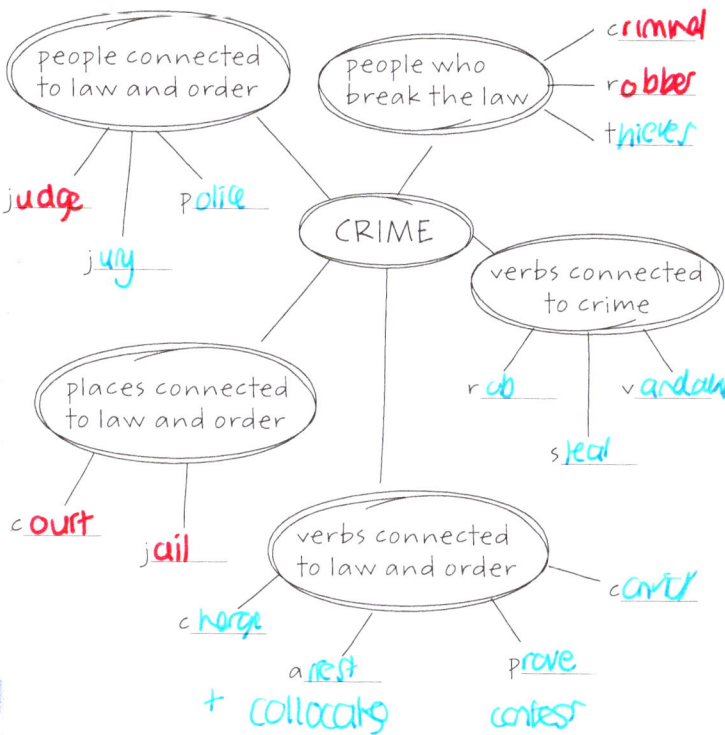

1
In Ontario, Canada, police charged Daniel Glenn with robbing a convenience store. Unwisely, he telephoned ahead to ask the sales assistant how much money was in the cash register. **The assistant** called the police who arrested Glen nearby.

2
In England, brainless 18-year-old **Peter Addison** vandalised a children's campsite building. After smashing the building he chose to write 'Peter Addison was here' on the wall in black marker pen. When police tracked him down he was also wearing a T-shirt stolen from the crime scene, proving to police they had the right man.

3
Police in California charged a daft 37-year-old San Francisco man with stealing a Lexus SUV. Unfortunately, after stealing the car, he chose to drive it to court. On the same day, a jury had to decide if they should convict him of another unrelated car theft charge. They found him guilty of both crimes.

4
In Vancouver, Canada, an **armed robber** held up a petrol station. The half-witted 22-year-old was chased by the police after the hold-up, got lost and so stopped at a petrol station to ask for directions. It was the one he had just robbed.

5
Two useless car thieves were caught when they couldn't understand how to drive a manual car. After holding up the owner of the Honda in the state of Georgia, USA, they spent several minutes trying to work out how to drive the car. Before they could escape, the police arrived and arrested them.

6
An inept criminal in Germany was sent to jail by a judge for four years after trying to rob a bank. The problem was he couldn't see out of the mask he was wearing, so he lifted it to demand money from **the cashier**. This allowed the police to identify him.

7
Two foolish criminals in Colombia face armed robbery charges for trying to rob an internet café. When they came into the café, they seemed to be normal customers. They rented two computers and sat down for a while. When it came time to pay, they took out guns, refused to pay the bill, and stole money from the cash register. Unfortunately, one of the robbers had forgotten to log out of his Facebook account. **Police** used the data to look up his home address, where they found him, and took him to jail.

6 Work with a partner. Talk about a recent crime you know about. Try and use some of the vocabulary from Exercise 5. Continue the following sentence.

Recently, I heard about …

7 In groups, discuss these questions.
1. What is the author's opinion of the criminals?
2. Which adjectives indicate this? Underline them in the text.
3. Do you think all of the criminals deserve a punishment? If so, what?

SPEAKING

8a Work with a partner. Check that you know the meaning of the following crimes. Use a dictionary to help you. Now decide how you could divide these crimes into different categories. What connects the crimes in each category?

shoplifting   blackmail   cyber-stalking   bribery   speeding
smuggling   pickpocketing   vandalism   mugging

8b Work with another pair and explain your choices.

8c Work in your groups of four to discuss these questions.
1. Which is the most serious crime in your opinion?
2. Which crimes are common in your country?

 ▶ MEET THE EXPERT

Watch an interview with Stefanie Bierwerth, a publisher, about the appeal of crime fiction.
Turn to page 154 for video activities.

12.2 THE CAUSES OF CRIME

LISTENING

1 Work with a partner. What are the main reasons why people commit crime? Make a list.

2a 12.1 Listen to three extracts from interviews with criminals. Which of the reasons you thought of in Exercise 1 are mentioned?

2b Listen to the extracts again. Take notes about each speaker under the following headings:
- Crime
- Age of criminal
- Reasons for crime
- Plans for the future

3 Comparing and contrasting Discuss these questions in small groups.
1. What are the reasons why these three people became criminals?
2. Do people become criminals in your country for the same reasons?

READING

4a Read the text and match one of the three causes of crime mentioned in the text (genetic, environment, choice) with each speaker from Exercise 2.

4b Read the text again. Look at the summary statements of the main ideas below and match them with the causes in the text.

1. Anti-social adults often produce anti-social children.
2. Criminals think carefully before they decide on a life of crime.
3. Young people who behave badly tend to become criminals.
4. People used to think that someone's physical features were a cause of crime.
5. Some experts now believe that people commit crimes because of their genes.
6. Criminals consider what they can lose and gain by committing a crime.

4c Which reason in the text do you think is the most common cause of crime?

WHY DO WE COMMIT CRIMES?

All adults at some time or another commit a crime, sometimes by accident, but why do some people intentionally commit crimes? Sociologists have put forward three theories that try to explain the causes of criminal behaviour.

GENETIC CAUSES
The idea that some people commit crimes because of biological factors has a long tradition. This theory suggests that criminals are born, not made. In the 19th century some people even thought brain size and skull shape could explain criminal behaviour. Although experts today no longer believe this, they do argue that human behaviour can be linked to an individual's genes. Studies of adopted children who show criminal behaviour suggest that their behaviour is more similar to their biological parents' behaviour than their adoptive parents', showing a genetic link.

ENVIRONMENT
This theory states that a person's surroundings influence their behaviour. Just as children learn good behaviour from their parents and siblings, so children can learn bad behaviour from their families and other close relationships. Researchers in this area argue that early anti-social behaviour in childhood often leads to a future of criminal behaviour. It is a vicious circle, as one expert states: 'Problem children tend to grow up into problem adults, and problem adults tend to produce more problem children.'

CHOICE
The central idea of this theory is that crime is a career decision, an alternative way of making a living. Supporters of this theory argue that most criminals are rational people, who know what they want and the different ways of getting it, i.e. work or crime. They are able to balance the risks of committing a crime, such as going to prison, against its benefits, i.e. what they gain if they aren't caught. The conclusion is if there are more benefits than risks, do it, but if there are more risks than benefits, don't do it.

In conclusion, we can say that research suggests there are three main reasons why people commit crimes: the genetic argument (biological factors); the environmental argument (people's surroundings) and the choice argument (as a career decision). Although researchers attach different weight to the importance of these three factors, most would agree that there is no one cause for criminality. The causes are complex and will vary from person to person, and in most cases there will be more than one reason for any particular criminal's behaviour.

THE CAUSES OF CRIME 12.2

VOCABULARY
COLLOCATIONS (4)

5a Find words in the text that go with the nouns below.
1. _____ behaviour (x5)
2. long tradition
3. genetic link
4. close relationships
5. vicious circle
6. career decision

5b Complete the sentences with phrases from Exercise 5a.
1. He spent many years in prison because of his criminal b***
2. Her parents were away from the house so often that she was unable to form close with either of them.
3. The USA has a long of allowing its citizens to own guns.
4. There are some teenagers in our town whose anti-s is beginning to annoy us – they write on walls and shout at people all the time.
5. Some people make a career at an early age, but others need time to decide what to do in their lives.

GRAMMAR
THIRD CONDITIONAL

· Regrets
· What if...? (past)

6a Look at these examples and answer the questions.
1. If they *had done* the job more quickly, they *would have left* in time.
   a Did they do the job quickly? ✗
   b Did they leave in time? ✗
2. If I *had wanted* to, I *could have become* a top businessman.
   a Did he want to become a top businessman? ✗
   b Did he become a top businessman? ✗
3. If I *had learnt* to control my temper when I was a kid, I *wouldn't have hit* the police officer.
   a Did he learn to control his temper? ✗
   b Did he hit the police officer? ✓
4. I *might have tried* harder if I *hadn't been* unemployed.
   a Was she unemployed? ✓
   b Did she try harder? ✗

> **GRAMMAR TIP**
> We use the third conditional to talk about unreal situations in the past, i.e. situations that are contrary to the facts.

6b Look at the examples of the third conditional in Exercise 6a and complete the rule.
We form the third conditional with *if* + past **perfect**, *would(n't)* **have** + **past** participle. We can also use **could** or *might* in the main clause.

→ Language reference and extra practice pages 148–149

7 Complete the sentences using the correct form of the verbs in brackets. Use *could* or *might* if possible.
1. If they **had planned** (plan) the robbery better, they _____ (succeed).
2. If the police **had acted** (act) more quickly, they _____ (prevent) the robbery.
3. If he **hadn't** (not drive) so fast, he _____ (not have) an accident.
4. The crime rate _____ (not increase) if the last government's policy **had been** (be) more efficient.
5. The police _____ (not catch) him if he **had not left** (not leave) his fingerprints on the door.

8 Make a conditional sentence beginning with *if* for each of the situations below.
1. The negotiator did not react to the hostage crisis quickly. The hostage died.
2. The police did not act decisively. The criminal escaped.
3. The police did not apologise. Mr Wesley was not satisfied.
4. The robber forgot to take a map. He got lost.
5. The thief did not run fast. The police caught him.
6. The court released the prisoner early. He injured two police officers.

SPEAKING  + 3rd conditional activity

9a Read the following statements. Decide if you agree or disagree with each statement. Make notes to support your position.
· Criminals are born, not made.
· Most criminals are either greedy or lazy.
· Crime doesn't pay.
· Petty crimes lead to serious crimes.
· Once a criminal, always a criminal.
· Television programmes are a major cause of crime.

9b In small groups, discuss the statements above.

12.3 SPECTACULAR ROBBERIES

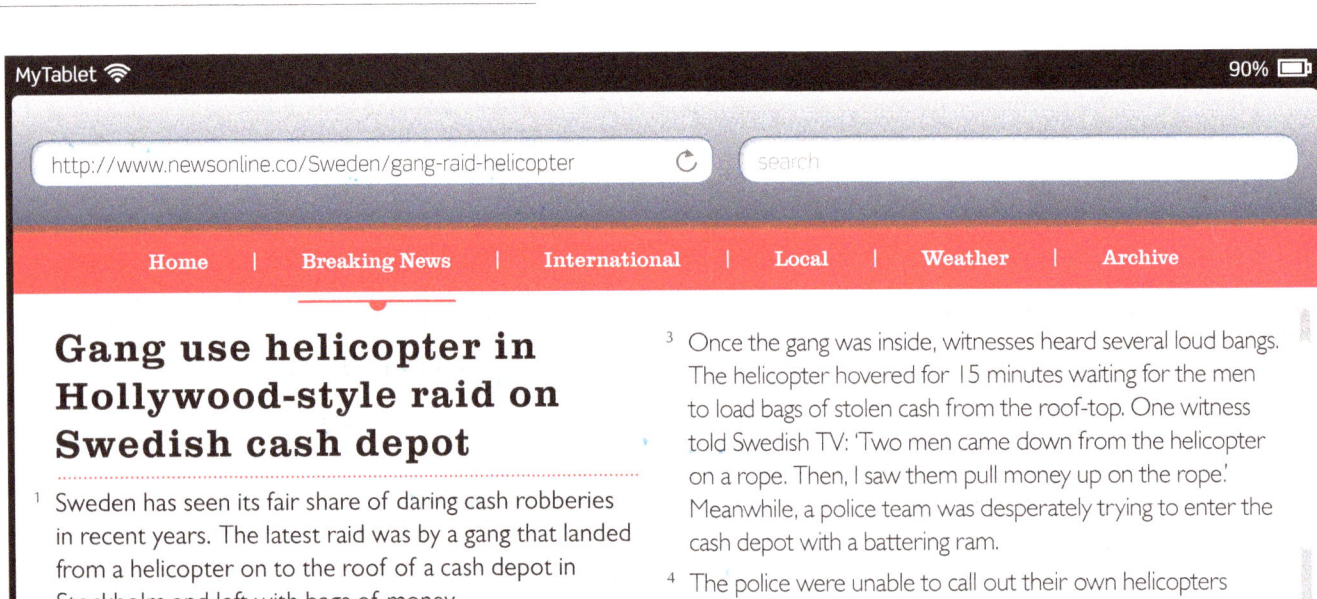

Gang use helicopter in Hollywood-style raid on Swedish cash depot

[1] Sweden has seen its fair share of daring cash robberies in recent years. The latest raid was by a gang that landed from a helicopter on to the roof of a cash depot in Stockholm and left with bags of money.

[2] The masked gunmen jumped out on to the roof of the G4S cash depot in the Västberga area just after 5 a.m., smashed windows and made their way inside. Around 20 staff were in the building at the time of the attack, and many had probably been involved in counting money.

[3] Once the gang was inside, witnesses heard several loud bangs. The helicopter hovered for 15 minutes waiting for the men to load bags of stolen cash from the roof-top. One witness told Swedish TV: 'Two men came down from the helicopter on a rope. Then, I saw them pull money up on the rope.' Meanwhile, a police team was desperately trying to enter the cash depot with a battering ram.

[4] The police were unable to call out their own helicopters because explosives had been put at the aircraft hangar in a bag marked 'bomb'. 'We've found what we believe is a live bomb,' a police spokesman, Rikard Johansson, said. Small sharp objects had also been placed on the road near the depot to stop the police from approaching the scene. 'I've never experienced anything like it,' said a police officer, Kjell Lindgren. Another officer added: 'What we know is that they broke down some kind of wall to get in. We don't want to comment on how they did it.'

[5] No staff were injured in the robbery. Investigators said the thieves wore masks, probably carried automatic weapons and set off explosives during the 20-minute raid. A stolen Bell 206 JetRanger helicopter was later found near a lake north of Stockholm, about 15 miles from the cash depot.

[6] The British-based G4S, one of the world's largest security companies, did not say how much money was in the depot at the time of the raid. A representative said the gang had made off with 'an unconfirmed sum of money'. Swedish media believe that the depot could have been holding several million Swedish kronor. G4S offered a reward for information.

Adapted from *The Guardian*

READING

1 Describe the photo. What do you think is happening?

2a Read the newspaper report quickly. Then, without looking back at the text, put the events below in the correct order.
a   Bags of money were loaded into the helicopters.
b   There were several loud bangs.
c   The company offered a reward.
d   Robbers smashed windows.
e   Robbers landed on the roof of the G4S cash depot.
f   Police found the stolen helicopter 15 miles from the crime scene.

2b Good journalists try to answer the following questions when writing a news report:
Who? What? Where? When? Why? How?
Find the answer to these questions in the report.

2c Looking at genre The following language features are often found in newspaper reports: present perfect, reported speech, direct speech. Find examples of these features in the report.

3 Work with a partner to discuss these questions.
1   Have there been any spectacular robberies in your country?
2   Do you think it is wrong when films and the media glamorise spectacular crimes?

SPECTACULAR ROBBERIES 12.3

4a Find words in the text that mean the following.
1. money in the form of coins and notes (para 1)
2. a surprise attack on a bank or shop to steal things (para 1)
3. a group of criminals who work together (para 1)
4. people who see a crime or accident and can say what happened (para 3)
5. people who try to find out about a crime or accident as part of their job (para 5)
6. money that is given to someone to thank them for doing something (para 6)

4b Complete the report below with the words in Exercise 4a.

Insurers have offered a large ¹_____ for information about the ²_____ who stole about £2m from a ³_____ processing centre. Up to seven men were involved in the ⁴_____. Police ⁵_____ hope that the reward will encourage people to contact them with key information to add to the ⁶_____ statements they have taken so far.

LISTENING

5a 12.2 Listen to eight speakers talking about the same incident. What are they talking about? What details can you remember?

5b Listen again. Which speaker (1–8):
a talks about people in this country and abroad knowing about the crime?
b says how much money was stolen?
c talks about someone who found some money?
d says that some members of staff weren't careful enough?
e says how big the reward was?
f says too many people were involved?
g talks about someone who worked there being involved?
h talks about tracing bank notes?

GRAMMAR
MODALS (PAST DEDUCTION)

6a Look at these opinions from Exercise 5. From the speaker's point of view, answer *yes*, *no* or *not sure* to the question that follows each opinion.
1. *They might have wanted to use the money in Europe.* Did they want to use the money in Europe?
2. *They shouldn't have stolen such a large amount of money.* Did they steal a large amount of money?
3. *Basically, they can't have planned it properly.* Did they plan it properly?
4. *They should have involved fewer people.* Did they involve fewer people?
5. *The £2 million reward might have got some informers and other criminals very interested.* Did the reward get some informers and other criminals interested?
6. *Someone with inside knowledge could have been involved.* Was someone with inside knowledge involved?
7. *They must have been very careless.* Were they careless?
8. *It couldn't have been more successful.* Was it successful?

6b Look at the sentences in Exercise 6a. Match them with the meanings a–e below. There may be more than one sentence for each meaning.
a This wasn't a good idea, but it happened.
b This was a good idea, but it didn't happen.
c It is possible, but not certain, that this happened.
d It is logically certain that this happened.
e It was not possible for this to have happened.

6c Complete the rule.
The modal perfect is formed with a modal verb (*must/should*) + _____ + past participle.

➡ Language reference and extra practice pages 148–149

7 What are your opinions of the robberies described in this lesson? Write five sentences using modal perfects, then discuss them with a partner.
The robbers in Sweden shouldn't have used a helicopter.

SPEAKING

8 *The perfect murder!* You are going to try and solve a crime. Work in groups of six. You are police detectives and each of you knows only the information on your card. Read the newspaper report below, and the information on your card, and discuss who committed the crime and how it was committed.

Student A: Turn to page 158.
Student B: Turn to page 155.
Student C: Turn to page 156.
Student D: Turn to page 162.
Student E: Turn to page 163.
Student F: Turn to page 160.

25 September | NEWS

This morning the body of beautiful millionairess Susan Shapiro was found on the banks of Lake Minoria. The police know from the autopsy report that the victim died last night between 8 p.m. and 10 p.m. The small lake and surroundings have been searched extensively by police and divers and no murder weapon has been found. It appears that she was stabbed in the chest.

12.4 SCENARIO
YOU, THE JURY

SITUATION

1 Read the situation below. Is this system similar to the one in your country?

In England criminal cases usually go to a Crown Court. In this court there is a judge and a jury. The jury is made up of 12 people. The jury listens to the arguments and evidence presented by the prosecution and defence lawyers. The jury then delivers a verdict: guilty or not guilty. The jury have to reach their verdict by discussing the case together. During the trial the judge is like a referee, making sure that both sides act fairly. The judge also decides on a punishment if the defendant is found guilty by the jury.

2a You are going to listen to members of a jury discussing a court case. First read a summary of the case.

A young well-educated homeless man went into a bookshop to get out of the cold and to read for a while. At some point he put two books into his pocket, and was seen by a witness doing this. He left the shop and sat on a nearby bench reading one of the books. He was accused by the manager of stealing and the police were called. He had enough money to pay for one of the books.

2b 12.3 Listen to the discussion and answer these questions.
1 What do Mr Davis (D), Ms Cornish (C) and Mrs Taylor (T) think about the case? Do they each think the accused guilty, not guilty or are they undecided?
2 Do they manage to agree on a verdict?

KEY LANGUAGE
REACHING A DECISION

3a Listen again and complete the phrases below.
1 You can look at it in two _____, I think.
2 It _____ to me that he's innocent because …
3 He _____ to be an honest person to me.
4 … there's some _____ from one witness to suggest he was stealing the books.
5 Personally, I'm not _____ he's guilty because …
6 Well, I've made up my _____.
7 There's very little _____, as far as I'm concerned.
8 It's _____ to me that he didn't intend to steal the books.
9 I'm not sure it's as _____ cut as that.

3b Which of the above expressions show strong certainty, and which expressions show weak certainty?

12.4 YOU, THE JURY

TASK
DISCUSSING COURT CASES

4 Read the information about three court cases on the right. Which crime:
a involved people eating something?
b involved someone taking pictures?
c took place in the countryside?
d went on for a number of months?
e took place at night?
f involved a vehicle?

5 Work in groups of three, Students A, B and C. You are going to discuss the cases and reach a verdict. For each case, turn to the correct page and use the information in your discussion. After your discussion, agree on a verdict as a group – guilty or not guilty. If you reach a guilty verdict, decide on one of these punishments.
- prison (how long?)
- a fine (how much?)
- community service (unpaid work in the local area) (number of hours?)

For Case 1:
Student A: Turn to page 158.
Student B: Turn to page 155.
Student C: Turn to page 156.

For Case 2 change roles:
Student A: Turn to page 158.
Student B: Turn to page 162.
Student C: Turn to page 157.

For Case 3 change roles again:
Student A: Turn to page 158.
Student B: Turn to page 161.
Student C: Turn to page 162.

Case 1
A burglar broke into the home of a woman who lives in a remote rural area. The burglary took place at 2 a.m. The woman, who is a martial arts expert, woke up and realised someone had broken into her house. She went downstairs quietly and, without warning, attacked the burglar. She knocked him unconscious and then, losing control, she kicked him repeatedly. The burglar was badly injured and spent a long time in hospital recovering. The burglar is now permanently disabled. The woman was arrested and charged with using excessive force.

Case 2
A woman in her late 30s became obsessed with a younger man of 25 who lives in the same town. He moved to the area a year ago and she first noticed him at the railway station as they both take the same train to work. They talked briefly on the platform on several occasions. More recently, she started following him, appearing outside his work and visiting places where he meets his friends. She found his address and started taking photographs of him. She also started phoning him at work, and at home, and when he answered she hung up. The man found out that she is planning to move into a flat opposite him. After several complaints the woman was arrested and charged with stalking the man.

Case 3
A 35-year-old man was driving his two children (aged five and six) to a theme park. The son and daughter were in the back of the car. The man gave them a packet of sweets to eat during the journey. They started fighting and one of the children began to choke on the sweets. The child could not breathe and was in difficulties. The driver turned round to help and lost control of the car. It crashed into a group of people sitting at tables outside a café. Five people were injured, two seriously. The man was arrested and charged with dangerous driving.

12.5 STUDY AND WRITING SKILLS

STUDY SKILLS
SUMMARISING

1 Read the extract from a writing guide about summarising. What are the most important things to remember when you summarise?

> **S** You often need to **summarise** something you have read, heard or seen. In each case you should pick out the main points. If you need to summarise something written, for example an article or an extract from a book, it is important to use your own words to express the ideas. After writing a summary it is a good idea to read the original again to make sure you have not missed any key points. A summary is not notes. It is a shorter version of the original text.

2a 12.4 Listen to part of a lecture on home security. What does the speaker say about the following?
1 windows
2 notes
3 ID cards
4 safety chains
5 burglar alarms

2b Read two sample summaries of the lecture. Work with a partner to decide which summary is better.

> **a** On the topic of home security, the expert mentioned a number of methods to protect you and your home, ranging from methods that cost nothing to some that are quite expensive. The methods, from the cheapest to the most expensive, were: keeping front doors and windows closed; not leaving signs that you are not at home; asking for identification; fitting window locks; installing and using a safety chain on the front door; fitting more secure locks to all doors; and installing a burglar alarm. Using these methods will prevent most burglaries. [91 words]

> **b** There are a number of methods you can use to prevent security problems in your house. You can do simple things like closing your windows and putting a security chain on the front and back door or you can put plenty of locks on the windows and install a burglar alarm that makes a lot of noise if someone is trying to break into the house. Never let anyone into the house unless you know them well. [76 words]

2c Listen to the lecture again. Work with your partner and read either Summary A or Summary B while you are listening. Check that the points in the lecture are covered in the summary. Compare with your partner and decide if your original decision about the better summary is still true.

3 Which pieces of information are in the lecture and which does each writer use in making the summary? Put ticks (✓) in the appropriate places in the table. Look at Audio script 12.4 on page 175 to check your answers.

	Lecture	Summary A	Summary B
1 Gives the name of the speaker.			
2 Gives the main topic (home security).			
3 Gives the order in which the information is/will be presented.			
4 Points out that people don't always use safety chains.			
5 Lists the methods for creating security.			
6 Finishes with a conclusion.			

4a 12.5 Listen to a lecture on car security and make notes. Use these headings.
- Topic
- Main points
- Conclusion

4b Use your notes to write a summary. Remember to use only the main points and note if there is a conclusion.

WRITING SKILL
A CAUSE AND EFFECT ESSAY

5 Read the essay on the causes of world poverty quickly and identify the three main causes of world poverty.

6 Read the essay again and outline the structure of the essay.

7 Cause and effect Underline all the words and phrases in the essay that refer to cause and effect and complete the two statements below.

Some of the words and phrases we use to explain the effects of a cause are: _____, as a consequence, consequently, so, _____, _____.
Other words and phrases are used to introduce the factors that are responsible for a cause, e.g. _____, as, _____, _____, one reason why ... , one of the most important reasons why ..., _____, the main reason why ... .

STUDY AND WRITING SKILLS 12.5

WHAT ARE THE CAUSES OF WORLD POVERTY?

There have been many studies of world poverty and how to reduce it. However, writers often have different definitions of the term. This essay focuses on absolute poverty. This can be defined as a state where people do not have access to basic human needs such as food, shelter, clothing and adequate health care. The essay aims to highlight the three main causes of poverty in the world. If these can be identified, government efforts to reduce it will be more effective.

It can be argued that the most important reason for poverty is over-population. There are simply too many people in some countries, or in areas of those countries. As a result, there are not enough resources to support the population. In many developing countries, people live by farming, hunting and gathering food. However, the land can only support a certain number of people. If there are too many people, the result is hunger and poverty. It is a vicious cycle: poor families are often big families because children are a source of labour and additional income. However, big families increase the population and create more poverty.

A second reason for world poverty is lack of education. A large number of people living in poverty are illiterate, as they must concentrate on making a living and have no time to educate themselves. Or it may be that they have no opportunities to learn to read and write. In many countries, there are no elementary or secondary schools, therefore their rates of illiteracy are very high. Without education, it is very difficult for people to get jobs and earn money, so they fall into the poverty trap. Nelson Mandela once said, 'Education is the most powerful weapon which you can use to change the world.'

Finally, the third main cause of poverty is a poor or non-existent health service in a country. In many poor countries, people who are sick cannot get good health care. Because of this, they become unhealthy and contract serious diseases. Without good health, people cannot work well or learn new skills. Studies have shown that if a health system in a country is improved, more people are able to move away from poverty.

It is possible to find many other causes of world poverty in academic literature, for example, unequal income distribution; the high cost of living; economic trends, to name but a few. Since the resources to reduce poverty are limited, it is, therefore, essential to focus on the main causes of poverty. If governments concentrate on controlling population growth, increasing educational opportunities and providing a high quality health service, the resources will be used efficiently.

8 Match 1–4 with a–d.
1 The number of violent crimes committed by juveniles has increased.
2 One reason why juvenile crime has increased
3 Crime has risen recently
4 The family unit has broken down recently.
a As a result, crime has risen.
b because of a breakdown of the family unit.
c is the decline in the number of community centres offering activities for young people.
d Consequently, many youth correction centres are overcrowded.

Dislike of authority

Juveniles ignore the instructions of teachers, the police, etc.

↓

As a result they take greater risks when cautioned by authority figures.

9 Look at the diagram above. It shows how a cause (first box) can have effects (second and third boxes). These boxes can be linked using some of the words and phrases from Exercise 7. Complete the paragraph from an academic essay about rising juvenile crime below. Use words and phrases from Exercise 7.

¹_____ of rising juvenile crime is the dislike of authority shown by young people. ²_____ of this dislike of authority, juveniles ignore the instructions of their teachers, the police or other people in authority. ³_____, they take greater risks with the law even when they have been cautioned by these authority figures. They get into trouble and commit crimes.

10a You are going to write an academic essay with the title: *What are the main causes of rising juvenile crime?* In groups, discuss these possible causes for the rise in juvenile crime. Can you think of any others?
- Poverty
- Breakdown of the family unit
- Single parents
- Rises in truancy
- The rise of materialism – wanting expensive toys and gadgets
- Gang culture
- Dislike of authority

10b Write the essay using the following structure.
Outline Structure: Introduction; Three paragraphs for the main body of the essay; Conclusion
Introduction: State what the essay is about, define any difficult terms, show the current relevance of the topic and say how you are going to organise your essay.
Three main paragraphs: Select three causes for the rise in juvenile crime from the ones you discussed in Exercise 10a. Using one paragraph for each cause, describe the effect they have had on juvenile crime. Start with the cause you feel has had the greatest effect.
Conclusion: Using two or three sentences, summarise what you have written about.

11 In small groups, read each other's essays. Mention the good points of the essays and say how the essays could be improved. Comment on both the content and language of the essays.

1 LANGUAGE REFERENCE

GRAMMAR

G1 QUESTION FORMS

PRESENT SIMPLE QUESTIONS

Use present simple questions to ask about regular or habitual actions and general truths or states. In questions with the verb *to be* and with modal verbs, put the verb before the subject.

Am I a suitable person for the job?
Can they take the test today?

With other questions in the present simple, use the auxiliary verb *do/does*.

Do you feel happier about college now?
How often do they travel to work together?

PAST SIMPLE QUESTIONS

Use past simple questions to ask about a past action. Form this question in the same way as the present simple, but put the auxiliary verbs in their past form.

Was she very intelligent when you knew her?
Did you feel embarrassed when it happened?

PRESENT CONTINUOUS QUESTIONS

Use present continuous questions to ask about an action happening at the moment or around the time of speaking or about a changing situation. Form this question by putting the verb *to be* before the subject.

Is he interviewing students at the moment?
Are they considering what to study at university?

PRESENT PERFECT QUESTIONS

Use this question to ask about the recent past or an event at an unknown time. Form this question by putting the verb *has/have* before the subject.

Has Martin found out his score?
Have they ever measured their intelligence?

! Don't use the auxiliary *do/does* with questions in the present continuous and present perfect.
Do you working at the moment? ✗
Do you have finished your work? ✗

G2 SUBJECT AND OBJECT QUESTIONS

Subject questions ask about the **subject** of a sentence.

subject
↓
Who designed the IQ tests?
Philip Carter designed the IQ tests.

Object questions ask about the **object** of a sentence.

object
↓
What did Philip Carter design?
He designed the IQ tests.

For subject questions, don't add an auxiliary verb.
Who gave you that present? ✓
Who did give you that present? ✗

We usually only use *who*, *what* and *which* to ask subject questions.

Who wrote the test?
What happened last night?

G3 PRESENT SIMPLE AND PRESENT CONTINUOUS

Use the present simple to describe:
- a regular or habitual action.
  She usually takes the train to work.
  We often use adverbs or time expressions of frequency with this use of the present simple: *often, usually, sometimes, once a week, twice a month*.
- a fact or general truth.
  Many people don't believe in horoscopes.
  Bill Clinton spends most of his time in the USA.

Use the present continuous to describe:
- an action happening around now (often temporary).
  Sorry, she's speaking to someone at the moment.
  We're currently looking for new people.
- a trend or changing situation.
  Prices are rising steadily at present.
  More and more people are learning English.
- a photograph or a scene.
  In the photograph, the two people are talking.

G4 STATE VERBS

State verbs describe something passive or a state (for example, the verbs *be, like, believe, understand, know, prefer, depend*). We rarely use state verbs in the continuous.

I know lots of ambitious people. ✓
I'm knowing lots of ambitious people. ✗

KEY LANGUAGE

KL GIVING OPINIONS, AGREEING AND DISAGREEING, MAKING SUGGESTIONS

In my opinion, ...   I suggest ...   I suppose ...
I don't know.   Why don't we ... ?
OK, how about ... ?   I accept that.   (Well,) it's true.
I can't agree, ...   No, that's out of the question.

VOCABULARY

V1 PERSONALITY ADJECTIVES

adventurous, ambitious, assertive, bossy, cautious, creative, easy-going, energetic, enthusiastic, even-tempered, generous, hard-working, level-headed, likeable, moody, open-minded, organised, quiet, reliable, reserved, self-confident, sensible, sensitive, serious, shy, sociable, strong-willed, talkative, thoughtful, warm-hearted

V2 PREFIXES

antisocial, bicycle, bilingual, discomfort, dislike, ex-baseball player, ex-boss, ex-president, ex-tycoon, misbehave, misunderstand, misuse, monorail, outperform, outrun, overconfident, overshadowed, redefine, redo, rewrite, semicircle, underrated, underuse

EXTRA PRACTICE 1

G1 **1** Write the missing words in sentences 1–10.
1. A: _____ he the right person for the job?
   B: Yes, I'd say so.
2. A: _____ you feel better about taking the test?
   B: Yes, I'm less nervous now I know what it is.
3. A: _____ he work well in a team?
   B: Yes, he's good with other people.
4. A: What exactly _____ your horoscope say?
   B: The same as usual. That I'll be lucky this week.
5. A: _____ they _____ all their homework?
   B: Yes, they have.
6. A: What _____ you working on at the moment?
   B: I'm working on a proposal for a film.
7. A: _____ we ask you a few questions?
   B: Yes, of course.
8. A: When _____ Carl Jung born?
   B: In 1875.
9. A: What _____ he study at university?
   B: Medicine, from 1894 to 1900.
10. A: _____ he _____ his final exam?
    B: Yes, he took it last week.

G2 **2** Read the sentences and complete the questions. The underlined word(s) should be the answer.
1. Bill Clinton is an ex-President.
   Who *is Bill Clinton* _____?
2. Myers Briggs designed the test.
   Who _____?
3. Oprah Winfrey owns several houses.
   What _____?
4. Marilyn Monroe married Joe DiMaggio.
   Who _____?
5. He can speak three languages.
   How many _____?
6. Spring is my favourite time of the year.
   What _____?
7. My boss is the reason I'm leaving.
   What _____?

G3, 4 **3** A university lecturer is interviewing a new student. Write the verbs in the present simple or present continuous.
A: How ¹_____ you _____ (study)? What's your approach?
B: Well I ²_____ (work) really well early in the mornings. Most of my friends stay up late, but I ³_____ (prefer) to go to bed early.
A: So do you find it difficult to work with others?
B: Not necessarily. It ⁴_____ (depend) what the task is. For example, at the moment I ⁵_____ (work) with a group of people. We ⁶_____ (set up) a club for young kids in the town centre.
A: Really? That's good. Now, ⁷_____ you _____ (know) about the exam at the end of every term?
B: Yes, I read about that.
A: How do you find exams?
B: Well! I ⁸_____ (get) worried before exams, but I think I ⁹_____ (get) better at staying calm.

KL **4** Complete the dialogue with phrases a–f. There is one extra phrase.
a I can't agree   d I don't know
b I suggest   e it's true
c I accept that   f In my opinion

A: ¹_____ we employ Sandra. She's the most cheerful.
B: Well, ²_____ that she was the happiest of everyone, but ³_____ – she has absolutely no previous experience.
A: But you don't need experience to answer the phone.
B: ⁴_____. How you answer the phone can make the difference in business.
A: Do you think we could train her?
B: I'm not sure. ⁵_____, that will take too much time and money.

V1 **5** Write the missing vowels in the adjectives.
1. You need to be an _dv_nt_r_ _s sort of person to go climbing in the mountains.
2. Don't be too c_ _t_ _ _s about saying what you think in meetings.
3. Running at 6 a.m. looks a bit too _n_rg_t_c for me. I prefer sleeping.
4. Don't talk to him. He's always m_ _dy on a Monday morning.
5. Gill is one of our most r_l_ _bl_ employees. She's always on time.
6. You look rather th_ _ghtf_l. What are you considering?
7. People who are _p_n-m_nd_d are often good listeners.
8. This job needs someone who is s_lf-c_nf_d_nt.

V2 **6** Complete the words with the prefixes in the box.

out bi anti over re under dis mis
mono ex-

1. _____ social   6. _____ shadowed
2. _____ cycle   7. _____ define
3. _____ comfort   8. _____ perform
4. _____ understand   9. _____ president
5. _____ rail   10. _____ rated

7 Complete the sentences with words from Exercise 6.
1. Can I borrow your _____? It's too far to walk.
2. Every time I ask you to do something, you seem to _____ what I say.
3. This new film is _____. The critics said it was boring, but I thought it was great.
4. My brother was always better than me at school and completely _____ me.
5. At the airport, take the _____ from one terminal to the other. It's faster than the bus.

8 Make five more sentences with the other words.

127

2 LANGUAGE REFERENCE

GRAMMAR

G1 PAST SIMPLE

Form the past simple of most regular verbs by adding *-ed* to the end of the verb.
jump – jumped
last – lasted

With verbs ending in *-e*, add *-d* only.
dance – danced
die – died

With verbs ending in *-y*, remove *-y* and add *-ied*.
carry – carried
hurry – hurried

Where a verb ends with the letter *t* or *d*, the *-ed* is an extra syllable and is pronounced /ɪd/.
lasted /ˈlɑːstɪd/
landed /ˈlændɪd/

For other verbs the *-ed* is pronounced either /t/ or /d/, depending on the sound at the end of the verb.
jumped /dʒʌmpt/
received /rɪˈsiːvd/

Many commonly used verbs have an irregular past simple form. For example:

become – became	*lead – led*
begin – began	*take – took*
write – wrote	*go – went*

Use the past simple to refer to finished actions that are in the past.
*I **began** school in 1989.*
*He **set** out across Europe in 1271.*

We often use the past simple when we know or say the exact time of the action and with time expressions such as *yesterday, last week, in 1271*.

G2 PRESENT PERFECT

Form the present perfect with *has/have* (*'s/'ve*) + past participle of the verb.
*She's **sailed** round the world.*
*They've **climbed** Mount Everest.*

Use the present perfect to talk about:
- finished actions in a time period that continues up to now. We often use time expressions such as *today, this week, this year*.
  *We've been really busy **all week**.*
  *You've worked hard **all year**.*
- experiences in our lives when we don't say when they happened. We often use adverbs such as *never, ever, already, yet, just*.
  *Have you **ever** visited their house?*
  *They've **never** climbed Mont Blanc.*

ALREADY, YET AND EVER

These three adverbs are often used in conjunction with the present perfect:
- *ever* is used in questions to refer to any time up to the present.
  *Have you **ever** been to Germany?*
- *already* is used in affirmative sentences and questions to refer to an event close to the present that has happened.
  *We've **already** done that. What's next?*
- *yet* is used in questions and negative sentences to refer to an event that is planned or expected, but not completed.
  *I haven't had time to do it **yet**.*

! We use *already* and *ever* before the main verb, but *yet* comes at the end of the sentence.
*I have **already** finished it.*
*Sorry, I haven't finished it **yet**.*

G3 PRESENT PERFECT AND PAST SIMPLE

The present perfect and past simple both refer to the past, but the present perfect doesn't necessarily say or imply when something happened.
We've already found someone suitable.

The present perfect and past simple can both refer to finished actions, but the past simple refers to a specific past time and the present perfect to a time continuing up to now.
*We **looked** for someone suitable last year.*
*We've **looked** for someone suitable this year.*

! We rarely use adverbs such as *ever, already, yet* with the past simple.

KEY LANGUAGE

KL DISCUSSING ADVANTAGES AND DISADVANTAGES, MAKING SUGGESTIONS

There are arguments for and against.
On the one hand …
On the other hand …
Another disadvantage of … is that …
I think we should …
It'd be a good idea to …
I suggest we …
How about …
Another drawback of …
That's a big bonus for them.

VOCABULARY

V1 TRAVEL

abroad, destination, home, journey, package holiday, travel (n), trip

V2 TRAVEL EXPRESSIONS

become more independent, become more self-confident, broaden your horizons, broadens the mind, do voluntary work, earn money, escape poverty, experience different cultures, explore new places, find yourself, get away from it all, learn a new language, learn new skills, meet new people, see new sights, study for qualifications abroad

V3 PHRASAL VERBS

break down, carry on, check in, get back, lift off, look around, set out, stop off

EXTRA PRACTICE 2

G1 **1** Complete the text with the past simple form of the verbs in the box.

lead   start   have   cross   run   stop   be
fly   complete

Sir Ranulph Fiennes ¹_____ born in 1944. In the army he ²_____ several expeditions, including a hovercraft expedition on the White Nile and crossing from the North to the South Pole. He ³_____ the Antarctic on foot, but seven years later illness ⁴_____ his solo trek to the North Pole and in 2003, he ⁵_____ heart surgery to save his life. Only four months after the operation, he ⁶_____ seven marathons in seven continents in seven days. He ⁷_____ in Santiago, Chile and then ⁸_____ to the Falkland Islands, Sydney, Singapore, London and Cairo. He ⁹_____ the marathons in New York.

2 Speaking practice Work with a partner to talk about:
- one thing you did last weekend.
- how you celebrated your last birthday.
- what you learnt in your last English lesson.

G2 **3** Put the word in brackets in the correct place in each sentence.
1. Have you been to France? (ever)
2. I've told you that – don't ask me again. (already)
3. Bill and Martin have seen it so let's watch it now. (never)
4. Haven't you finished it? (yet)
5. Have you finished your lunch? (already)
6. Why haven't you told me? (ever)
7. I haven't had time to speak to her. (yet)
8. Has he been late for class? (ever)

G3 **4** Write the words in brackets in the past simple or the present perfect.
1. They _____ (climb) Mount Everest twice before and are going for a third time this year.
2. _____ you ever _____ (ride) on a camel?
3. When _____ he _____ (die)?
4. _____ he _____ (have) time to see Martin last week?
5. He _____ (just announce) another attempt to reach the South Pole.
6. She _____ (raise) money for charity last year by crossing the desert.
7. I _____ (never live) abroad. What's it like?
8. We _____ (meet) loads of wonderful people when we went to Ethiopia last year.
9. How many exams _____ you _____ (have) so far this month?
10. I _____ (visit) so many countries in my life that I can't remember them all.

KL **5** Put the words in the correct order to make expressions.
1. On the _____ cold.
   one / hand / it's
2. On the _____ beautiful.
   it's / other / hand
3. There are _____ for _____.
   arguments / against / and
4. Another _____ is that _____.
   expensive / disadvantage / it's
5. It'd be _____ to _____.
   a / idea / ask / people / other / good
6. I think _____ see _____.
   should / what / we / say / they

V1 **6** Match the words in the box with the meanings below.

abroad   travel   destination   journey   trip
package holiday

1. going to different places _____
2. in a different country _____
3. the time spent travelling from one place to another, often over a long distance _____
4. a short journey, often for work _____
5. where you're trying to get to _____
6. a holiday that has a fixed price and includes travel, accommodation, etc. _____

V2 **7** Match the sentence halves.
1. They say travel helps you to find
2. You should broaden
3. I prefer to explore
4. Most people just go abroad to
5. Travel makes you become
6. I like places where you experience different
7. We saw some incredible

a. more independent.
b. yourself, but I think it's just running away.
c. new sights.
d. your horizons with a journey.
e. get away from it all.
f. cultures.
g. new places and meet new people.

V3 **8** Choose the correct answer.
1. Did you have time to look *out/around*?
2. We set *out/in* on our adventure as the sun was rising.
3. Ask the taxi driver to carry *on/along* to the end of the road.
4. Let's stop *out/off* at the temple on the way.
5. How do you get *out/to* the market?
6. What time does he get *return/back* from work?
7. How many hours before we fly do we have to check *out/in*?
8. What time is she going to get *back/away* from her trip?

129

3 LANGUAGE REFERENCE

GRAMMAR

G1 PRESENT PERFECT CONTINUOUS

Form the present perfect continuous with *have/has* (*'ve/'s*) + *been* + *-ing*.
   He**'s been working** from home.
   Employers **have been investing** in video conference technology.

We use the present perfect continuous to talk about actions and situations that continue into the present.
   I've been studying at Oxford University for two years (and I am still studying there).
   They**'ve been talking** on the phone for two hours (and they are still talking).

We often use the present perfect continuous with the time expressions *since* and *for*. Use *since* to refer to a point in time and *for* to indicate a period of time.
   I**'ve been studying** at Oxford University **since 2006**.
   I**'ve been studying** at Oxford University **for two years**.

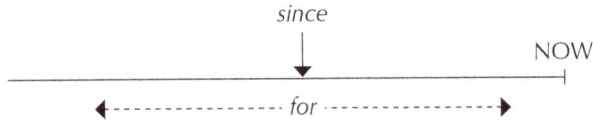

We don't usually use state verbs with the continuous form.
   I've ~~been knowing~~ John for years. ✗
   I've known John for years. ✓

G2 PRESENT PERFECT SIMPLE AND PRESENT PERFECT CONTINUOUS

We use the present perfect simple to emphasise:
- that an action started in the past and is completed.
   I**'ve prepared** the leaflets you asked for.
   They**'ve interviewed** everyone.
- the result of the activity (for example, by telling us how much or how many).
   We**'ve asked** over five hundred people.
   He**'s done** all his homework.
   How many people **have** you **interviewed**?
   How much of your work **have** you **done**?

We use the present perfect continuous to emphasise:
- that an action started in the past and is still continuing.
   She**'s been working** here for over three years.
   We**'ve been writing** letters to all the candidates.
- the activity and its duration (for example, by telling us how long).
   Roger **has been playing** tennis for years.
   Roger **has been playing** tennis since he was a boy.
   How long **have** you **been working** here?

KEY LANGUAGE

KL ASKING QUESTIONS, GIVING ANSWERS

FRAMING QUESTIONS
I'd also like to know …
I'm (also) interested in knowing …
A question we like to ask all our …
I was wondering what/if/when …
A question now about …
Let me follow that up with another question.
Moving on, can/could you tell me …
Just one last/final question …

FRAMING ANSWERS
I'm glad you asked me that.
That's a very good question.
Without going into too much detail, …
Let me just think about that for a moment.
I thought you might ask me that.
I haven't really thought about that.
I'm not an expert, but …
I'm afraid I don't know the answer to that.

VOCABULARY

V1 WORK ADJECTIVES

challenging, exciting, flexible, glamorous, monotonous, repetitive, rewarding, satisfying, stressful, stimulating, tedious

V2 DEPENDENT PREPOSITIONS

ability to, depend on, expected to, experience of, fluency in, knowledge of, look for, motivated by, prospects for, report to, responsible for, suitable for

V3 EXPRESSIONS CONNECTED WITH TIME AND WORK

spend time, time-consuming, time management, work–life balance, workstation

EXTRA PRACTICE 3

G1 **1** Complete the sentences with *for* or *since*.
1 I've been trying to call you _____ hours – where have you been?
2 _____ the last six years he's been living in France.
3 She's been studying English _____ she left school.
4 _____ 1990, the council have been spending much more on public transport.
5 I've been looking for that _____ weeks – where did you find it?

2 Complete the sentences with the words in the box.

you	since	watching	been	long	haven't
has	for	hasn't	teaching	having	

1 Rose _____ been building this house _____ 1995.
2 I've _____ reading all day.
3 How _____ have _____ been working here?
4 They _____ been studying hard enough. They must work harder.
5 We've been _____ at this school _____ two years. The kids are great.
6 He _____ been getting enough sleep. He's really tired.
7 She's been _____ guitar lessons for ages, but she still can't play a tune.
8 I don't know what happened in the series. I haven't been _____ the TV recently.

G2 **3** Choose the correct verb form.
1 We've *prepared / been preparing* three boxes and they're all ready to be sent.
2 Can you take over? I've *packed / been packing* these all morning. I need a rest.
3 Have you *waited / been waiting* long?
4 How long have we *driven / been driving* now?
5 I've *written / been writing* fifty letters so far today.
6 We've only *seen / been seeing* the first five minutes of the film, so sit down.
7 How long have they *been / been being* here?
8 I've *worked / been working* all morning, so I'm really tired.

KL **4** Write the missing prepositions in sentences 1–6.
1 I'm also interested _____ knowing about your last job.
2 A question now _____ your long-term ambitions.
3 Moving _____, can you tell me why you want the job?
4 Let me follow that _____ with another question.
5 Without going _____ too much detail, can you tell us why?
6 I'm afraid I don't know the answer _____ that.

5 Put the words in the correct order to make expressions.
1 one / last / question / just / .
2 I'm / you / asked / that / me / glad / .
3 question / good / that's / a / very / .
4 just / think / for / a / let / about / that / moment / me / .
5 thought / that / really / I / about / haven't / .
6 you / might / me / thought / ask / I / that / .

V1 **6** Match the descriptions of people's jobs with the adjectives in the box.

flexible   glamorous   stressful   challenging   rewarding

1 'I'm a Hollywood actress. I'll be at the Oscars next month.' _____
2 'We work long hours and take complaints from members of the public. I need to see a doctor!' _____
3 'As long as I work 35 hours a week my boss doesn't mind when I work. So some days I start at 9 a.m. and some days at midday.' _____
4 'I work with a children's charity. It's hard work but I really feel I'm helping people.' _____
5 'The next expedition is through the Amazon rainforest by boat.' _____

V2 **7** Match the sentence halves.
1 We're looking
2 I wouldn't depend
3 We need someone with fluency
4 Knowledge
5 My experience
6 You'll report
7 There's good prospects

a in Polish.
b to me.
c on her to remember.
d of management is limited.
e for promotion.
f of Java programming would be helpful.
g for a candidate with a degree.

V3 **8** Complete the sentences with either *work* or *time*.
1 Don't spend too much _____ on this.
2 We don't have our own offices where I work, but I have my own _____ station.
3 You can improve your _____ management with proper planning.
4 Nowadays more and more people are trying to get a good _____–life balance.
5 Meetings are really _____-consuming and not always useful.

131

4 LANGUAGE REFERENCE

GRAMMAR

G1 FUTURE FORMS

WILL

Use *will* (*'ll*) to:
- make decisions and promises at the time of speaking.
  He hasn't arrived yet, so we'll just have to go without him.
  Sorry, I'm a bit busy. I'll call you back in five minutes.
- make predictions about the future.
  Don't worry, I'm sure you'll pass your exam.

We often introduce the *will* future with words and expressions like *think, probably, it's (un)likely, I'm certain*.
  I (don't) think you'll be able to learn Spanish.
  They'll probably call us before they leave.
  It's (un)likely that we'll stop for a meal somewhere.
  I'm certain Rachel will be there.

GOING TO

Use *going to* to talk about plans or intentions (something which you have already decided).
  We're going to visit my friends next week.
  They're going to watch a film tonight.

THE PRESENT CONTINUOUS

Use the present continuous to talk about fixed future arrangements, usually involving other people.
  I'm meeting Peter at the cinema at seven.
  Nobody else is coming to the party.

G2 FIRST CONDITIONAL

Form the first conditional in the following way:

if-clause	+	main clause
if + present simple		will/may/might/should, etc.

*If people only **learn** English at school, other languages **will die** out.*
*If you **come** to my house first, we **can go** together.*
*If he **asks** you for help, you **should say** 'yes'.*

We don't use *will* in the *if*-clause.
  If people will only learn English at school, other languages die out. ✗

Use the first conditional to talk about real possibilities.
  *If they **don't hurry**, they'll miss the plane!*
  *I'll revise more if it **helps** me pass the exam.*

We can put the main clause first. If we do this, we don't use a comma.
  I might buy a car if I save enough money.

UNLESS

Unless means the same as *if not*.
  Unless we protect languages, they'll become extinct.
  = *If we don't protect languages, they'll become extinct.*

! We don't use a negative structure in the *unless*-clause.
  Unless we don't protect languages, they'll become extinct. ✗

WHEN AND AS SOON AS

When and *As soon as* can replace *if* in the first conditional. We use them when we are very certain that something will happen.
  ***When** they arrive, call me and I'll meet them.*
  ***As soon as** they arrive, we'll start the meeting.*

! We never use a future tense with these time expressions.
  When the train will arrive, I'll give you a call. ✗

KEY LANGUAGE

KL ACCEPTING AND REJECTING IDEAS, CONSIDERING CONSEQUENCES

ACCEPTING IDEAS

I think you're right.
It's an interesting thought.
That's a great idea.
OK, good idea.
Mmm, maybe you're right.
Mmm, well, yes.
That's a good point.
Yeah, right.

REJECTING IDEAS

(Mmm,) I don't know about that.
I'm not sure about that.
I'm afraid I don't like that idea.
I'm not in favour of it.

CONSIDERING CONSEQUENCES

If we do that, what will happen?
What will the effects be?
Let's think this through.
OK? What's the problem?
Maybe, but think about the consequences if we leave them out.

VOCABULARY

V1 LANGUAGE LEARNING

accent, bilingual, dialect, false friend, foreign language, grammar, native (adj), pronunciation, second language, slang

V2 PHRASAL VERBS

catch on, fall behind, get by, keep up with, let down, pay off, pick up, take up, take off

V3 BRITISH AND AMERICAN MONEY IDIOMS

go on a spending spree
look like a million dollars
splash out on
be broke
rip (someone) off / be ripped off
pass the buck
a cheapskate
tighten your belt

V4 LANGUAGE STYLE

appropriate, context, familiar, formal, friendly, humorous, informal, medium, polite, register

EXTRA PRACTICE 4

G1 **1** Write the words in brackets in the correct tense: *will, going to* or *present continuous*.

1 A: I bought this phone here, but it doesn't work.
   B: OK. Leave it here and I _____ (look) at it as soon as I have time.
2 It's all arranged. We _____ (meet) at 2 p.m. in the market square.
3 We've discussed it and we _____ (get) married!
4 I don't think I _____ (do) anything on Monday. Can we meet then?
5 A: What do you intend to do about Lillian?
   B: We _____ (offer) her an extension on the essay.
6 I haven't made up my mind yet, but I _____ (probably go) to the lesson tonight.
7 You should go to the party. I'm certain that Frank _____ (be) there.
8 Thanks for the offer, but I think I _____ (stay) at home tonight.

G2 **2** Complete the second sentence so that it has a similar meaning to the first, using the words given.

1 If you don't revise, you won't pass your exams.
   If you revise, _____.
2 If we see your teacher, we should ask him for the correct answer.
   We should ask your teacher for the correct answer when _____.
3 The world might only have one or two languages in the future if we don't protect them.
   The world might only have one or two languages in the future unless _____.
4 I won't go if you don't go.
   I won't go unless _____.
5 I'll be there at about 5 p.m. unless there's lots of traffic.
   If _____, I'll be there at about 5 p.m.
6 We'll go for coffee as soon as the class ends.
   When _____.
7 I'll give you a call if I'm not busy this afternoon.
   Unless _____, I'll give you a call.
8 You shouldn't go out so much if you don't have much money.
   If you don't have _____ stay in.

KL **3** Complete the words in the conversation.

A: So we all agree our staff need English lessons. But the problem is when? What about at lunch time?
B: No, I'm not ¹s_____ about that. Staff won't like it. They'll complain.
C: I ²t_____ you're right. When are they supposed to eat? I think after work is better.
A: I'm ³a_____ I don't like that idea. I think that will cause some problems because people finish at different times.
B: Maybe, but think about the ⁴c_____. If we have them during working hours, it'll cost us money.
C: Yes, but they would work harder. Let's think this ⁵t_____.
A: I'm not in ⁶f_____ of it. Money isn't the only problem. How can we have everyone joining the class in the middle of the day?

V1 **4** Match the words in the box to their definitions below.

foreign   dialect   grammar   accent   bilingual   native

1 the way you say words in a language _____
2 from another country _____
3 able to speak two languages fluently _____
4 a way of speaking in a particular region of a country _____
5 from or belonging to a particular country _____
6 the rules of language _____

V2 **5** Choose the correct word.

1 When I'm nervous, my English lets me *off/down*.
2 Don't fall *behind/ahead* with your homework.
3 I have a friend who just seems to pick languages *off/up*. I think she knows six!
4 I can get *by/on* in Spanish – in restaurants, for example.
5 Children tend to catch *on/along* more quickly.
6 Have you ever thought of taking *off/up* Chinese?
7 Slow down! I can't keep up *at/with* you.

V3 **6** Match idioms a–f with situations 1–6.

1 We shopped and shopped for hours – I think we have everything for the house now!
2 I think we can afford the holiday if we are careful with what we buy in the next couple of months.
3 You look absolutely amazing – you could be a celebrity!
4 I can't believe how much they charged. I have never paid that much before.
5 I think I'm going to treat myself to that designer jacket.
6 I don't know how I'm going to pay my bills this month – I have no money.

a to look like a million dollars
b to be broke
c to splash out on
d go on a spending spree
e to be ripped off
f to tighten your belt

V4 **7** Complete the text with the words in the box.

appropriate   context   formal   informal   polite   register

In my opinion, you always need to think about the ¹_____ of your material and where it is going. Some social media sites appear to be ²_____, but it is still important to be ³_____ because you don't know who will read your posts. However, when you send emails, thinking about ⁴_____ is very important. Even though it is an electronic message, you need to be more ⁵_____ if you are talking to your lecturer or boss and you should make sure you are using ⁶_____ language. For example, he/she may not be impressed if you start your email with 'Hey dude'.

5 LANGUAGE REFERENCE

GRAMMAR

G1 SECOND CONDITIONAL

Form the second conditional in the following way:

if-clause	+	main clause
if + past simple		would/could/might, etc.

If she **knew** the answer, she **could help** you.
If they **gave** a discount, **would** you **buy** it?

We use the second conditional to talk about an unreal situation in the present or future.

As with the first conditional, we can put the main clause first.
I'd help you if I **had** time.

WERE AND WAS

Both are possible in the second conditional, with no change in meaning.
If I **was** a politician, I'd make some big changes.
If I **were** a politician, I'd make some big changes.

When we give advice, we often use *were*.
If I **were** you, I'd take the job.

G2 COMPARISON

Form the comparative of one-syllable adjectives by adding *-er*, and the superlative of one-syllable adjectives by adding *-est*.
great – greater – greatest   big – bigger – biggest

With two-syllable adjectives ending in *-ow* and *-er*, add *-er* or *-est*. With adjectives ending in *-y*, remove *-y* and add *-ier* or *-iest*.
narrow – narrower – narrowest
clever – cleverer – cleverest
happy – happier – happiest

Form the comparative of other two-syllable adjectives and longer adjectives by adding *more* before the adjective, and the superlative by adding *most* before the adjective.
hopeful – more hopeful – most hopeful
interesting – more interesting – most interesting

! There are exceptions. Put *more/most* (not *-er/-est*) before one syllable adjectives which are past participles. For example:
tired – more tired – most tired
lost – more lost – most lost

LESS AND LEAST

Use *less* or *least* before any adjective. The number of syllables is not important.
It's **less** expensive.
It's **the least** expensive.

IRREGULAR ADJECTIVES

The adjectives *good* and *bad* are irregular and do not follow the rules above.
good – better – best   bad – worse – worst

MODIFIERS

Modifiers help us to comment on the size of the difference in the comparison. To talk about a large difference, use *a lot* or *much*. To talk about a small difference, use *a little* or *not much*.
China is **a lot** more populated than Norway.
Italy isn't **much** bigger than England.

AS … AS

Use *as* + adjective + *as* to say there is no difference.
The twins are **as tall as** each other.

Use *not as* + adjective + *as* to make the adjective weaker.
I'm **not as sure as** you that this is a good idea.
The film was**n't as good as** I expected it would be.

KEY LANGUAGE

KL THE LANGUAGE OF PRESENTATIONS

BEGINNING A PRESENTATION
I'd like to introduce my colleagues …

STATING THE MAIN PURPOSE OF THE PRESENTATION
Our purpose today is to …

GIVING THE PLAN/STRUCTURE
My presentation is divided into three/four parts.
If you have any questions, we'd be pleased to answer them at the end of the presentation.

TALKING ABOUT A NEW POINT
Moving on now, …
This brings me to my next point.

REFERRING TO A VISUAL AID
Please look at the screen.

ENDING A PRESENTATION
Now, let me summarise our main points.
Thank you very much for your attention.
Are there any questions?

VOCABULARY

V1 ADJECTIVES, ADVERTISING

attention-grabbing, catchy, commercial (n), dull, effective, endorse, exotic, eye-catching, humorous, intriguing, irritating, jingle, logo, misleading, original, persuasive, powerful, promote, recognisable, romantic, shocking, slogan, sophisticated, sponsorship, witty

V2 WORDS WITH A SIMILAR MEANING (CONNECTED TO CHANGE)

alter – change
enhance – improve
distort – change something's shape/sound
exaggerate – make something seem better/larger/worse
manipulate – skilfully control/move

V3 WORD COMBINATIONS

advertising manager, animated cartoons, attractive target, breakfast cereals, cartoon characters, fast food, food products, interactive websites, junk food, media analysis, persuasive message, school holidays, television advertisement, TV commercials, vast sums

EXTRA PRACTICE 5

G1 **1** Write the verb in brackets in the correct form to make second conditional sentences. Use *could* and *might* when possible.

1. If we _____ (advertise) more, we'd sell more.
2. What _____ (happen) if we put a poster up?
3. If I knew the number, I _____ (give) them a call.
4. If I _____ (be) you, I'd find a new USP.
5. Could you do it if I _____ (ask) you?
6. You _____ (not know) what this advert is for if you looked at it.
7. _____ you _____ (give) us a bigger budget if we needed it?
8. If we used the internet more, the company _____ (reach) more people.

2 Speaking practice Tell a partner what you would do in different situations. Use the phrases below.

If I had:
- more money, I'd …
- a new career, it …
- time, I'd …

If I was:
- President / Prime Minister, I'd …
- ten years younger, I'd …

G2 **3** Choose the correct form.

When I first started working in the business, advertising was much ¹*less important / the most important* than it is nowadays and our budgets weren't anything like as ²*big / bigger* as they are now. Companies now realise that marketing is ³*more complex / complexer* because there are so many different kinds of media. For example, the internet is one of the ⁴*fastest / most fast* ways of launching a new product, especially to young people. At the click of a button you can send out adverts. It's also ⁵*cheaper / cheapest* than television advertising, which takes months of planning and costs a fortune. It's true that television reaches the ⁶*higher / highest* number of people at once but in many cases internet advertising can be just as effective ⁷*than / as* TV. For example, by choosing the right websites you are ⁸*more / most* likely to reach your target market.

4 Complete sentences 1–5 with the words and phrases in the box.

| as interesting | a little | much better | much more |
| the least | | | |

1. My exam results weren't _____ than yours, so don't worry.
2. We can make the product _____ cheaper than it is now, but not much.
3. His new book isn't _____ as his first one.
4. This is a _____ attractive design than the last one – well done.
5. This is _____ important problem – let's discuss the other points first.

KL **5** Match the sentence halves.

1. Our presentation is divided into
2. Please look
3. I'd like to introduce
4. Let me summarise our
5. Are there
6. Thank you very much for
7. If you have any questions, we'd be pleased to answer them

a. your attention.
b. my colleagues.
c. any questions?
d. main points.
e. four parts.
f. at the screen.
g. at the end.

V1 **6** Complete the words.

1. We've got a famous singer to e_____ our new soft drink.
2. That's a really e_____-c_____ image. Where was it photographed?
3. We've just agreed a s_____ deal with a Formula 1 racing team.
4. If we make a radio advert, we'll need to have a c_____ song that everyone knows.
5. Coca-Cola must have the most famous l_____ in the world.
6. It's a rather dull s_____. Can we make it wittier?
7. How about having the actors drinking the product in a really e_____ location with a beach, islands and palm trees?

V2, 3 **7a** Match the words to make word combinations.

1. advertising   a. food
2. TV   b. message
3. vast   c. websites
4. manipulate   d. images
5. animated   e. manager
6. enhance   f. features
7. fast   g. food
8. junk   h. cartoons
9. persuasive   i. commercials
10. interactive   j. sums

7b Write definitions for the word combinations in Exercise 7a. Then check your answers in a dictionary.

an advertising manager: The person in charge of things like TV commercials and slogans.

6 LANGUAGE REFERENCE

GRAMMAR

G1 DEFINING RELATIVE CLAUSES

Use defining relative clauses to identify or define things, ideas, places, time and possessions.
*Children like subjects **which** interest them.*

> Don't repeat the noun from the main clause or introduce a personal pronoun to replace it.
> *Have you ever been to that museum which we just drove past it? ✗*
> *That's the man who he helped me yesterday. ✗*

A defining relative clause begins with a relative pronoun or adverb.

RELATIVE PRONOUNS

Use *that* to refer to things, people or ideas.
*That's the book **that** I was looking for.*
*Are you the person **that** I spoke to yesterday?*
*You're ignoring the point **that** I was making.*

Use *which* to refer to things or ideas.
*Yesterday we went to the restaurant **which** you recommended to us.*

Use *who* to refer to people.
*That's the man **who** I bought my car from.*

Use *whose* to refer to possession.
*He's the teacher **whose** students get the best grades.*

RELATIVE ADVERBS

Use *where* to refer to places.
*He studies at a university **where** some of our politicians got their degrees.*

Use *when* to refer to time.
*I still remember the day **when** we first met.*

If we use a relative adverb we don't normally use a preposition in the relative clause.
That's the house where I was born in. ✗
That's the hotel where we stayed last year. ✓

SUBJECT/OBJECT RELATIVE CLAUSES

The relative pronoun can be the subject or the object of the relative clause.
What's the name of the film that we saw yesterday?
*(We saw **the film**.)*
That's the shop which has the dress I want to buy.
*(**The shop** has the dress.)*

If the relative pronoun is the object of the relative clause, then it can be omitted.
What's the name of the film (that) we saw yesterday?

G2 NON-DEFINING RELATIVE CLAUSES

Non-defining relative clauses give information about something in the main clause but do not help to identify or define it. They must have a comma before and after the clause. Non-defining relative clauses are not common in spoken English.
*The President, **who is currently on a trip to the USA**, said he disagreed with the decision.*
(We know who the President is without the information in the relative clause.)

> Do not use *that* in non-defining relative clauses. Use *who* or *which* instead.
> *The course, that was also started by Professor Smith, is ending next year. ✗*
> *The course, which was also started by Professor Smith, is ending next year. ✓*

We can also use a non-defining relative clause at the end of a sentence.
Last year we visited Rome, which we thought was a really beautiful city.

KEY LANGUAGE

KL DISCUSSING POSSIBILITIES AND OPTIONS

THINKING ABOUT POSSIBILITIES
There are several ways to deal with this.
Let's look at our options.
The good thing is … the bad thing is …

MAKING SUGGESTIONS
How about (+ *-ing*)   Supposing we …

CHANGING YOUR APPROACH
Let's see, what other things can we do?

MAKING A DECISION
That's the best solution.

DECIDING WHAT TO DO NEXT
The best way is to …   So, the next thing to do is …
Why don't you send me notes on all the problems … ?

VOCABULARY

V1 EDUCATION AND STUDYING

approach, bullying, compulsory education, continuous assessment, criticise, curriculum, drop out, elementary school, easy-going teacher, environment, exam, fail, formal learning, friendly teachers, graduate, hand in, higher education, informal learning, method, mixed-sex schools, pace, pass, primary school, private education, punctual, secondary school, single-sex schools, state (public) education, statistics, strict, truancy, unique, well-prepared

V2 EDUCATION COLLOCATIONS

do homework/coursework/your best/an exam; drop out of school; fail an exam/a course; get a good grade/a good result/a place at university/a degree; go to school/college/a seminar; graduate from university/from high school (US, Australian English); hand in an essay/an assignment; leave primary school; make progress/mistakes; pass an exam/a course; revise for an exam/a subject/a test; sit an exam; study a subject/a language; take or retake an exam/a course

EXTRA PRACTICE 6

G1 **1** Complete the sentences with a relative pronoun or adverb. If it is possible to omit the pronoun, do not include it.

1. He's the person _____ I told you about.
2. Is this the place _____ you grew up?
3. She's the one _____ sister goes to the same school as us.
4. Do you remember the day _____ we went there?
5. Is this the book _____ we need to buy?
6. Do you still remember the first house _____ you lived in?
7. We need to hire someone _____ can really help the business grow.
8. It's the story of a man _____ life changes forever the day he meets a stranger in a café.

2 Combine the two sentences to make one sentence with a defining relative clause.

1. The school gets good results. I studied there.
   The school _____ gets good results.
2. The people are friendly. They live next door.
   The people _____ are friendly.
3. The girl works at the library. She was at the meeting.
   The girl _____ was at the meeting.
4. This is the station. I met John there.
   This is the station _____ I met John.
5. The idea is a good one. You suggested it yesterday.
   The idea _____ is a good one.
6. I bought the band's CD last week. They're playing here tonight.
   The band _____ CD I bought last week are playing here tonight.

G2 **3** Correct the mistake in each sentence.

1. Maria Montessori who was an Italian educationalist, developed the Montessori method.
2. This course, that is run by Professor Jones, is my favourite.
3. His theory, whose is really nothing new, says we learn best by doing.
4. The university, which was founded in 1803 is the most famous in our country.
5. The Prime Minister, who he was a student at this university, is going to make a visit here next month.
6. The manager of Westtown Bank, who we spoke to her yesterday, gave us the wrong information.
7. I gave the book to my friend John, which always likes to try new authors.
8. They want to knock down King's Hospital, where I was born in.

KL **4** Complete the gaps in the dialogue.

A: I don't know which university to apply to.
B: Well, there are several ¹_____ to _____ with that problem.
A: Really?
B: Of course. ²_____ _____ visiting both before deciding?
A: I've done that. London seems more fun, but the ³_____ _____ about Oxford is that everyone has heard of it.
B: OK, well make a list of pros and cons for each.
A: Yes, that's the ⁴_____ _____.
B: So the ⁵_____ thing to _____ is to fill in the application forms.

V1 **5** Complete the sentences with the words in the box.

graduate   criticise   unique   exams   approach
hand in

1. Did you _____ your essay on time?
2. Do you _____ this year or next?
3. How many _____ have you got this term?
4. What's your _____ to teaching?
5. People never _____ teachers in my country.
6. He has a _____ method of learning English.

V2 **6** Make phrases using one word from each box. Then fill in the gaps with the correct collocation. You may need to change the tense.

do   get   graduate   hand   revise   retake

all his exams   for the exams   from university
good grades   in the assignment   my best

1. I hope I get a good job after I _____ _____.
2. 'How was the exam?'
   'It was hard but I _____ _____. I couldn't have done any more.'
3. You need to _____ _____ to get a place at that university.
4. If you don't _____ _____ on time, you will fail the course!
5. He's very upset! He has to _____ _____ because he missed so many classes this year.
6. She's _____ every day this week. She really wants to pass them.

137

7 LANGUAGE REFERENCE

GRAMMAR

G1 MODALS (NECESSITY AND OBLIGATION)

CAN/CAN'T
Use *can/can't* to talk about present ability and possibility.
> We **can** ask him if he'd like to join us.
> I **can't** ski. I don't know how to.

COULD
Use *could* to say something is possible or likely in the future.
> Your work on this **could** be useful later on.
> That table **could** be good for my office.

SHOULD/SHOULDN'T
Use *should/shouldn't* to say if something is advisable or not.
> I think we **should** ask customers what they want.
> We probably **shouldn't** wait any longer to start work on this.

HAVE TO/MUST
We use both *have to* and *must* to talk about something that is necessary and important, but there are some differences in meaning.

Use *have to* to say something is essential or that it is a general rule.
> When you develop a new design you **have to** try it out a number of times.
> It **has to** be strong enough to carry eight people.

Use *must* to say something is necessary or important in your personal opinion.
> I feel that we **must** make the design more modern.
> It **must** be on my desk by the end of the day.

! We do not normally use *you must* or *you mustn't* in face-to-face conversation. Use *should* instead.
You ~~must~~ be more careful. ✗
You **should** be more careful. ✓

DON'T HAVE TO/MUSTN'T
Use *don't have to* to say something is not necessary.
> It **doesn't have to** be made of metal. Plastic is fine.
> They **don't have to** be here. We can decide ourselves.

Use *mustn't* to say it is necessary or important not to do something.
> We **mustn't** forget to tell them about the party.
> They **mustn't** find out about our plans. They wouldn't like them.

G2 MODALS (PRESENT DEDUCTION)

Use modal verbs to make guesses (deductions) about the present, based on evidence. The different modal verbs express different levels of certainty.

MUST
Use *must* to say that you are certain something is true.
> The door is open so Michael **must** be home.
> Jane was ill, but she's running around, so she **must** be a lot better!

CAN'T
Use *can't* to say that you are certain something is not true.
> This painting **can't** be by Rembrandt. It's much too modern.
> The police say he attacked someone at 7 p.m., but it **can't** be true because he was with me at that time.

COULD/MIGHT
Use *could* or *might* to say something is possible.
> It **could** be true that it was all his own work. It's definitely possible.
> The package **might** be from David. Open it and find out!

We can also use modal verbs with a continuous form.
> He **must be feeling** better!
> They **might be coming** later.

KEY LANGUAGE

KL DESCRIBING QUALITIES
Another strong point is …
It's aimed at …
It looks very (stylish/modern/functional/strong) …
It's functional/innovative/excellent value for money.
It's made of (wood/metal/leather).
It's made from (a new material) which is (waterproof/strong/heat resistant).
It has several (special/unique) features.
It will appeal to …
One of the best qualities is …
There are several (special/unique) features I really like.

VOCABULARY

V1 WORD BUILDING, ADJECTIVES
art, artist, artistic, design (n/v), designer, well-designed, develop, developer, development, developing, engineer (n/v), engineering, innovate, innovator, innovation, innovative, invent, inventor, invention, inventive, manufacture, manufacturer, manufacturing, produce, producer, product, productive, scientist, science, scientific, use (n/v), usable, user

V2 DESIGN
elegant, functional, futuristic, handmade, innovative, mass-produced, retro, simple, streamlined, stylish, traditional, up-to-date

V3 MATERIALS, SHAPES AND TEXTURES

MATERIAL
aluminium, canvas, leather, paper, plastic, steel, straw, wooden

SHAPE
angular, circular, curved, square

TEXTURE
hard, polished, rough, smooth, soft

V4 ABSTRACT NOUNS
advertising, communication, consumerism, industrialisation, recycling, streamlining

EXTRA PRACTICE 7

G1 **1** Complete the second sentence so that it has a similar meaning to the first, using a modal verb and any other words necessary.

1. Sorry but I'm unable to help you with this.
   Sorry but _____ you with this. **I can't**
2. I think it's important that we make it stronger.
   We _____ it stronger. **must**
3. Is it possible for you to come with us tonight?
   _____ with us tonight? **Can**
4. It isn't necessary to ask for his permission.
   You don't _____ for his permission. **have to**
5. I'm able to use steel in this design.
   I _____ in this design. **can use**
6. I'd advise you not to bother him until after lunch.
   You _____ him until after lunch. **shouldn't**
7. Keep that wood. It's likely to be useful later.
   Keep that wood. It _____ later. **could be useful**
8. The new law says that it's essential that you use recyclable products.
   You _____ recyclable products because of the new law. **must**

G2 **2** Match replies a–f with sentences 1–6.

1. I heard that it never rains in England.
2. My son is eating again now.
3. The front door is open.
4. He said if he was free, he'd be here by nine at the latest. It's midnight now.
5. There was a rumour about them getting married and then I saw them buying an engagement ring together.
6. Just because it's specially designed, this tiny pen cost over €200.

a My flatmate must be home.
b You must be joking! It never stopped when I was there.
c He must be feeling better.
d So what they say about them must be true.
e That can't be true. It's only plastic.
f He can't be coming.

G1, 2 **3** Complete the sentences with the modal verbs in the box.

have to   must (x2)   don't have to   shouldn't
can't   could   can

1. You _____ do that now – we'll have time tomorrow.
2. You _____ speak to her like that – she's very sensitive.
3. Don't forget that you _____ buy a ticket before you get on the train.
4. I _____ start working harder or I'll fail the exams.
5. This _____ be the right way. Let's stop and ask someone.
6. Our new secretary _____ speak two foreign languages – she's really clever.
7. He's not answering the phone – he _____ be out somewhere.
8. Take something to read – there _____ be delays at the airport.

KL **4** Complete the sentences with the words in the box.

appeal   point   value   looks   qualities   made
aimed   several

1. There are _____ features I really like.
2. It's _____ from a combination of metals.
3. It will _____ to business people.
4. It's excellent _____ for money.
5. It _____ very stylish.
6. It's _____ at the younger market.
7. One of the best _____ is its flexibility.
8. Another strong _____ is the innovative design.

V1, 2 **5** Complete the words with -ic, -er, -ive or -al.

1. I don't think he'll like the idea – he has very tradition_____ views.
2. My nephew is a software design_____.
3. This new keyboard layout is very us_____ friendly.
4. This plan of yours is very innovat_____. Will it work?
5. He's a very artist_____ person with great skill in painting.
6. One scientif_____ theory says there's no such thing as global warming, but no one takes it seriously.
7. For that spare part we'll have to contact the manufactur_____.
8. That new science fiction film is really futurist_____, with spaceships and lasers.
9. I'd like a kitchen that's function_____ rather than fashionable.
10. I'm an engine_____ specialising in bridges.

V3, 4 **6** Complete the sentences with the words in the box.

industrialisation   polished   recycling   efficiency
consumerism   aluminium   streamlining (x2)

1. I think our society is completely based on _____ these days. All we do is shop!
2. We need to improve the _____ of these machines. They currently use too much energy.
3. This all used to be countryside, but the _____ in the late eighties destroyed the landscape.
4. The _____ of this car makes it go faster and also looks great.
5. I love the way the artist has used _____ to create something new and beautiful. Normally these materials would be thrown away.
6. They are looking at _____ the business to make it more efficient.
7. It is impressive to see the way the artist has combined _____ and wood for a really modern look.
8. He believes _____ metallic surfaces are essential in a professional kitchen.

LANGUAGE REFERENCE

GRAMMAR

G1 PAST CONTINUOUS

Form the past continuous with *was/were* + verb + *-ing*.
> I **was working** on a project for six months.
> The children **weren't working** very hard.

Use the past continuous:

- to talk about background actions
  It was a beautiful day – the sun **was shining** and the birds **were singing**.

  ◄----- sun was shining, birds were singing -----► NOW

- to talk about a longer background action in the past when a shorter action interrupts it or happens during it.
  We **were talking** about you when you rang.
  (the background action is interrupted and stops)

  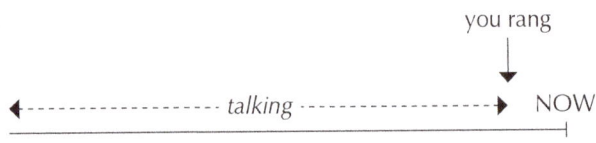

  I **was having** a staff meeting when Julia arrived five minutes late.
  (the action happens during the background action)

  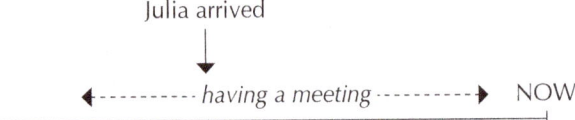

- to talk about repeated actions in the past that take place over a temporary period of time.
  People **were coming in** all day to buy this item.

  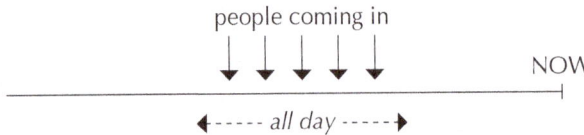

- to emphasise the duration or continuity of a past action.
  For the whole of last month we **were trying** to solve this same problem.

  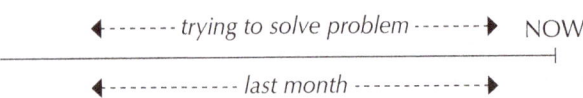

! We rarely use state verbs such as *be, like, know, believe, understand* in the continuous form.
  I ~~was liking~~ the fish soup. ✗
  I **liked** the fish soup. ✓

G2 PAST PERFECT SIMPLE

Form the past perfect simple with *had* + past participle.
> I called but he**'d** already **left**.
> When I checked, it was obvious they **hadn't understood** the instructions.

Use the past perfect simple to emphasise that one action happened before another in the past.
> The film **had** already **started** when we arrived at the cinema.

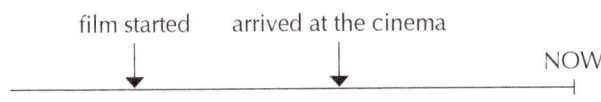

The past perfect simple is often used with the conjunctions *when, before, after* and *by*.
> I had left **when** he called.
> She had been to Australia twice **before** we went together.
> We went out **after** we had eaten breakfast.
> **By** the age of 80, he had written over a hundred books.

If the sequence of events is clear, we can also use the past simple.
> I called my friend after I finished work.

KEY LANGUAGE

KL THE LANGUAGE OF NEGOTIATION

How many would you like to order?
We are thinking of placing a large order.
I'm afraid that would be a bit/very difficult.
What about if we paid earlier? Would you be able to … ?
Let me check if I understand you.
How do you feel about that?
That sounds fine.

VOCABULARY

V1 BUSINESS TERMS AND ROLES

business, charge (v), community, competitor, customer, entrepreneur, invest, investor, law, loss, manufacturer, manufacturing, owner, partner, prices, profit, retail, retailer, staff, supplier, taxes, wages, wholesaler

V2 COLLOCATIONS

BEFORE
do some market research, make a business plan

START
do the first year accounts, go into partnership, set up a company

DURING
launch a new product range / an advertising campaign, make money / a profit, recruit a new manager / talented employees, reduce production costs, run a factory, set up an overseas branch

END
go out of business, reduce the number of staff, run the business badly

EXTRA PRACTICE 8

G1 **1** Write the verbs in brackets in the past continuous or the past simple.

When I ¹ _was_ (study) at university, I took a part-time job as a security guard at a factory to earn some extra money. I often ² _worked_ (work) at night, and one evening I ³ _____ (check) the warehouse when I heard a noise. I was really scared so I ⁴ _____ (call) the police. They arrived and while they ⁵ _____ (search) the area they found someone asleep in a small cupboard next to the warehouse. The person ⁶ _____ (be) the daytime security guard, who ⁷ _____ (live) in the factory because he couldn't afford to rent a flat. He ⁸ _____ (wear) pyjamas produced in the factory. The factory owners were furious at first and ⁹ _____ (plan) to sack the young man, but in the end they found him a cheap flat and he ¹⁰ _____ (keep) his job.

G2 **2** Match the sentence halves. _past perfect_
1 By the time they got to the cinema **c**
2 He stayed out late **a**
3 By the end of his first year at university **e**
4 I'd just gone to sleep **b**
5 After I'd booked the tickets **d**

a after I'd told him not to.
b when the phone rang and woke me up.
c the film had already started.
d she changed her mind and said she wanted to eat out instead.
e he'd already decided he didn't want to be a doctor.

G1, 2 **3** Choose the correct tense.
1 We launched the second version once we (**had seen**) / were seeing how successful the first one was.
2 By the time he was applying / (**'d applied**), the job had already gone.
3 He called while I tried / (**was trying**) to finish this essay.
4 After he (**had invested**) / was investing more money, the business took off.
5 The entrepreneur (**gave**) / had given another billion dollars to charity after he had already given three billion.
6 We didn't need to clean the house, because he (**had already done**) / already did it.
7 I studied business in the evening while I (**was working**) / had worked in a kitchen.
8 She left before anyone (**had had**) / was having a chance to explain the situation.
9 The business (**went**) / was going bankrupt last month and they couldn't save it.
10 All last year, the company had looked / (**was looking**) for ways to survive the crisis.

G2 **4** Speaking practice Tell a partner about yourself, using the phrases below.
By the age of five, I had …
By the age of ten, I had …
By the age of fifteen, I had …

KL **5** Complete the sentences with the words in the box.

placing   would   sounds   afraid   feel
paid   check

1 How many _____ you like to order?
2 We are thinking of _____ a large order.
3 I'm _____ that would be very difficult.
4 What if we _____ earlier?
5 Let me _____ if I understand you.
6 How do you _____ about that?
7 That _____ fine.

V1 **6** Complete the words.
1 How many s_____ do you have working here?
2 The first rule of business is that the c_____ is always right.
3 How much money did you i_____ in the company?
4 We made a huge p_____ last year.
5 Malcolm is my p_____ in the business.
6 The p_____ of computers keeps going down.
7 This government keeps putting up t_____ .
8 It's much cheaper to buy products from a w_____ than from a shop.

V2 **7** Choose the correct verb(s). There may be more than one possible answer.
1 make / go out of / ~~found~~ business
2 launch / ~~do~~ / go into a company
3 introduce / ~~found~~ / launch a product
4 make / ~~go into~~ / ~~launch~~ a profit
5 reduce / make / ~~run~~ costs
6 ~~go into~~ / set up / ~~make~~ another branch

141

9 LANGUAGE REFERENCE

GRAMMAR

G1 THE PASSIVE

We form the passive with the verb *to be* + the past participle of the main verb.
> The test **is carried** out.

Form the passive for each tense as follows:

tense	example
present simple	The Earth **is struck**.
past simple	Meteorites **were discovered**.
present perfect	The theory **hasn't been agreed** on.
future	Mars **will be explored**.
modal	The rock **must be destroyed**.

If we include the person who does the action, we introduce them with the preposition *by*.
> The test is carried out **by scientists**.

Use the passive when the person doing the action is not important, not known or is obvious.
> A strange message about an object in the sky **was left** on a police answering machine.
> The space shuttle **will be flown** twice around the moon.

We also use the passive when we want to start a sentence with information that is known or has been mentioned before.
> Twenty scientists are currently on the team. By the end of the year, they **will be joined** by 25 more.

G2 ARTICLES

Use articles in the following ways:

- **first and second mention**

Use *a/an* when you mention a singular noun for the first time.
> Tokyo has **a** major problem with space.
> **An** alternative idea has been suggested.

Use *the* when we refer to something that has been mentioned before.
> (Tokyo has **a** major **problem** with space.) At last city planners are trying to solve **the problem**.

Don't use an article with general plural countable nouns, and when we mention a plural noun for the first time.
> **Scientists** still haven't found a way to deter meteorites.
> **Satellites** will be launched into space. (Scientists will then use **the** satellites to look for alien life.)

- **known things**

Use *the* when there is only one of something.
> **The** Earth's moon is a natural satellite.
> Engineers are designing a train which will travel under **the** city.

- **set uses**

Use *the* with the names of some countries.
> **the** United States, **the** United Kingdom, **the** Netherlands

Use *the* with the names of geographical features.
> **the** Baltic Sea, **the** Pacific Ocean, **the** Amazon, **the** Alps

Use *the* with superlatives.
> It's **the** largest engineering project of its kind.

Use *a/an* when talking about a job someone does.
> I'm **a** teacher.
> She works as **a** lawyer.

Don't use an article with the names of towns and cities, and most countries.
> Venice, Paris, Tokyo, Japan, China

KEY LANGUAGE

KL DISCUSSING OPTIONS, MAKING DECISIONS

What about calling (it/them/that) … ?
There are other possibilities …
It sounds good to (me/us).
Well, one option would be to …
If (we/I/they) called it X, (people) would like that name.
Mmm, nice idea.
Are we all agreed then?
Have we reached a decision?
I'll recommend (that) to …
We're all agreed.

VOCABULARY

V1 COLLOCATIONS

build a model/prototype, do (some) research, do safety tests, find a solution, make a breakthrough, meet deadlines, solve a problem, test a theory

V2 GLOBAL THREATS

asteroid, alien invasion, collide, collision, comet, deflect, devastation, drought, earthquakes, extinction, famine, genetic engineering, hazardous, hurricanes, impact, infectious diseases, meteor, meteorite, overpopulation, probe, superbugs, threat, tsunamis, volcanoes, wipe out

V3 PRODUCTION

aircraft, aviation, flight test, limited number, mass-produce, modify, modification, model, prototype, simulation, test drive, wind tunnel

EXTRA PRACTICE 9

G1 **1** Complete the second sentence using a passive form so that it has a similar meaning to the first.

1. Astronauts fly the shuttle into space.
   The shuttle _____ into space.
2. Scientists did the tests yesterday.
   The tests _____ yesterday.
3. The company has launched the new brand.
   The new brand _____.
4. They haven't answered our questions.
   Our questions _____.
5. Engineers built the new plane in Seattle.
   The new plane _____ in Seattle.
6. You can play tennis in the morning.
   Tennis _____ in the morning.
7. The President has announced a new environmental policy.
   A new environmental policy _____.
8. We fire the rockets from mission control.
   The rockets _____ from mission control.

2 Read the sentences and delete the agent if it is unnecessary.

1. She was sacked ~~by her employer~~ yesterday.
2. It was announced by the Prime Minister today that he would resign within the week.
3. It is the third time that the Earth has been hit by an asteroid in recent years.
4. The bridge was built by people in the 1920s.
5. The emergency meeting was organised by our managing director.
6. The criminal was sent to prison by the judge for three years.

G2 **3** Complete the gaps with *the*, *a* or *an*, or leave a space if no article is necessary.

1. I'm _____ engineer for a large building firm.
2. The flight stops in _____ Tokyo.
3. There's _____ major problem with this idea.
4. We're going skiing in _____ Swiss Alps this winter.
5. We thought we might go to _____ Canada for our next holiday.
6. She wants to become _____ nurse when she finishes school.
7. I think _____ cars are the most serious cause of pollution in the world.
8. This is one of _____ slowest trains I've ever been on.
9. The tunnel passes under _____ sea from England to France.
10. Now _____ trains run several times a day between London and Paris. Tickets for _____ trains cost from £25 for a single.

KL **4** A local council is discussing what to call a new bridge across the city's river. Complete the discussion with phrases a–e.

a Well, one option would be
b We're all agreed
c I'll recommend
d It sounds good
e What about calling

A: ¹_____ to call it Peterson Bridge, after Gerald Peterson, who did so much for the city in his life?
B: Hmmm, I'm not sure if that's the best idea. The park in the centre is already called Peterson Park, so it might be confusing. ²_____ it Broad Bridge. Then people will know you go down Broad Street to get to it.
A: ³_____ to me.
C: Yes, I like that idea, too.
A: ⁴_____. We'll call it Broad Bridge. ⁵_____ that to the mayor, then we can look at changing the street signs and maps.

V1 **5** Choose the correct verb.

1. Finally, they've *solved/made* a breakthrough.
2. We've been *doing/finding* some research into it.
3. Did you *make/do* the safety tests?
4. Have they *built/met* the prototype yet?
5. I'd like to *make/test* your theory.
6. We still haven't *found/done* a good solution.
7. I've *met/solved* the problem with the machine.
8. Do you think we'll *meet/do* the deadline?

V2,3 **6** Choose the correct word, a, b or c, to complete each sentence.

1. There was a terrible _____ between the two football players.
   a collision
   b devastation
   c threat
2. Can we make some _____ to the designs?
   a modifications
   b simulations
   c impact
3. The _____ industry needs to reduce pollution from its engines.
   a comet   b wind   c aviation
4. Can we _____ the asteroid so it doesn't hit us?
   a modify   b deflect   c test
5. Let's run another _____ on the computer to see what will happen in a real situation.
   a modification
   b devastation
   c simulation
6. We're doing another flight _____ on the prototype.
   a tunnel
   b test
   c mass-produce

10 LANGUAGE REFERENCE

GRAMMAR

G1 EXPRESSIONS OF QUANTITY

Use expressions of quantity to comment on the quantity of a noun. They can be used with subjects and objects.

*I only have **a couple of shirts** left.*
***Plenty of people** want to go there.*

COUNTABLE AND UNCOUNTABLE NOUNS

Some quantifiers can only be used with a countable or uncountable noun.

Use these quantifiers with countable nouns:
a couple of, a few, many

Use these quantifiers with uncountable nouns:
a little, much

Use these quantifiers with both countable and uncountable nouns:
a lot of, no, none, some, plenty of, enough

GENERAL AND SPECIFIC NOUNS

Use *some* and *no* with general nouns without an article.

***Some people** aren't interested in sport.*
*I'd like **some meat**.*
***No bikes** are allowed on the pathway.*

Use *some of, none of, plenty of, a couple of, a lot of* with specific plural or uncountable nouns.

***Some of the people** we were expecting didn't come.*
*You can use **some of the meat in the fridge**.*
***None of them** wanted to go.*
***A couple of my friends** live there.*
***A lot of the students** are getting good marks.*

G2 INFINITIVES AND -ING FORMS

When one verb follows another, it may appear in the infinitive or -*ing* form. The form depends on the first verb, and the following structures are possible:

- verb (+ object) + infinitive with *to*
  *Most people **want to live** for a 100 years.*
  *Everyone **wants the champion to win** again.*

Other verbs include: *allow* (object + *to*), *decide, hope, manage, promise, teach* (object + *to*).

We also use the infinitive with *to* with *would* + verb.
I like to play tennis. ✓
I like playing tennis. ✓
I'd like to play tennis. ✓
I'd like playing tennis. ✗

- verb + -*ing*
  *We **prefer watching** comedies.*
  *They **enjoy playing** tennis on Saturdays.*

Other verbs include: *practise, recommend, suggest, understand.*

We also use the -*ing* form after a preposition.
*I'm going to give **up learning** Spanish.*
*I'm good **at making** friends.*

- verb + infinitive with *to* or -*ing*
  I like to travel.
  I like travelling.

Other verbs include: *advise, begin, continue, love, hate.*

KEY LANGUAGE

KL RAISING AND RESPONDING TO ISSUES

STATING THE PURPOSE OF THE MEETING
We're here to discuss …
I want to talk (to you) about …

ENCOURAGING PEOPLE TO SPEAK
Go ahead please.
Please make your point.

MAKING A POINT
It's about the …
I'm very unhappy with … / about it.
It's not acceptable – I'm sure you understand that.
Sorry, could I just say something please?
What are you going to do about it?

THANKING PEOPLE FOR THEIR IDEAS
Thank you / Thanks very much for your comment.

RESPONDING TO POINTS
Mmm, I understand how you feel, …
It's a serious problem …
We're very concerned about this problem.
We're taking it seriously …
I'm sorry that you're thinking of … , because of …

SAYING YOU WILL TAKE ACTION
I'll look into the matter.
We're thinking about various options to deal with it.
We're looking at various ways of dealing with it.

STATING THE KEY POINTS THAT HAVE BEEN AGREED
Well, to sum up …

VOCABULARY

V1 PHRASAL VERBS

buy into, catch on, die out, find out, keep up with, pick up on, slow down, take over

V2 FASHION

designer, fashion, fashionable, fashion blogger, fashion-conscious, fashion show, fashion statement, fashion victim, high street fashion, unfashionable, stylist, trendsetter

V3 DESCRIBING TRENDS

be down, be up, decline (n/v), decrease (n/v), dramatic, drop (n/v), fairly constant, fall (n/v), go up, gradual, greatest fall/rise, grow, improve (v), increase (n/v), level off, marked fall, peak, remain (relatively) stable, rise (n/v), sharp rise, sharp drop, significant, slight, slow, stabilise, steady, sudden, top out (at)

EXTRA PRACTICE 10

G1 **1** Choose the correct answer.
1 Sorry, I only have *a lot / a couple* of hours to do this and I won't have time tomorrow.
2 We never have *a little / enough* money for holidays.
3 *A few / A little* people couldn't come this evening.
4 We still have *plenty of / many* sugar in the cupboard.
5 *Some / Much* of you need to stay late, but most of you can leave.
6 *No / None* of them know about our secret. Shall I tell them?
7 *A lot / A couple* of customers – nearly 80 percent – complained about the price, so I suggest we lower it.

2 Write in the missing words in sentences 1–6.
1 A few my old friends work in the fashion industry. They all really like it.
2 Plenty people I know only wear black, but I prefer different coloured clothes.
3 Can I talk to you about something for couple of minutes?
4 Give him little more time – I'm sure he'll finish it.
5 There are lot of students in my class that want to study English.
6 None the people in my family went to university. I was the first.

G2 **3** Match the sentence halves.
1 I really enjoyed
2 You're not allowed
3 Most people want
4 He's not good at
5 They started
6 We advise you

a to use a dictionary in the exam. It's against the rules.
b making friends. That's why he's so lonely.
c to make a booking before you travel.
d working here before I did.
e playing tennis. Let's do it again sometime.
f to live to 100.

4 Complete the sentences with the verb in brackets in the correct form.
1 Most people want _____ (live) in this part of town.
2 She decided _____ (cancel) the appointment.
3 Do you enjoy _____ (watch) nature films?
4 He taught me _____ (play) chess.
5 They're really good at _____ (help) with problems.
6 We should carry on _____ (drive) for another hour.
7 Are you allowed _____ (come) with me?
8 They suggested _____ (take) the train.
9 I'd love _____ (see) that new film about Shakespeare.

KL **5** Complete the phrases with the words in the box.

acceptable   matter   unhappy   point   here
say   sum   comment

1 Please make your _____.
2 I'll look into the _____.
3 Sorry, could I just _____ something please?
4 Thank you for your _____.
5 We're _____ to discuss transport.
6 Well, to _____ up, we are all agreed about the solution.
7 It's not _____ – I'm sure you understand that.
8 I'm very _____ with these plans.

V1–3 **6** Complete the gaps with a preposition.
1 I don't buy _____ this new trend.
2 Enthusiasm for the new sports hall died _____ when they saw the price.
3 The growth in the population has slowed _____ in recent years.
4 I just can't keep _____ with high street fashions these days.
5 Do you think this fashion for pink will catch _____ ?
6 Did you pick up _____ the anger in his voice?
7 Life expectancy will top _____ at 100 by the end of the century and stop rising.
8 The new craze for red hair is taking _____ the population!
9 I should buy it before the prices go _____ .
10 The company's share price levelled _____ at $50 today.

V3 **7** Choose the correct answer.
1 There's been a *gradual/dramatic* fall in unemployment figures. They dropped by over half a million in only one month.
2 His condition has remained *stable/sudden* overnight, so the doctors are feeling happier.
3 Share prices have remained *steady/dramatic* recently, with prices staying the same.
4 Life expectancy is set to *rise/remain* sharply over the next century, with many more of us living until we're well over 100.
5 There's been a *big/slight* fall in the number of car owners, but nothing significant.
6 Sales have *declined/grown* recently, so shop owners are very worried.

11 LANGUAGE REFERENCE

GRAMMAR

G1 REPORTED SPEECH

Use reported speech to report someone's words.

'I want to become a famous singer.'
She said she **wanted** to become a famous singer.

'I always hoped to become an actor.'
He said he**'d always hoped** to become an actor.

When we use reported speech, we make changes to the tense of the verb, to pronouns and to time adverbs. The table shows the most common changes:

Direct speech	Reported speech
Tenses	
present simple	past simple
present continuous	past continuous
present perfect	past perfect
past simple	past perfect
will	would
can	could
Pronouns	
I	he/she
we	they
my	his/her
our	their
Time adverbs	
today	then/that day
yesterday	the day before
tomorrow	the next day/the day after
last week	the week before

'I work as a teacher.'
He said he **worked** as a teacher.

'We left our bags at the station.'
They said **they had left their** bags at the station.

'I start my new job today.'
Rita said **she started her** new job **that day**.

'They were with me yesterday.'
Laurie said they **had been** with **her the previous day**.

TELL AND SAY

Use *tell* with an object before the reported speech.
He told **me** that he couldn't come out. ✓
He told that he couldn't come out. ✗

Never use *say* with an object before the reported speech.
She said ~~me~~ that she would be late. ✗

COMMANDS

Use the infinitive with *to* to report a command.
'Leave my house!'
He told the journalist **to leave** his house.

G2 REPORTED QUESTIONS

To report a question, use expressions like *He asked me …* , *She wanted to know …* .

For Yes/No questions (questions which require *yes* or *no* as an answer) use *if*.

'Do you know Peter?'
They asked me **if** I knew Peter.

'Have you worked on a newspaper before?'
He wanted to know **if** I had worked on a newspaper.

For other questions, use the *wh-* word.

*'**Why** are you interested in TV?'*
He asked me **why** I was interested in TV.

*'**What** experience do you have?'*
I wanted to know **what** experience she had.

As with reported speech, the verb in the direct question often changes in the reported question by moving back a tense and there are changes to pronouns and time adverbs.
*'Is Rachel **coming** to stay **today**?'*
Mum asked me if Rachel **was coming** to stay **that day**.

In reported questions, use the same word order as a statement.
Sarah asked me ~~did I want~~ to visit her. ✗
Sarah asked me if I wanted to visit her. ✓

! Don't use question marks with a reported question.

KEY LANGUAGE

KL COMPARING AND CONTRASTING

different from …, the same as …, similar to …, much better than …, less important than …, a lot worse than …

VOCABULARY

V1 DESCRIBING BOOKS AND FILMS

atmosphere, audiences, breathtaking, brooding, cast, chapter, character, classic, dark, disturbing, dramatic, entertaining, episode, gripping, groundbreaking, heavy going, hilarious, magnificent, novel, out-of-this-world, outstanding, page-turner, plot, series, sketch, stunning

V2 MEDIA GENRES

animation, autobiography, crime, current affairs programme, documentary, drama series, folk, garage, hip hop, horror, hospital drama, opera, quiz show, R&B, rap, reality, reggae, romantic comedy, science fiction, sitcom, soap, soul, thriller

V3 WORDS CONNECTED WITH THE ARTS

bestseller, biography, blockbuster, critic, epic, hit, household name, masterpiece, movie rights, royalties

V4 FILMS

action scenes, choreograph (v), dub (v), full-length, genre, hero, heroine, lead actor, lead character, location, main role, pitch, sequel, set (n), special effects

EXTRA PRACTICE 11

G1 **1** Rewrite the sentences as reported speech.
1. 'I travel 50 miles a day.'
   She said _____.
2. 'I don't want to talk about it.'
   He told us that _____.
3. 'I've called three times.'
   He said he _____.
4. 'Go home!'
   My father told me _____.
5. 'Mel is going to Australia.'
   Jemma said that _____.
6. 'They lived here from 1863 to 1899.'
   The tour guide said _____.
7. 'I'm leaving.'
   She said _____.
8. 'Stop talking!'
   The teacher told the class _____.

2 Read the conversation between two people who work for a music magazine and complete the report of their meeting below.

PETER: We're having this meeting to decide who we'll feature in the next issue.
BRYAN: I've spoken to James Blunt and he isn't available until next month. I'm also trying to contact Jennifer Lopez, but I can only get her agent.
PETER: I spoke to Paul McCartney at a Music Awards show. He said he can do an interview.
BRYAN: We can't do another issue on The Beatles! Try calling the Kings of Leon.

Peter and Bryan had the meeting to decide who they ¹_____ feature in the next issue of the magazine *Music Now*.

Bryan said he ²_____ to James Blunt but he ³_____ until the following month. He ⁴_____ also _____ to contact Jennifer Lopez, but he ⁵_____ only get her agent. Peter said he ⁶_____ to Paul McCartney and he ⁷_____ he ⁸_____ do an interview.

However, Bryan told Peter they ⁹_____ do another Beatles' issue. He told him ¹⁰_____ the Kings of Leon instead.

G2 **3** Put the words in the correct order to make sentences with reported speech.
1. Thierry asked me _____.
   had / I / if / seen / you
2. Your boss wanted to know _____.
   if / late / were / you
3. They asked me _____.
   why / didn't / take / I / the / job
4. She wanted to know _____.
   hadn't / you / called / why
5. Your parents asked me _____.
   you / were / where

4 Rewrite the questions as reported questions.
1. 'Can I help you?'
   The shop assistant asked _____.
2. 'Why are you here?'
   The receptionist wanted to know _____.
3. 'Do you live in London?'
   The tourist asked _____.
4. 'Is this your car?'
   The police officer wanted to know _____.

KL **5** Match the sentence halves.
1. For some reason the sequel was a lot worse
2. All his films are similar
3. The sequel is very different
4. Special effects are less important
5. Isn't there something better
6. It's the same plot as

a. the first one.
b. than the first one.
c. than a good plot.
d. from the other one.
e. to that other one we saw.
f. than that on TV?

V1, 2 **6** Complete the table with the words in the box.

chapter documentary folk novel reggae
page-turner reality sitcom soap hip hop
soul autobiography episode

Music	Books	TV programmes

V1–4 **7** Choose the correct answer.
1. The *plot/genre* of this film is so complicated I can't understand who is who.
2. I hate it when they *pitch/dub* movies. I prefer to hear the original language.
3. The first episode of that new detective *sequel/series* is on tonight.
4. There's this *hilarious/gripping* comedy series set in a hotel.
5. The lead actress gave a(n) *outstanding/full-length* performance. She deserves an Oscar.
6. The *soap/documentary* follows the lives of three real-life police officers in New York.
7. The *special/romantic* effects in that film set in space are breathtaking.
8. The *sets/characters* in Shakespeare are never just as simple as good and evil.

12 LANGUAGE REFERENCE

GRAMMAR

G1 THIRD CONDITIONAL

Form the third conditional in the following way:

if-clause + main clause
if + past perfect   would/could/might + have + past participle

*If Sarah **had asked** me, I **would have helped** her.*

Use the third conditional to talk about unreal situations in the past, i.e. situations that are contrary to the facts.
*If he **hadn't driven** so quickly, the police **could have caught** him.* (He drove quickly, the police didn't catch him.)
*If she'**d been** a little nicer, I **might have gone** to her party.* (She wasn't nice, I didn't go to the party.)

We often use the third conditional to:
- talk about regrets.
 *If I'**d worked** harder, I **might have got** better results.*
- criticise.
 *If you'**d listened** to me, you **wouldn't have got** into trouble with the police.*
- make excuses.
 *Sorry, but if the plane **had left** on time, I **wouldn't have been** so late!*

As with the first and second conditional, we can put the main clause first.

G2 MODALS (PAST DEDUCTION)

Use modal perfects to make guesses (deductions) about things in the past. The modal perfect is formed with a modal verb (e.g. *must, can, should*) + *have* + past participle.
*They **must have climbed** in through the back window.*
*They **should have checked** the car before they left.*

Use *should have* to say something was a good idea, but it didn't happen.
*To finish the job more quickly they **should have asked** more people to help.*

Use *shouldn't have* to say something wasn't a good idea, but it happened.
*He **shouldn't have driven** over the speed limit.*

Use *might have* to say that it is possible, but not certain, that something happened.
*He **might have decided** to ask the police for help.*

Use *must have* to say it is logically certain that something happened.
*There's a broken window at the back so the robber **must have climbed** in there.*

Use *couldn't have* to say that it is not possible that something happened.
*The judge **couldn't have given** any other sentence but 20 years in prison for a crime like this.*

➥ page 138 for present deduction.

KEY LANGUAGE

KL REACHING A DECISION

The evidence clearly shows …
I am sure that you will find my client innocent.
The facts of the case are clear.
I'm not certain he's guilty because …
There should be no doubt in your minds that this man is guilty.
I am confident that you will find the defendant guilty.
You can look at it in two ways.
I will bring witnesses to confirm that …
I believe he's innocent because …
It's clear to me that …
It seems to me that …
I've made up my mind.
It's obvious to me that …

VOCABULARY

V1 CRIME

CRIMES
blackmail, bribery, cyber-stalking, dangerous driving, kidnapping, mugging, pickpocketing, (armed) robbery, shoplifting, smuggling, speeding, (car) theft, vandalism

PEOPLE CONNECTED TO CRIME
the accused, attorney, burglar, captor, criminal, the defence, defendant, detective, gang, hostage, investigators, judge, jury, lawyer, (juvenile) offender, police, prisoner, the prosecution, prosecutor, (bank) robber, suspect, (car) thief/thieves, victim, witnesses

THINGS CONNECTED TO CRIME
case, court, crime scene, evidence, explosives, false pretences, fingerprint, fraud, getaway, guilty, guns, jail (US) / prison (UK), a job (= a crime), legal, mask, punishment, raid, ransom, reward, verdict

VERBS
arrest, catch, charge (with), chase, convict, escape, face charges, hold up, identify suspects, investigate, offend, prove, rob, smash, stalk, steal, suspect, track (someone) down, vandalise, witness

V2 WORD COMBINATIONS

antisocial behaviour, bad behaviour, career decision, close relationship, criminal behaviour, genetic link, good behaviour, human behaviour, long tradition, vicious circle

EXTRA PRACTICE 12

G1 **1** Correct the mistake in each sentence.
1 If Dmitry has asked me to help, I would have.
2 If he hadn't left so much evidence, the police wouldn't caught him.
3 I might have become a solicitor if I would worked harder at school.
4 If you'd had listened to me, you wouldn't have taken the job.
5 Sorry, but if the plane would had left on time, I wouldn't have been so late!
6 You could come if you had wanted to.
7 We wouldn't have missed the deadline if everyone had been done what they promised.
8 If I hadn't have heard the news, I wouldn't have known.

G2 **2** Complete the second sentence using a modal perfect form so that it has a similar meaning to the first.
1 The lock was smashed. I'm certain the thief did it.
 The thief _____ smashed the lock.
2 It's possible that the owner forgot where he parked the car.
 The owner _____ forgotten where he parked the car.
3 The lights weren't on at the house. I'm certain they were still out.
 They _____ been home because the lights weren't on.
4 It's possible that they left a message on your voicemail.
 They _____ left a message on your voicemail.
5 The kids ate everything – they were really hungry.
 The kids _____ been really hungry because they ate everything.
6 There isn't a door at the back. It wasn't possible for the burglars to get in from there.
 They _____ got in from the back because there isn't a door there.
7 It was wrong of them to take the book without asking me.
 They _____ taken the book without asking me.
8 The project went completely wrong. It wasn't planned properly.
 They _____ planned the project properly because it went completely wrong.
9 We didn't take out insurance when we went on holiday and we had a car accident.
 We _____ taken out insurance when we went on holiday.

KL **3** Complete the sentences with the pairs of words in the box.

facts + case   look + ways   evidence + shows
find + client   doubt + minds   you + defendant
believe + innocent   certain + guilty

1 The _____ clearly _____ that you were at the scene of the crime.
2 The _____ of the _____ are clear.
3 I'm sure you will _____ my _____ innocent.
4 There should be no _____ in your _____ that this man is guilty.
5 I am confident that _____ will find the _____ innocent.
6 You can _____ at it in two _____.
7 I'm not _____ she is _____.
8 I _____ he's _____ because the witness said he was in a different city at the time.

V1 **4** Complete the sentences with the words in the box.

fingerprints   getaway   kidnapping   lawyer
suspect   investigate   witness

1 You are accused of _____ a ten-year-old boy.
2 The police are holding the _____ for more questions.
3 The _____ car was waiting outside for the robbers.
4 I'd like to speak to my _____ before I speak to the police.
5 The detective is trying to _____ the disappearance of the jewels.
6 My first _____ is a woman who was walking past the park at the time of the murder.
7 The police found the thief's _____ on the window.

V1, 2 **5** Match the words to make phrases.
1 career   a relationship
2 long   b link
3 false   c circle
4 antisocial d crisis
5 close   e pretences
6 genetic   f tradition
7 vicious   g decision
8 hostage   h behaviour

149

▶ MEET THE EXPERT

1 PERSONALITY

1 Discuss these questions with a partner.
1 What technique do actors Daniel Day-Lewis and Johnny Depp both use?
2 How do they prepare for roles?

2a Michael Gould is a British actor. Read these six topics he discusses in an interview. In what order do you think he will discuss them?

a A technique Michael always uses
b A technique people misunderstand
c Companies he has worked for
d How another actor prepares
e How he prepared for a particular role
f A director he has worked with

2b ▶ 1 Watch the interview with Michael. Put the topics in the correct order.

3 Watch the interview again and decide if these statements are true (T) or false (F).
1 Method actors lose their own personalities in a role.
2 Michael thinks Daniel Day-Lewis is a good actor.
3 Daniel Day-Lewis told Michael an interesting story about acting.
4 Michael uses some method-acting techniques.
5 Psychiatrists helped Michael to understand a particular character.

4 Work with a partner. How can acting techniques help you become a more successful language learner? Think about the various techniques that Michael talked about in the interview. How might they help you improve your English?

Michael Gould in the 2009 Royal Shakespeare Company's production of Othello.

3 WORK

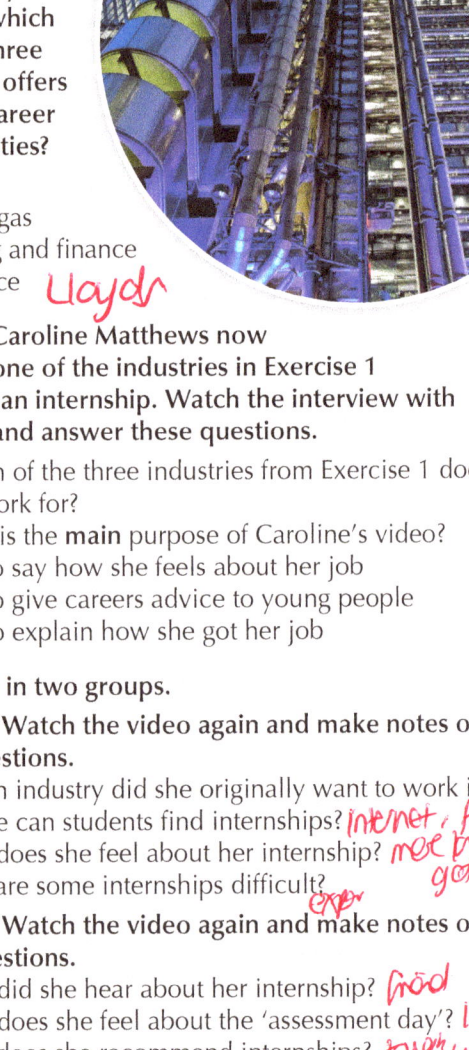

1 Work in small groups. In your opinion, which of these three industries offers the best career opportunities? Why?
- oil and gas
- banking and finance
- insurance

2 ▶ 3 Caroline Matthews now works in one of the industries in Exercise 1 following an internship. Watch the interview with Caroline and answer these questions.
1 Which of the three industries from Exercise 1 does she work for?
2 What is the **main** purpose of Caroline's video?
   a To say how she feels about her job
   b To give careers advice to young people
   c To explain how she got her job

3a Work in two groups.
Group A: Watch the video again and make notes on these questions.
1 Which industry did she originally want to work in?
2 Where can students find internships?
3 How does she feel about her internship?
4 Why are some internships difficult?

Group B: Watch the video again and make notes on these questions.
1 How did she hear about her internship?
2 How does she feel about the 'assessment day'?
3 Why does she recommend internships?
4 What should you do in an interview?

3b Compare your notes with other students in your group.

3c Now work in pairs (A and B) and share information with a student from the other group.

4 Work in small groups and discuss these questions.
1 Have you ever had advice on your education or career? Who gave you the advice? How good was the advice?
2 What careers advice would you give to a university student?

4 LANGUAGE

1 Discuss these questions with a partner.
1 Does your first (or main) language have many different accents or dialects? If yes, how do people in your country feel about them?
2 Is your first language spoken in any other countries? Which ones?
3 Is there a standard form of your first language? If yes, how do you know it is the standard form?

2 ▶ 4 Henry Hitchings is an author and expert on the English language. Watch the interview with Henry. Does he believe that British English is the best language for global communication? *No, not necessarily*

3a Read these six opinions from different people about the English language. Do you think Henry Hitchings would agree (A) or disagree (D)?
1 'A language belongs to every person who can speak it.' *A*
2 'Globish is a good word for the international English that business people use.' *D*
3 'In the future, people will learn to speak two forms of English.' *A* — *local / international*
4 'Native speakers of English should simplify their language in international communication.' *A*
5 'English will not be the only language of global communication in the future.' *A*
6 'In the future, the most important changes in the English language will come from the USA.' *D*

3b Watch again and check your answers to Exercise 3a. What differences are there between the sentences in Exercise 3a and Henry's opinions? What additional information does he give?

4 Work in small groups and discuss. People today speak one or more of the world's 6,000–7,000 languages. However, around 500 languages may soon become extinct.
- Is it important to have a variety of different languages in the world? Why?/Why not?
- Should governments spend money on protecting traditional languages? Why?/Why not?
- Would you learn a foreign language even if you didn't have to? Why?/Why not?

5 ADVERTISING

1 You are going to watch an interview with Vena Raffle, Head of Investigations at the Advertising Standards Authority (ASA) in the UK. Look again at the text on page 158. Why did the ASA ban an advertisement with American actress Julia Roberts?

2a Before you watch, what do you think Vena Raffle might talk about? Choose four topics from this list.
a What the ASA is, and why it exists
b What kind of people make complaints
c What happens to a complaint at the ASA
d Examples of bad adverts
e The name of a specific company (e.g. Lancôme)
f Advice on how to make a good advert
g The future of the ASA

2b ▶ 5 Watch the interview. Which four topics above did Vena discuss? What can you remember about each one?

3a Match these key words from the interview with their meanings 1–5.

claim   council   department   evidence   ruling

1 a group of people that are chosen to make rules, laws or decisions, or to give advice
2 acts or signs that show clearly that something exists or is true
3 a statement that something is true
4 an official decision
5 one of the groups of people who work together in a particular part of a large organisation such as a university or company

3b Watch again and make notes to help you complete these sentences.
1 If the complaint is quite simple, the _____ Department will deal with it.
2 If the council agrees with a report from Vena's department, _____ will be made.
3 If an advert is misleading, it will be _____ to make a decision.
4 If an advertiser does not _____, the ASA will put a ruling on their website.

4 Work in small groups. In your opinion, why might a company choose to make an advert that they know will offend some people?

MEET THE EXPERT

6 EDUCATION

1 Work with a partner and answer these questions.
1. What can you remember about Maria Montessori?
2. What is the Montessori method?

2a ▶ 6 You are going to watch an interview with Rob Gueterbock, who works at a Montessori school. Watch the interview and complete sentences 1 and 2 with phrases a–h. Which phrase can go in both sentences?

1. In traditional education, children …
2. In Montessori education, children …

a. are able to follow their own interests.
b. learn by doing, not by listening.
c. learn according to a curriculum.
d. learn with the whole class.
e. learn individually and in small groups.
f. form mixed age communities.
g. learn only with children of the same age.
h. learn at their own pace.

2b Watch the interview again and take notes on the following.

1. Reasons for becoming a Montessori teacher
2. The Montessori method of learning
3. Why Montessori schools call teachers 'guides'
4. Montessori education in different countries
5. What Rob thinks about children and technology

2c Compare your notes with a partner.

3a Imagine that you have been asked to give a report to the Ministry of Education in another country. The Ministry wants to improve the level of education of school children aged 6–16. Work in three groups. Each group should give a short report on the advantages of three different approaches to education. Decide on a definition for your group's approach to education. Then decide on the advantages of your group's approach to education.

- Group A: traditional education
- Group B: Montessori education
- Group C: digital education

3b Take turns to give your reports. Decide which group gave the best reasons.

7 DESIGN

1 Work in groups of three. Look at the photos of the 'hush pod chair' by product and furniture designer Freyja Sewell, then discuss the five questions in the extract below from a book about design.

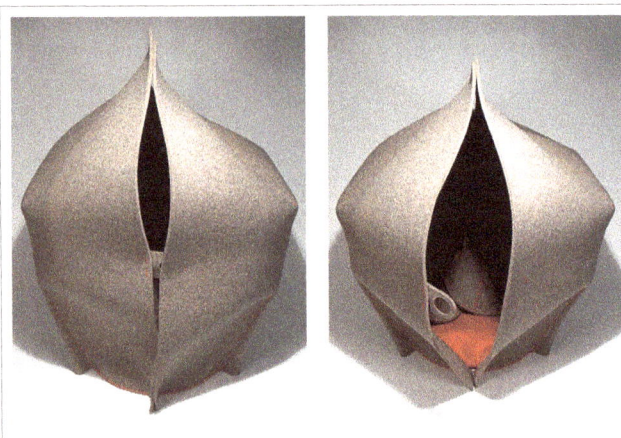

Designers have to ask themselves questions such as:
'Is the product really wanted?',
'How is it different from everything else on the market?',
'Does it fulfil a need?',
'Will it cost too much to manufacture?'
and 'Is it safe?'.

2 ▶ 7 Watch the interview with Freyja. Tick (✓) the adjectives you hear.

- sustainable
- elegant
- innovative
- natural
- mass-produced
- renewable
- careful
- traditional
- rigid
- disposable

3a Watch the interview again. Match each object or material (1–6) to its description in the video (a–f).

1. a light bulb
2. a chair
3. wool felt
4. wool
5. starch
6. starch-bound wool

a. something connected to a particular country
b. something used because it was hard
c. something used because it was soft
d. something used because it was natural
e. something developed in another country
f. something that is an example of a good design

3b How do we know that materials are important to Freyja?

4 Do you own a mobile phone, smart phone or tablet computer? Work in groups. Compare the designs of your phones or tablet computers by discussing these features.

- form (style and beauty)
- sound design (e.g. does it 'click' or 'whistle'?)
- function and efficiency

8 BUSINESS

1 You are going to watch an interview with Teresa Le, chef and owner of Ládudu, a Vietnamese restaurant in London. Before you watch, read these extracts from the interview and discuss questions a–f with a partner.

[2] 'Why don't I just go about and teach people how to make good Vietnamese food at home?'
a What are the advantages of teaching people to cook in their own homes? *cheap*

[4] 'Running a restaurant is actually very different to running a mobile home-cooking business.'
b What do you think 'a mobile home-cooking business' is? *cook in own home*
c How is running a restaurant different from running a mobile home-cooking business? *bigger, demanding, more staff*

[3] 'The business is Ládudu. La in Vietnamese means "leaf" and dudu means "papaya", so together it's "papaya leaf".'
d How did you choose the name of a business? *meaning*

[5] 'I do quite like Jamie Oliver. I admire him for his passion. To me, he's more than a chef.'
e How might Jamie Oliver (a well-known British chef) be 'more than a chef'? *businessman, book*

[1] 'I wanted to start my own business because …'
f Why do you think Teresa wanted to start her own business? *lost job, something for herself, lack of V. restaurants in London, enjoyed cooking*

2a ▶ 8 Watch the interview with Teresa. In what order do you hear the extracts in Exercise 1? Write 1–5 in the boxes.

2b Work with a partner. Look at questions a–f again. Can you remember Teresa's answers?

2c Watch the interview again and check Teresa's answers to questions a–f. *publishing, career, caring, social reform*

3 Teresa's friends gave her money to help open her restaurant. Work with a partner to discuss the following.
What are the advantages and disadvantages of starting a business:
- with friends?
- with family?
- using a bank loan?

10 TRENDS

1 Work with a partner. Read these situations, then discuss the questions below.
a The owner of a fashion magazine in Los Angeles wants to find out which styles are popular in youth subcultures of big cities. For example, she would like to find out if young people in Moscow or London have similar styles to youth in Istanbul or Berlin.
b The owners of a luxury hotel in Kraków would like to give their guests a better experience. They want to find a way of showing visitors why they should always choose their hotel.
c The owners of a clothing company in Manchester are preparing their business plan. They want to make clothes for only one of the following: children (0–17), young adults (18–30), adults (31–64) or pensioners (65+). They want to find out which is best.

1 Why might trends be important to the owners of each of these businesses?
2 What advice would you give them? Why?

2 ▶ 10 You are going to watch an interview with Cate Trotter, Head of Trends at a London-based trend-spotting consultancy. Watch the interview and do the following. *Watch once through.*
1 While watching, decide which businesses in Exercise 1 Cate can help. Circle the letter (a–c) if you think she can give them advice and help. *Not a. b. c.*
2 After watching, work with a partner. How does Cate help businesses? *understand trends / what happens next*

3 Decide if these statements are true (T) or false (F). Then watch the interview again to check your answers.
1 The history of a trend is important to Cate's work. **T**
2 Cate gives presentations and reports to her clients. **F**
3 Trend tours help her clients understand a trend from a customer's point of view. **T**
4 Sustainability affects the food business more than other types of business. **F** *all*
5 Understanding trends gives companies an advantage over others. **T**
6 Global trends usually appear in different countries at different times. **T**

4 Work in small groups. Cate says that she helps businesses find new opportunities. What opportunities might come from the following trends?
- More and more people getting a university education
- Higher prices for food, especially meat and fish *vegetarian, insects*
- A larger number of adults who choose to be single and live alone *singles events, housing / furniture, ready meals*

▶ MEET THE EXPERT

12 CRIME

1a What is/are your favourite genre(s) of films and fiction? Give a score from 0 to 5 to each of these genres (0 = I have no interest in this; 5 = I love this).

crime, thriller and mystery   science fiction   fantasy
horror   romance   humour   historical

1b What is most important for a good crime story – the plot, the setting or the characters? Why?

2 You are going to watch an interview with Stefanie Bierwerth, a publisher of crime fiction. Before you watch, match these words with their meanings (1–5) below.

crucial   detective   psyche   psychological   solve

1 relating to the way that your mind works and the way that this affects your behaviour
2 extremely important because everything else depends on it
3 a police officer whose job is to discover information about crimes and catch criminals
4 to find the correct answer to a problem or the explanation for something that is difficult to understand
5 someone's mind, or their deepest feelings, which control their attitudes and behaviour

3a ▶12 Watch the interview and answer these questions. According to Stefanie:
1 why is crime fiction such a popular genre?
2 what different types of crime fiction are there?
3 what makes a great thriller?

3b Watch the interview again and complete these notes from a summary of it. Write between one and three words from the interview in each gap.

According to Stefanie:
1 crime fiction is more popular than _____ and _____.
2 many readers enjoy reading about the _____ of the mind.
3 there are many _____ crime fiction.
4 female readers are more likely to prefer _____ crime stories.
5 _____ are very popular with publishers because they sell well.
6 readers are becoming more interested in crime fiction from _____.

4 Work in small groups. What are the benefits for language learners of the following?

- Reading fiction in English
- Using an eReader rather than a book

COMMUNICATION ACTIVITIES

LESSON 10.4 EXERCISE 4A (PAGE 103)
RESIDENT 1

Think about the problems and make notes of your ideas for solving them. You want:
- all clubs and bars to close at midnight.
- a new, underground car park to be built in the town centre
- the Sandy Cove project to be cancelled – it's expensive and not good for the environment.
- more flats and houses to be built for students.

LESSON 2.3 EXERCISE 11B (PAGE 21)
STUDENT A

Read about jobs 1 and 2 below and tell Student B a little about them. Ask questions about your partner's experience to find out if he/she is suitable for either of the jobs.

Have you ever done any voluntary work?
– Yes, I have.
Oh, when did you do that?
– Well, I worked for Save the Children last summer.

VACANCY

Vacancies for speakers of two languages to accompany small groups of fourteen-year-old students to major European cities such as Paris, London and Rome. The ideal person will:
- have experience of looking after groups of children.
- have knowledge of at least two major European cities.
- be reliable and well-organised.

VACANCY

We require four active, strong and enthusiastic young adults to accompany a trip for older people to the foothills of the Himalayas. The ideal person will:
- have experience of working with or looking after older people.
- have experience of working in a foreign country.
- be responsible and reliable.

Answer Student B's questions about jobs 3 and 4.

LESSON 3.2 EXERCISE 10B (PAGE 29)
STUDENT A

Listen and correct Student B, using the prompts below. Repeat the whole sentences.
1. Poland
2. for nine months
3. Spanish

Say the sentences below. Your partner will correct you.
1. So, you've been working from home for two years?
2. So, you've been studying computing since January?
3. So, you've been driving for six years?

LESSON 4.4 EXERCISE 5A (PAGE 43)
STUDENT D

You think the best option is to send senior and middle managers to the UK and the USA for crash courses, and to provide as many one-to-one classes as possible. Try to persuade the other members to accept your ideas. Use the ideas below and your ideas from Exercise 2b.
- Managers will learn English quickly.
- Crash courses in the UK / the US are the most effective way of learning English.
- One-to-one teaching means that managers can learn English at a time that is convenient for them.
- You do not want to have online courses. In your opinion, they are not effective. You need face-to-face contact with a teacher.

LESSON 12.3 EXERCISE 8 (PAGE 121)
STUDENT B

Julie Barriskell used to be a school friend of the victim, but became jealous of her success. Julie was the last known person to see the victim. She sent a text message to the victim and invited her to the lake at 5 p.m. Police have a record of the text message. She is a friend of Dr Drake Ramorey. She has an alibi from 8 p.m.

LESSON 12.4 EXERCISE 5 (PAGE 123)
STUDENT B CASE 1

The following information is for you to use in the discussion to help you reach a decision.
- Woman got angry and lost control.
- Man already unconscious and no danger.
- Burglar had no weapon.
- Woman gave no warning.
- Burglar was small and light.

LESSON 3.4 EXERCISE 8 (PAGE 33)
CANDIDATES

Evaluation sheet

Name of interviewer

For each category, write a number from 1 to 5.
(1 = excellent, 5 = poor)
1. Did the interviewer make you feel relaxed?
2. How good/fair were the interviewer's questions?
3. Did the interviewer give you enough time to answer the questions?
4. How carefully did the interviewer listen to your answers?
5. How appropriate were the follow-up questions?
6. How effective was the interview?

Overall quality of interviewer

COMMUNICATION ACTIVITIES

LESSON 3.4 EXERCISE 8 (PAGE 33)
INTERVIEWERS

Evaluation sheet

Name of candidate ....

For each category, write a number from 1 to 5.
(1 = excellent, 5 = poor)
1 Personality (outgoing? friendly?)
2 Communication skills (good? poor?)
3 Enthusiasm (enthusiastic? energetic? motivated?)
4 Experience (experienced? lacks enough experience?)
5 Answers to questions

Overall quality of candidate ....

LESSON 4.2 EXERCISE 8A (PAGE 39)
GROUP A

Here are some notes to help you prepare for the motion: The English-speaking world should adopt American English.
- American spelling easier
- American bigger influence – films, TV, music, youth culture
- One English form – makes communication easier, and easier for students
- America largest economy in world

LESSON 4.4 EXERCISE 5A (PAGE 43)
STUDENT A

You think the best option is to send as many staff as possible to the language school near Head Office. Try to persuade the other members to accept your ideas. Use the ideas below and your ideas from Exercise 2b.
- Staff will be away from their offices so they can focus on learning English without interruptions.
- The courses are not expensive.
- The teachers are well trained and professional.
- You do not want English classes at Head Office because staff won't attend regularly.

LESSON 12.3 EXERCISE 8 (PAGE 121)
STUDENT C

Martha Smith is seventy-five years old and walks her dog by the lake every morning. She found the body and police have not been able to find any connection between her and the victim. She was a judge before she retired and is a well-respected member of the community.

LESSON 5.1 EXERCISE 7A (PAGE 47)
STUDENT A

LESSON 5.3 EXERCISE 8A (PAGE 51)
FATHER

You understand that your son wants a cool, fast bike, but you don't want to pay a lot of money. However, you think that the smallest, cheapest bike is too small.

LESSON 6.3 EXERCISE 10A (PAGE 61)
STUDENT A

Education in China
- In China, children begin primary school at the age of seven, except in Beijing, Shanghai and major cities where children can begin school at six and a half years.
- Compulsory education lasts for nine years.
- Children go to primary school for six years and then junior middle school for three years.
- They can complete their secondary education by studying a further three years but that is not compulsory.
- 7.5 percent of the population enrol in higher education.
- A wide variety of four- to five-year undergraduate programmes are available and there are also some special two- to three-year special programmes.
- All education in China is free, including university accommodation.

LESSON 12.4 EXERCISE 5 (PAGE 123)
STUDENT C   CASE 1

The following information is for you to use in the discussion to help you reach a decision.
- The woman was extremely frightened.
- Felt that she was in great danger in her own home.
- Didn't know how many burglars there were.
- There had been several burglaries with violence in the area recently.
- The defendant had no confidence in the police.

LESSON 8.4 EXERCISE 6A (PAGE 83)

DOMINO REPRESENTATIVES

Read the information below and prepare for the negotiation. When there are options, make a decision about what are the most important points for you. Try to get a good deal. You want:

- Quantity: 50,000 units.
- Designs: Oasis – 10,000 units; Mirage – 15,000 units; Horizon – 25,000 units; you make a much bigger profit on the Mirage and Horizon designs.
- Delivery: 7 August, 21 August or end of August; best date is 7 August – important because retailers will start selling the winter range in September.
- Payment: after 60 days (best time), after 30 days or on delivery
- Discount: 10% (high), 5% (usual discount for wholesalers), 3% (low)

LESSON 9.2 EXERCISE 8A (PAGE 89)

Make as many present or past simple sentences from the table as you can. Make guesses if necessary. You have ten minutes. (You will need to add prepositions, eg *by*, *in* or *to*.)

1	The ballpoint pen		Carl Benz in 1884
2	Nokia mobile phones		South Africa
3	Diamonds	make	Alexander Fleming
4	The World Wide Web	create	Sri Lanka
5	The telephone	manufacture	Muslim mathematician Al-Khwarizmi
6	Tea		
7	Toyota cars	invent	Isaac Newton
8	The first motor car	discover	Laszlo Biro
9	The Republic of Turkey	grow	Mark Zuckerberg
10	Gravity	mine	Tim Berners-Lee
11	Algebra		Japan
12	The first mercury thermometer	develop	Finland
13	Facebook		Ataturk
14	Penicillin		Fahrenheit
			Alexander Bell

LESSON 12.4 EXERCISE 5 (PAGE 123)

STUDENT C CASE 2

Your job is to briefly summarise the case so that everyone in your group is clear about the details of the case. Then join in the discussion and express your opinion about what the others say to reach a decision.

LESSON 9.3 EXERCISE 8A (PAGE 91)

FOR THE MOTION

Think about:

- how big projects affect local communities in a negative way. Think of three different ways.
- how and why the money should be spent on important essential things like housing. Think of two other essential things.
- who the projects mainly benefit? The local people? Or just the building companies, the politicians and the rich?
- how some big projects can damage the environment.
- how these projects are very expensive and who pays for them.
- your own ideas for the motion.

LESSON 10.4 EXERCISE 4A (PAGE 103)

MAYOR

Lead the discussion. Listen to people's opinions and suggestions, and respond to them. You want:

- increased parking fines so that more people use the buses.
- part of the beach to be private and heavy fines for people leaving rubbish on the beach.
- the Sandy Cove project to go forward. It will create jobs and provide extra parking space.
- the universities to build more student accommodation.

LESSON 1.2 EXERCISE 8 (PAGE 9)

STUDENT B

Sigmund Freud was born on 6 May 1856 in [1]_____. He went to the University of Vienna and studied [2]_____. He graduated in 1881 as a Doctor of Medicine. He lived in Vienna for [3]_____ years. In 1907, the psychiatrist [4]_____ was introduced to Freud and together they formed the International Psychoanalytical Association. Jung was its first president. [5]_____ emigrated to London. His brother lost all his property when he left Vienna. Freud lived in a house in [6]_____. He died in 1939.

LESSON 3.4 EXERCISE 7A (PAGE 33)

CANDIDATES

1 Review and discuss what type of person the club is looking for.

2 Think of some adjectives to describe your personality.

3 Think of three questions you think they will ask at your interview.

4 Think about your answers to the questions in Exercise 3 above. You may use information from your own life and experience or you may invent any information you wish.

COMMUNICATION ACTIVITIES

LESSON 12.3 EXERCISE 8 (PAGE 121)

STUDENT A

Rex Peterson, an army veteran, has been hacking into the victim's computer and monitoring the victim's whereabouts for the last year. He has many photos of the victim and the victim has complained about him to the police.

LESSON 12.4 EXERCISE 5 (PAGE 123)

STUDENT A CASE 1

Your job is to briefly summarise the case so that everyone in your group is clear about the details of the case. Then join in the discussion and express your opinion about what the others say to reach a decision.

CASE 2

The following information is for you to use in the discussion to help you reach a decision.
- The woman is making the man's life impossible.
- He is stressed and receiving medical treatment.
- He is in danger of losing his job.
- He feels like a prisoner in his own home.
- He is worried about what she might do next.

CASE 3

The following information is for you to use in the discussion to help you reach a decision.
- It was an accident.
- He was not speeding.
- The car was in good condition.
- The road was narrow and needed repairs.
- The people outside the café were sitting in a dangerous position.

LESSON 5.1 EXERCISE 7A (PAGE 47)

STUDENT B

LESSON 5.2 EXERCISE 2 (PAGE 48)

AGAINST

Advertisers regularly edit and touch up images to make their models more attractive so that consumers will spend more money on their products and services. However, this manipulation of images has been attracting increasing criticism from the general public and also from celebrities. There is a feeling that photoshopping has gone too far and that it is harmful to society, and especially to young people.

The argument is simple. Constant exposure to digitally-enhanced pictures that show apparently 'perfect' people is distorting children's and young adults' view of the world. It can cause young people to have unrealistic expectations about their body image and can lead to eating disorders and emotional problems. No wonder that fifty percent of women between sixteen and twenty-one say they would consider cosmetic surgery. And some teenagers are even having their school photographs airbrushed to make them appear like models.

Thankfully, governments are beginning to put pressure on the advertising industry. In the United Kingdom, the Advertising Standards Authority banned an advertisement by Lancôme featuring the actress Julia Roberts. They said that the flawless skin seen in the photo was too good to be true. Other governments are proposing that all digitally-enhanced images should have a warning label.

There have also been developments in the celebrity world, with a number of famous people taking action. Kate Winslet famously took action against GQ magazine for digitally altering her body in its photographs, making her unrealistically thin. When Brad Pitt appeared on the cover of W Magazine, he requested that there should be no retouching and selected a photographer, Chuck Close, who was well known for his detailed portraits that showed skin flaws. Britney Spears agreed to show 'un-airbrushed images of herself next to the digitally-altered ones.' Her aim was to 'highlight the pressure put on women to look perfect'. The 'before' and 'after' images of Britney Spears were striking. Some of the changes made to her original photographed body included slimmer hips, a smaller waist, and the removal of cellulite.

Manipulating images of people in commercials is not acceptable because it is particularly damaging to young people. They are being set impossible standards of body image by the widespread use of this technique – photoshopped images destroy young people's self-esteem. We need to follow the example set by some celebrities and refuse to accept this practice. And we need to put pressure on our government to introduce more legislation.

LESSON 5.3 EXERCISE 8A (PAGE 51)

MOTHER

You feel very strongly that your son should have a bike that is very safe, not too big and not too fast. You have heard stories about terrible accidents with quad bikes. You don't want one with a big engine.

LESSON 10.4 EXERCISE 4A (PAGE 103)
STUDENT

Think about the problems and make notes of your ideas for solving them. You want:
- free travel for students on buses. More council accommodation for students at low rents.
- the council to cancel the Sandy Cove project. It will destroy the beauty of the beach.
- the police to be more friendly and understanding.
- all young people be able to stay out late at night and have fun in clubs.

LESSON 5.3 EXERCISE 8B (PAGE 51)

Name	Dolphin x300	Barracuda x100	Shark x400	Dirt Monster x700
Length	1,100 mm	1,600 mm	1,700 mm	2,300 mm
Engine size	50 cc	125 cc	250 cc	300 cc
Top speed	22 kph	28 kph	75 kph	80 kph
Price	€300	€550	€3,000	€3,200
Safety rating	★★★★★	★★★★★	★★★★	★★

LESSON 6.3 EXERCISE 10A (PAGE 61)
STUDENT B

Education in France
- Since 1967, school attendance has been compulsory for those from six to sixteen years of age.
- Many children enter voluntary kindergartens at the age of three.
- Primary schooling lasts for six years.
- Secondary schooling is divided into two stages:
- Stage 1 – from eleven to fifteen years; almost all children now attend a *collège*.
- Stage 2 – from fifteen to eighteen years they study in a general, technical or vocational *lycée*.
- 53.6 percent of the French population enrol in higher education.
- There are two kinds of universities in France: public universities and Grandes Ecoles (that set higher standards).
- Higher education is primarily paid for by the French taxpayers so tuition fees are very low.

LESSON 4.2 EXERCISE 8A (PAGE 39)
GROUP B

Here are some notes to help you prepare against the motion:
The English-speaking world should adopt American English.
- All differences – fun and interesting
- British English – language of Shakespeare and famous British authors/poets
- Not just American English – other varieties (e.g. Australian, Irish, Indian)
- You cannot regulate language. It develops naturally.

LESSON 1.4 EXERCISE 5A (PAGE 13)

Rashid: Indian, aged 25

A calm person. Speaks in a soft voice with an Indian accent.
Serious at all times during the interview. Has strong opinions about everything. Likes discussing economics and politics.

Your three best qualities? 'reliable, hard-working, knowledgeable'
Your worst quality? 'I get very impatient if people don't do their job properly.'
Your ideal boss? 'Someone who praises you whenever you do good work.'
Why choose him? 'I will do my best for your company at all times.'
Non-smoker, vegetarian and doesn't drink alcohol.
Interests: art, philosophy and current affairs.
Dressed unfashionably in a dull, grey suit.

Mitsuo: Japanese, aged 20

Family emigrated to Australia when he was 14 years old. Speaks English with a strong Japanese accent. Thoughtful, polite, sociable.

Your three best qualities? 'calm, strong sense of duty, will put company interests first'
Your worst quality? 'I get upset and angry if people are not polite to me.' 'I don't like people criticising me.'
Your ideal boss? 'Someone who is understanding and asks for my opinion frequently.'
Smokes cigars in the evening.
Interests: motorbike riding, tango dancing, entertaining friends
Smartly dressed in a suit, white shirt and designer tie.

LESSON 8.4 EXERCISE 6A (PAGE 83)
SUNSPEX SALESPEOPLE

Read the information below and prepare for the negotiation. When there are options, make a decision about what are the most important points for you. Try to get a good deal.

You want to sell:
- Quantity: 50,000 units.
- Designs: Oasis – 25,000 units; Mirage – 15,000 units; Horizon: 10,000 units; you make a much bigger profit on the Oasis and Mirage designs.
- Delivery: 14 September (best time), 7 September or by the end of August (bad time)
- Payment: on delivery, after 30 days or after 60 days; important to get your money quickly because you need to pay interest on a large bank loan.
- Discount: 0% (best), 2% (for cash on delivery), 8% (for orders over 60,000)

COMMUNICATION ACTIVITIES

LESSON 5.3   EXERCISE 8A (PAGE 51)

SON

You want the biggest, fastest bike with the biggest engine. Your friends will think you are silly if you have a bike with a really small engine. You think you are responsible and will drive safely.

LESSON 6.3   EXERCISE 10A (PAGE 61)

STUDENT C

Education in Argentina

- Argentina has nine years of compulsory schooling.
- Basic education is divided into three-year phases corresponding to junior and senior primary school and middle (or lower secondary) school.
- After this period of compulsory education, students have the choice of studying further or not for three years in upper secondary.
- 48% of the population enrol in higher education.
- First degrees for teachers and technicians last for three years but there are longer degrees for four to six years for engineering, medicine and law.
- University education is free but students have to pay for accommodation, transport and materials.
- Argentina has one of the most educated populations in Latin America.

LESSON 7.2   EXERCISE 3A (PAGE 68)

STUDENT B

1930–1939

In the 1930s designers increased the efficiency of boats and aircraft by giving them smooth and curved shapes. Then, in 1934, Chrysler launched its new streamlined car, the Airflow. This was the start of the use of aerodynamics in car design. Streamlining, as it was called, was about speed, efficiency and, most of all, the modern world. Designers realised that consumers were attracted to other streamlined products, and so they began to use streamlining in a wide range of domestic appliances, such as refrigerators.

The designer Henry Dreyfuss helped to develop a new theory about design called ergonomics. He believed that machines worked better if they were adapted to people's needs. His reputation was based on the Bell 3000 telephone. Because of its ergonomic design, it was easy for people to use.

At this time a number of new materials were used in design, such as Bakelite (an early type of plastic). It was a perfect material for producing smooth, streamlined products.

LESSON 12.3   EXERCISE 8 (PAGE 121)

STUDENT F

Encourage people to talk about how the crime was committed. Do not reveal this information till near the end: ice melts.

LESSON 8.3   EXERCISE 2 (PAGE 80)

3

OBITUARIES

Mark McCormack

[1] Mark Hume McCormack, sports agent, died on 16 May, aged seventy-two. Mark McCormack started the industry of sports marketing. He was the first person to realise that sports personalities could earn extra money from endorsements and sponsorship. The company which he founded, International Management Group (IMG), represents many of the most famous sports people in the world such as Tiger Woods, Pete Sampras, the Williams sisters and Michael Schumacher.

[2] McCormack had been a promising college golfer. However, after graduating from Yale Law School he worked as a lawyer. Later, he realised that sports marketing had great potential. His first client, in 1960, was Arnold Palmer, the famous golfer. Thanks to his energy and entrepreneurial skills, he built up a highly profitable business. By 1990 he had become the most powerful person in sport.

[3] IMG expanded to include a television production company sports academies and a branch representing top models such as Kate Moss.

[4] By the end of his life, he had also published several books, including the best-selling *What they don't teach you at Harvard Business School*.

[5] He will be remembered for his ability to negotiate huge contracts for a wide range of sports personalities and celebrities.

[6] He leaves three children from his first marriage and one from his second to former tennis professional, Betty Nagelson.

Mark McCormack, born 6 November 1930; died 16 May 2003

Chaleo Yoovidhya

4

OBITUARIES

[1] ChaleoYoovidhya, inventor of the popular energy drink 'Red Bull' died on 17 March. By the time of his death he had become one of Asia's richest men and one of the 250 wealthiest people in the world.

[2] The third son of a Chinese father and a Thai mother, he grew up in northern Thailand. The family was poor and made a living selling ducks and fruit. Chaleo worked from a young age and did not complete his secondary education. He later earned a living as a bus conductor and a salesman, as well as by helping in his brother's pharmacy in Bangkok.

[3] Always interested in science, in the 1960s he set up a company called TC Pharmaceuticals. He worked on his own formula for an energy tonic which was given to truck drivers to help them stay awake. He named it 'Krating Daeng', meaning Red Buffalo in Thai, and began selling it around the country during the 1970s.

[4] In 1982, an Austrian toothpaste salesman, Dietrich Mateschitz, was in Thailand and drank a can of the drink to help his tiredness and jetlag. It worked well and he went into partnership with Chaleo. The launch of the new product, 'Red Bull', as it was now called, was in Austria in 1987. It is now sold in over seventy countries around the world. The market research done at the time of the launch suggested it was going to fail. It has annual sales of 4.6 billion cans.

[5] Although extremely successful, Chaleo remained a private man and had not given an interview or made a public appearance for over thirty years. He was married twice and had eleven children.

Chaleo Yoovidhya, born 17 August 1923; died 17 March 2012

LESSON 4.4 EXERCISE 5A (PAGE 43)
STUDENT B

You think the best option is to hire two English language teachers to give courses at Head Office. Try to persuade the other members to accept your idea. Use the ideas below and your ideas from Exercise 2b.
- The teachers will teach British English and American English.
- You will be able to control closely the language training they provide.
- Staff will attend classes when it is convenient for them.
- You do not want to use the nearby English language school. You think staff will take too much time after classes returning to Head Office.

LESSON 10.4 EXERCISE 4A (PAGE 103)
RESIDENT 2

Think about the problems and make notes of your ideas for solving them. You want:
- immediate action to reduce pollution in the city.
- severe penalties for young people who behave badly at weekends.
- the Sandy Cove project to go forward. It will attract more visitors and bring income to businesses.
- more police officers to deal with the increase in the crime rate – your car was stolen recently.

LESSON 2.3 EXERCISE 11B (PAGE 21)
STUDENT B

Read about jobs 3 and 4 below and tell Student A a little about them. Ask questions about your partner's experience to find out if he/she is suitable for either of the jobs.

Have you ever done any voluntary work?
– Yes, I have.
Oh, when did you do that?
– Well, I worked for Save the Children last summer.

VACANCY 3

We are looking for five people to accompany scientists on a trip to the Amazon Forests of Brazil. The ideal person will:
- have experience of working in a scientific environment.
- have experience of working with animals.
- be young, fit and enthusiastic.

VACANCY 4

Assistant travel agent required to help customers with their enquiries about foreign travel. The ideal person should:
- have some experience of travelling to a variety of places.
- have good communication skills.
- be a good team member.

Answer Student A's questions about jobs 1 and 2.

LESSON 12.4 EXERCISE 5 (PAGE 123)
STUDENT B CASE 3

Your job is to briefly summarise the case so that everyone in your group is clear about the details of the case. Then join in the discussion and express your opinion about what the others say to reach a decision.

LESSON 11.2 EXERCISE 2A (PAGE 108)
STUDENT C

Stanley Kubrick (1928–1999)

1. Stanley Kubrick is often described as a perfectionist genius. He is admired as one of cinema's greatest talents. As a director he made only thirteen feature films in a career of over forty years, but many of them are regarded as masterpieces, and he earned nine Oscars. Kubrick once said that a film was more like music than fiction, although all his films were adapted from novels.

2. He directed the Hollywood epic *Spartacus* in 1960, the most expensive film of its day, and the only all-Hollywood movie he ever made. Soon after finishing this film, unhappy with the pressure of Hollywood, he moved from America to Britain.

3. Kubrick spent five years developing his film *2001: A Space Odyssey* (1969). This is probably his most famous and influential film. It was a science fiction blockbuster which was popular with both the critics and the public. Often described as a masterpiece, its special effects won an Academy award and were a big influence on George Lucas when he came to make the *Star Wars* films. His final film was *Eyes Wide Shut* (1999), starring Tom Cruise and Nicole Kidman.

4. The film *A Clockwork Orange* (1971) was removed from cinemas in the UK after Kubrick felt it had been misinterpreted, and it was only shown again after his death.

5. He valued his privacy and worried about security. He certainly disliked travel after he moved to England, and he also had a well-known fear of flying. He once told a friend that he travelled to London four or five times per year, only for appointments with his dentist.

6. Kubrick was frequently unwilling to discuss personal matters publicly, and this gave rise to his reputation as an eccentric, reclusive genius. This image of him was denied by his family after his death. It was often reported that Kubrick was rude and unfriendly to the people he worked with. For example, he had a good friendship with the actor Malcolm McDowell during the making of *A Clockwork Orange*, but after the filming ended Kubrick never contacted him again.

7. Kubrick had little contact with the media, so few people knew what he looked like. Kubrick once told a reporter who came to his door that Stanley Kubrick wasn't at home.

COMMUNICATION ACTIVITIES

LESSON 11.2 EXERCISE 2A (PAGE 108)
STUDENT B

Syd Barrett (1946–2006)

1 Often called an eccentric genius, Syd Barrett formed the supergroup Pink Floyd in 1965 and wrote, sang and played guitar on all their early hits, including the 1967 masterpiece *Piper at the Gates of Dawn*. He left the band in 1968 after experiencing a kind of breakdown due to the pressures of stardom and touring. He made two solo albums, *The Madcap Laughs* and *Barrett*, both released in 1970, which continue to sell well.

2 Barrett then left the music business completely, deciding a musician's life was not for him. He did not make any music at all after 1974. Once a household name, he is now more or less forgotten except by his fans. He moved back to his home town of Cambridge and started to use his original name of Roger Barrett. He lived alone, quietly spending his time painting and gardening. He received a six-figure income from his Pink Floyd royalties, but had little contact with the outside world. Although he hadn't appeared or spoken in public since the mid 1970s, fans and journalists still tried to contact him.

3 In 1971 a journalist found him. Syd told the reporter that he walked a lot, painted, wasted time and was afraid of getting old. He also said that he felt full of dust and guitars. Another journalist reported that a bald, fat man answered the door and said that Syd couldn't talk. In 1992, Atlantic Records offered half a million dollars for any new Syd Barrett recordings.

4 After his return to Cambridge his family reported that he was content and quite healthy. In his later years, when fans or journalists called on him he was polite and coherent, but refused to discuss his past as a famous rock star. Talking to one journalist on his doorstep in 2001, Syd asked him to leave as he didn't do interviews any more.

LESSON 6.3 EXERCISE 10A (PAGE 61)
STUDENT D

Education in Germany
- Compulsory education in Germany lasts for nine to ten years (it varies between states). It usually remains compulsory for a further three years, at least on a part-time basis.
- Between the ages of three and five the majority of German children attend voluntary kindergarten school.
- They then take four years of primary education through to the age of ten.
- They proceed to one of three types of secondary school:
  – Hauptschule or a short-course secondary school focuses on preparation for a vocation.
  – Realschule or intermediate school is aimed at those targeting middle-level positions in government or business.
  – Gymnasium or grammar school give students the opportunity to apply to university.
- The majority of universities in Germany are funded by the federal government and charge little or no tuition fees. There are not many private universities, although the number has risen in recent years.
  For most undergraduate degrees, students are expected to complete their studies in four years, but actually most students take more time. In fact, the average length of study is seven years.

LESSON 12.3 EXERCISE 8 (PAGE 121)
STUDENT D

Professor Ewan Shapiro is the father of the victim. He has a water-tight alibi. He hosted a large dinner party from 6 p.m. till 11 p.m. last night and was seen by fourteen people. He will inherit a small amount (one quarter) of his daughter's money.

LESSON 12.4 EXERCISE 5 (PAGE 123)
STUDENT B   CASE 2

The following information is for you to use in the discussion to help you reach a decision.
- It's a free country and she is doing nothing wrong.
- He is exaggerating her behaviour.
- It is a small town so they go to the same places.
- She is just being friendly.
- Photography is her hobby.

LESSON 12.4   EXERCISE 5 (PAGE 123)
STUDENT C   CASE 3

The following information is for you to use in the discussion to help you reach a decision.
- A car is a weapon.
- A driver must concentrate on the road at all times.
- He shouldn't have given sweets to the children.
- None of the people in the car were wearing seatbelts.
- The driver should have stopped before helping the child.

LESSON 4.4   EXERCISE 5A (PAGE 43)
STUDENT C

You think the best option is to set up English language courses online for all staff. Try to persuade the other members to accept your idea. Use the ideas below and your ideas from Exercise 2b.
- Online courses are a relatively cheap way of teaching large numbers.
- You will be able to work with the language expert on the content of the courses.
- Online courses enable staff to learn English at a time which suits them.
- You do not want classes at Head Office. There are no suitable rooms for the purpose.
- One-to-one classes are expensive. You do not think senior staff will like them.

LESSON 3.4   EXERCISE 7A (PAGE 33)
INTERVIEWERS

1 Review the key personal qualities or skills you are looking for in the candidate.

2 Write out the six questions below to ask at the interview.
1 Why / want this job?
2 What / sort / person / you?
3 What / strengths / weaknesses?
4 What / think / can bring / this job?
5 What / interests / have / outside work?
6 Where / see yourself / five years' time?

3 Add two more questions to ask at the interview.

LESSON 1.2   EXERCISE 8 (PAGE 9)
STUDENT A

^{1}_____ was born on 6 May 1856 in Freiberg, Moravia. He went to the University of ^{2}_____ and studied medicine. He graduated in ^{3}_____ as a Doctor of Medicine. He lived in Vienna for forty-seven years. In 1907, the psychiatrist Carl Jung was introduced to Freud and together they formed the International Psychoanalytical Association. ^{4}_____ was its first president. Most of Freud's family emigrated to London. ^{5}__ lost all his property when he left Vienna. Freud lived in a house in Hampstead, London. He died in ^{6}_____ .

LESSON 3.2   EXERCISE 10B (PAGE 29)
STUDENT B

Say the sentences below. Your partner will correct you.
1 So, you've been working in Germany since graduating?
2 So, you've been living in Brazil for six months?
3 So, you've been studying French for a year?

Listen and correct Student A, using the prompts below. Repeat the whole sentences.
1 for four years
2 teaching
3 for two years

LESSON 12.3   EXERCISE 8 (PAGE 121)
STUDENT E

Dr Drake Ramorey was engaged to marry the victim. Surprisingly, he was already in the victim's will. He will inherit most (three quarters) of the victim's money. He is an expert on chest and lungs. He has a history of violence with his previous girlfriend.

LESSON 9.3   EXERCISE 8A (PAGE 91)
AGAINST THE MOTION

Think about:
- how big projects benefit local communities e.g. by providing a wide range of jobs. Think of some jobs that can be created.
- how big projects can stimulate the country's economic growth.
- how big projects can give the country a sense of pride.
- how some projects can help the environment. Give two examples.
- your own ideas against the motion.

LESSON 10.4   EXERCISE 4A (PAGE 103)
ENVIRONMENT OFFICER

Think about the problems and make notes of your ideas for solving them. You want:
- fewer cars in the city centre – the pollution level is higher than in many other European cities.
- more bus routes and cheaper fares.
- the council to invest in expensive equipment to clean the beaches.
- dogs and barbecues to be banned from the beach.

LESSON 7.2   EXERCISE 3A (PAGE 68)
STUDENT C

1990–1999

During the 1990s, many designers worried about the damage to the environment caused by industrialisation. They were especially worried about the rapid use of energy sources and raw materials. They wanted to find ways of slowing this down. These ideas influenced design in many areas. For example, solar-powered cars and electric cars were developed. The recycling of paper and other materials became popular, for example in designer Jane Atfield's plastic shelving unit. The material she used came from old washing-up liquid bottles. Designers created more energy-saving products and products which consumers could repair or recycle. The focus was on product durability. Another big influence on design was advances in communication, in particular the internet and mobile phone technology.

One product that connects the two big concerns of designers in the 1990s was Trevor Baylis' wind-up radio, launched in 1995. This product was particularly useful in Africa because it could work without having expensive batteries. People made the radio work by turning a handle to generate the power.

AUDIO SCRIPTS

LESSON 1.1 RECORDING 1.2

C = Christina, H = Helen, G = George

C: Oh, Helen, come on! You can tell a lot from a person's appearance. I mean, when people meet me for the first time, they can see I'm quite a sociable person – I love parties, going out, enjoying myself, that sort of thing. I always try to have a good time and not take life too seriously.

H: I don't know, Christina. It's certainly not the same for me. Look, I've got quite a lot of friends, but most of them say they thought I was really quiet and serious when they first met me. Maybe it's the way I dress. But you know me, I think I'm quite energetic. And I'm interested in everything.

G: Mmm.

H: Maybe people think I'm strange because of my sense of humour, I don't know, or because I don't care what people think. I like to do things my way. Anyway, you always laugh at my jokes, George.

G: Yes, I think you're really funny.

H: What about you, George? You're very different from how you look.

G: How do you mean?

H: Well … you've got a really good job, running your internet company. You're hard-working, very focused on your career. You seem to know exactly what your aims are. People would never guess, just looking at you – they'd probably think you're an out-of-work actor or something.

G: Yeah, you're right, Helen. I suppose I do look a bit strange. The way I dress, I mean. I'm really a serious person, as you know, and people don't always realise that when they first meet me. I like to be in control, I plan everything very carefully, and I don't like too much change in my life. That's the way I am.

C: I suppose you are very different from your appearance, George, and you are a bit strange …

H: Christina!

C: … but you're a good friend, that's the important thing.

H: She's right. You're very reliable and you have high standards, I like that. I think you're a person with real principles, and there aren't too many people like that these days.

G: Thanks, Helen, I think that's a good description of me. You know me well, don't you?

LESSON 1.2 RECORDING 1.3

A = Anchor, P = Presenter, F = Frank Partridge

A: And now at 11 o'clock it's over to Jenny Mason and today's edition of *Changing World*.

P: Good evening everyone. Our guest tonight is Dr Frank Partridge, an expert in psychometrics and on personality. Dr Partridge – our listeners are very interested in personality tests, so can I ask a few questions about those before we talk about your current research?

F: Yes, certainly, and good evening everyone.

P: OK, my first question. What exactly does psychometrics mean?

F: Well, psychometrics is really related to the measurement of intelligence and personal qualities. It measures four things: the measurement of knowledge, the measurement of abilities, the measurement of attitudes and personality traits. It's really about the differences between individuals.

P: I see. How did psychometric testing start? I mean, who designed the early tests?

F: Well, the first psychometric tests were designed to measure intelligence. I think the first usable intelligence test was the Stanford–Binet test. The test was developed originally by a French psychologist called Alfred Binet.

P: Mmm, interesting. So, how useful are the tests? Are they reliable? That's what most people want to know.

F: Well, that's a good question. All tests must have reliability and validity. Let me explain what I mean. When you use a reliable test, you get the same results each time. If the test is valid, it measures what it's supposed to measure … and not something else.

P: Mmm. I wonder if you could you give us an example of what exactly you mean by validity?

F: An example? Well … if you test a teacher on how many books they can carry, that's not a valid measure of their ability as a teacher.

P: Right, I see. Well, what can personality tests tell you about a person?

F: Well, there's one test, called the Myers–Briggs test, which is widely used all over the world. It's based on a study of more than 20,000 people. Organisations think it's useful when you want to work out people's roles in a team. Some people say it's useful to decide your personality type. You can, for example, find out how organised, reliable and sociable you are.
I think the questions are quite interesting and people seem to enjoy doing them. There are questions like: 'Can you stay calm under pressure?' 'Are you a good team player?' 'How motivated are you?' And so on.

P: Have you taken any of these tests yourself?

F: Yes, I have. The results were very interesting.

P: OK, thanks for that. Now, let's get on to your research. What are you working on at the moment, Dr Partridge?

F: I'm currently carrying out research into the validity and reliability of lie detector tests and how far people can beat those tests. I am particularly interested in whether actors, such as method actors who thoroughly immerse themselves in a role … well, whether they could beat the tests.

LESSON 1.4 RECORDING 1.4

C = Chris, J = Jodie

C: Honestly Jodie, I don't understand it. Two assistants leaving us in the last three months. It's not about us surely, it's not our fault, is it?

J: I don't know. I suppose we are difficult at times.

C: Difficult? How do you mean?

J: Well … you expect quite a lot from staff, I'd say. You're ambitious and hard-working, and if the staff don't do things right, you often lose your temper. You speak your mind instead of being diplomatic. Maybe that's why Barbara's left us. I think you upset her quite often. Perhaps you didn't realise it.

C: Mmm, it's true, I do have a bad temper at times. But that wasn't the reason she was unhappy with me. She wanted to go shopping during office hours, to buy a birthday present for her mother. But we were really busy at that time so I said 'no'. She didn't say anything, but I could tell she wasn't happy with my decision.

J: Yes, but that wasn't the only reason. I don't think she really liked you. She just couldn't get on with you.

C: Yeah, but she didn't like me mainly because I'm a smoker. She always gave me funny looks when I went out of the office to have a cigarette. I tell you, Jodie, I'm really pleased she's left. I like open-minded people, you know, people who live and let others live. That's the kind of person I want to employ here.

J: Sorry, I can't agree with you about Barbara. In my opinion, she was a really hard worker, she did a good job for us. I've missed her a lot.

C: Well, she's gone and that's that. It's not my fault. What about the other one who left, Louise? Now, I got on really well with her, but you couldn't stand her.

J: That's not true at all, you're exaggerating as usual. OK, she wasn't my kind of person. She was too quiet and it really got on my nerves. I'm sociable, noisy at times, maybe too noisy. And it's true, I do have a very loud voice and a loud laugh, but I like to have a bit of fun with people. That's why I get on so well with Georgia, we're always joking with each other. Louise was jealous of my relationship with Georgia.

C: I accept that. But don't forget Georgia used to make fun of her a lot and she didn't like it. She was a sensitive person, Louise …

J: Yeah, without any sense of humour at all. I'm so glad she's gone. I haven't missed her at all.

C: Well, I liked her. And I have missed her … a lot. She was a great worker, she always did exactly what I asked her to do. You know, she was afraid of you, Jodie, you have such a strong personality.

J: Nonsense. Anyway, let's look ahead. The problem is we need to find someone who'll be a good match for both of us. Why don't we go for a man this time, instead of a woman?

C: No, that's out of the question. We're not allowed to say we prefer a man – it's against the law to do that. We want someone, male or female, who'll fit in here. I suggest we contact the agency again. Let's see who they can offer us. I think we should tell them exactly the kind of person we're looking for.

J: OK, how about you phoning them this time? I'm really busy, I've got a big order to deal with.

C: All right, leave it to me.

LESSON 2.1 RECORDING 2.1

N = Nadia, L = Lisa, A = Armando, J = Jacques, T = Tom

L: Hi, Nadia, my name's Lisa.

N: Hi, Lisa.

L: Nadia, what's the furthest you've travelled from home?

N: Mmm, let me think … well, I suppose the answer is Indonesia.

L: Indonesia? Did you enjoy it?

N: Yeah, it was fascinating. I went with a friend and we got on really well. And she's still a good friend, I'm pleased to tell you. The country's got thousands of islands and we visited quite a few of them. I must say, I'll

AUDIO SCRIPTS

never forget Komodo – they have the largest lizards in the world there, Komodo Dragons, and one of them chased us across the beach. It was absolutely terrifying, I can tell you!
L: Wow! What an experience!
N: Mmm, not to be forgotten. Who's next?
A: Hi, I'm Armando.
N: Hi, Armando.
A: What's the longest journey you've been on?
N: You mean, in time?
A: Yeah, in time.
N: Well, I've travelled for four months, three times. During those trips, I visited, erm … Mexico, Indonesia, India and many other south-eastern Asian countries, like Thailand and Vietnam. I loved Vietnam – the people were so friendly, and the food was wonderful. But it was a bit noisy in the streets – you know, a lot of people travel on motorbikes, and you hear them everywhere.
J: Hi, I'm Jacques. Erm … what are the most popular destinations for people from your country?
N: Depends a lot on the group, Jacques, but I'd say older people, say the over-fifties, they like to go to the Canary Islands, and young people prefer Thailand, to really get away from it all. Next question?
T: Hello Nadia, I'm Tom. People say that people travel to broaden their minds. Is that right? Do you think that travel broadens the mind? What are the reasons why people travel, in your opinion?
N: Hmm, interesting question, Tom. I suppose there are lots of reasons. Some want to see new sights and explore new places, erm … meet new people and experience different cultures. I certainly wanted to do all those things. But I also wanted to learn new skills, especially social skills, and to do some voluntary work. I wanted to become more self-confident. Oh, yes, and I was also interested in learning a new language, or at least getting some knowledge of an Asian language. Now my friend, Joanne, she just wanted to earn some money while she was abroad, to finance her studies. But there are lots of other reasons why people travel.
T: How do you mean, exactly?
N: Well, how can I put it, erm … some people travel to, erm … find themselves, I mean, to learn more about themselves, perhaps become more independent, or maybe just generally broaden their horizons. Other people may choose to do that by travelling abroad to study for a qualification. Sadly, some people may be forced to travel to look for work, to escape poverty which is not a good reason for travel, but perhaps becoming common. One thing's for sure, Tom, if you travel a long way from home, for a long time, you're a different person when you return. It makes you into a …

LESSON 2.2 RECORDING 2.2

1 Ibn Battuta travelled through most of the Islamic world.
2 He visited all the Arab lands.
3 He stopped off in Spain, Russia and Turkey.
4 In 1943, Cousteau and an engineer invented the aqualung.
5 Cousteau produced many films and books.
6 As a teenager she worked in a textile plant.
7 Tereshkova's spacecraft lifted off on 16 June 1963.

LESSON 2.3 RECORDING 2.3

I = Interviewer, M = Martin Wells
I: Martin, thanks for coming in today.
M: It's a pleasure to be here and to be able to tell people about the Universities Explorers programme.
I: So, Martin, could you tell us a bit about your last year?
M: Well, I've just returned from the forests of the Amazon River Basin in Brazil and I've had the most amazing year. Last year in January, I won a scholarship on the Universities Explorers Programme. Then I raised a large sum of money, with the help of some very generous friends. And then I started travelling. This year I've explored the ice-cut fjords of the South island in New Zealand, I've climbed the Himalayas in Nepal and I've met Inuit people in Nunavut in Canada. I've also helped with environmental projects near Hoi Anh in Vietnam, and I have to say it must be one of the most beautiful ancient cities in the world. I've never done so much in one year before.

LESSON 2.3 RECORDING 2.4

I: That's incredible Martin. What has been your greatest travel experience?
M: Well, in September… we travelled to the start of the Salween River. We wanted to do the same trip that Wong How Man, China's greatest living explorer, did. The river runs for almost 3,000 kilometres and it starts in Tibet. When we got near it I had to use a walking stick so as not to fall over. We climbed the last hill and saw the ice caves. At that moment it was the most beautiful sight in the world. On our return journey the weather was very bad. We survived because we found a hut to shelter in. I've learnt a lot about exploring since September.
I: This programme sounds amazing. Would you recommend it to other young adults?
M: Absolutely. I'm quite young and I've already done six expeditions. The programme has given me and others a chance to experience nature and discover its beauty. We've learnt about the cultures and traditions of all the places we've visited. I've had the best time of my life. But the most difficult bit is having to raise a lot of money at the start … and I haven't covered all my costs yet.
I: Thanks, Martin. I'm sure our readers will be fascinated by your experience.

LESSON 2.3 RECORDING 2.5

1 I've just returned from the forests.
2 I've had the most amazing year.
3 Last year in January, I won a scholarship.
4 Then I raised a large sum of money.
5 And then I started travelling.
6 I've climbed the Himalayas in Nepal.

LESSON 2.4 RECORDING 2.6

D = Douglas, K = Karen
D: Let's talk about the problems we had on the last trip. What went wrong, Karen?
K: Well, to start with, there was no team spirit in the group, was there? They didn't get on well with each other, and some of them ending up hating each other, there's no other word for it.
D: Mmm, that was a big problem, I agree. It took up a lot of our time to sort things out. The students were continually asking to change rooms and when I said 'No', they got really upset. You know, we're going to have to review rooming arrangements for this trip.
K: Well, how about this? I suggest we ask students if they want to share a room or not. And if they don't, they'll simply have to pay more.
D: Mmm, yes, that's worth considering. What about hotels? I think we chose the right ones, don't you?
K: Yes, definitely, no one complained about them. But you know, the hotel manager wasn't happy with the students, the way they behaved. Seems there were too many late-night, noisy parties in their rooms. Some of the other guests were upset about it.
D: Yeah, it's true. That was a problem for us. But you know, what upset me the most was when we talked to them after the trip?
K: Oh?
D: Well, they said we tried to do too much during the trip. They complained they didn't have enough free time. What do you think?
K: I think we talked about this before the trip. There are arguments for and arguments against, aren't there? On the one hand, it's good to give them free time, they get a chance to explore places. On the other hand, if you give them too much free time, they say we haven't organised enough trips for them. You just can't win.
D: True, and don't forget, Karen, another drawback of giving them a lot of free time is that they get into trouble. Remember what happened with the fire escape.
K: How could I forget that! Actually, I've got a few suggestions for this next trip.
D: Me too.
K: Good. Well, I think we should have more meetings with students before they leave. The good thing about this is that they'd get to know each other better.
D: Yeah. That's true. Also, it'd be a good idea to give students maps of the cities we visit. I suggest contacting the tourist boards and asking them to send us some.
K: And how about showing the students some restaurant menus before they leave? That'd be a big bonus for them. They won't get any surprises about the food then, will they?

LESSON 3.1 RECORDING 3.1

1 Well, the hours are very long and I have to work shifts, but I like my colleagues and I enjoy the variety of the work. You know, every day's different. I suppose the main reason I like the job is the contact with patients. I like to feel that I'm helping people, and my colleagues are great, so that makes the job very rewarding. It's certainly not the pay – that's terrible!
2 I really enjoy my job, although there can be a lot of routine paperwork and I have to attend a lot of meetings. Preparing cases takes up a lot of my time, and can be very challenging. The best parts of the job are meeting clients and going to court. I work for a big prestigious international firm, so there are good opportunities for promotion and I get to travel quite a lot, which is nice.

AUDIO SCRIPTS

3   Some people would say it's a glamorous job, and I suppose it is sometimes, but actually it's very hard work as well. There's also not much job security. The pay's good, but sometimes I don't work for a few weeks, so that can be a worry. I suppose I enjoy the travel – there's a lot of that – but sometimes there's a lot of waiting around for photographers and stylists, which can be really tedious.

4   Some parts of the job are not very interesting, like filling shelves, you know, very monotonous. Also, changing the window displays gets a bit repetitive. Really, it's dealing with people I like, on the phone and face to face. My boss is a lovely person, but he's so badly organised. He usually gets me to deal with problem customers who want refunds, that kind of thing. Some people think I'm a workaholic, and it's true I do a lot of overtime, but I like to do a job well and I'm proud of my work. It's a big chain so I hope I'll become assistant manager next year if I move to another branch.

5   What I particularly like is that it's a very flexible job. I can work from home some of the time. I find it stimulating, meeting and interviewing different people. It's also satisfying when you finish a long article and it's published. I've got a book coming out next year as well. One thing about working on a monthly magazine is that I have a lot of tight deadlines. That makes the job very stressful.

LESSON 3.2 RECORDING 3.2

1   I'm a language graduate and I've been translating from Italian to English for most of my career. We've been living in Milan for nearly five years and I've been working from home for two years, since our first child was born. I've found that my work–life balance has been easier to manage since I started working from home – and it needs to be easy to manage when you've got children!

2   I: How long have you been working from home for?
    S: I'm a writer and I've been working from home for the last 18 months, since I lost my job. It's been pretty tough. For one thing, I've been paying a lot more for heating. To be honest, it's quite lonely … and I've missed things like the office gossip. I wish I could go back to my old job. The only good thing is I can get up late. I've never been a morning person.

3   It's not for everybody, but I like working from home. I do contract work in design. The best thing is that I don't have to commute to work on crowded trains. I've had lots more time and I've been learning a new language since I started working at home in January. I've always wanted to learn Spanish. I've also bought myself a new guitar and I've been taking lessons for the last six months.

4   I: So, you've been working from home for eight years?
    P: No, actually I've been working from home for six years. I've been running a small business from home for a lock manufacturer. It's a Basque company based near Bilbao.
    I: And I see your husband is at home. Does he work from home as well?
    P: Yeah, about three days a week. He hasn't been working at home much recently as he's often needed in head office.
    I: Do you like working from home?
    P: Well, there are some disadvantages. I miss all my office friends and working in a team, and there's not enough space in the house. You also need to be good at time management. But basically, I love it. You have flexibility and you get to spend more time with the family. Also you save loads of money not commuting to the office. And the internet and social networking makes homeworking a more rewarding experience. And with my iPad and Skype I can now have meetings from the comfort of my home.

LESSON 3.3 RECORDING 3.4

A = Anna, J = Jan, Z = Zhang Li, S = Sylvie

A: Welcome back. This is Anna from 103.8 Oxford Lite FM and we've asked three students who are at Oxford Brookes University to join us. Welcome guys. Can you introduce yourselves?
J: Hi. I'm Jan and I'm Polish.
Z: Hello, I'm Zhang Li from Beijing, China.
S: And I'm Sylvie from Lille … erm … which is in France.
A: So what are you all studying?
Z: International Hospitality Management.
S: Yes. International Hospitality Management.
A: And what've you been doing recently?
Z: Well, we've all been doing our work placements.
J: Yeah, I've been working as a trainee concierge at the Marriott Beach Resort in Marbella in Spain.
Z: I've been doing that as well, but I've been at the Savoy in London.
J: Being a trainee concierge is great because you have to know about all the parts of the hotel.
Z: And it's really great training if you wanna be a hotel manager.
J: I agree and I've done so much. I've been on three trips. I've been to Seville, to Tangiers and Gibraltar.
Z: I haven't done any tours yet, but I've worked in four different parts of the hotel. I've booked trips, I've arranged transport and I've answered lots of questions about the local restaurants.
A: Sounds great. And Sylvie, let's bring you in here. What have you been doing?
S: Well, for the last three months, I've been working as a trainee chef at the Ritz hotel in London. I haven't been on any trips yet, but I've been working really hard learning all the skills I need to be an assistant chef. I've been in the kitchen or the restaurant every day. Also my tutor at university has given me lots of advice and encouragement and support. I can phone her when I want.
J: My concierge at the Marriott is fantastic. She speaks lots of languages and is Polish like me. She has treated me like a colleague from the start. She really makes me feel my input is valuable and has given me lots of confidence. She talks to me and doesn't talk down to me. I see her as my mentor.
A: Would you recommend your work placement to others?
J: Absolutely. The Marriott is famous for its work placements and its training. And I get paid, which is really good.
S: Yeah, we all get paid. All the placements organised through the university are paid placements. And the Ritz and the Savoy both have good training programmes.
A: And finally … who's the one who speaks all the languages?
J: That's me … I speak Spanish, English, German, and of course Polish. And I've been learning Italian since January. I was motivated by our concierge.

LESSON 3.4 RECORDING 3.5

H = Harry, M = Marta

H: I think you're right, Marta, educational qualifications and experience are not really so important as these are work placements – we've got to find young people with the right skills and personal qualities.
M: Exactly. The people we choose will get some initial training in New York, so that'll prepare them well for the placements. As you say, it's the personal qualities which are so important. It'll be pretty stressful, building up the club here. They'll have to work long hours and be very flexible. OK, we're not offering a competitive salary, but there are other benefits, and a nice working environment – that should attract some good candidates. There are great opportunities, but there will be some less glamorous parts of the work. We'll need someone who's very motivated, erm … enthusiastic, and has lots of energy.
H: Absolutely. And I think the best candidates will be very determined, people who have a real desire to succeed, because it won't be easy. We need outgoing people, I'd say, who can work with people from different cultures. Don't forget – a lot of our customers won't be English. All the candidates must also have an interest in health and fitness, don't you think?
M: Oh, definitely. And I agree – we need a fairly extroverted person, with really good communication skills. People skills are also very important to the company – so we want people who can adapt to different situations. If possible, they'll be fluent in another language – French, German, Japanese, whatever. Also, pretty good computer skills are important.
H: Yeah, I like the sound of those ideas. But most of all, we want people who are looking for a long-term career with us, and who'll stay with us afterwards.
M: OK, I've made a note of the points we mentioned. Now let's write the advert.

LESSON 3.4 RECORDING 3.6

I = Interviewer, C = Candidate

1   I: Now, looking at your CV. I'd like to know what you feel you learnt in your last placement?
    C: I'm glad you asked me that because I feel I developed some important skills while I was there.
2   I: I'm also interested in knowing your reasons for applying to our company.
    C: That's a very good question. Basically, because it is such a respected and famous organisation.
3   I: Now, a question we like to ask all our candidates. What are your strong points?
    C: Well, without going into too much detail, I have very good people skills.

AUDIO SCRIPTS

4 I: OK. Thank you. A question now about your computer skills. What software are you familiar with?
   C: I thought you might ask me something about that. Well, what I can say is, I have a good knowledge of Excel and Word, and can prepare excellent Powerpoint presentations.
5 I: Right, thank you. Moving on. Could you tell me what you think the growth areas in the leisure industry are?
   C: Well, I'm not an expert, but I think the boom in fitness centres will continue in the next few years.
6 I: OK. Just one final question. Where do you think you'll be in five years' time?
   C: Let me just think about that for a moment. Well, I hope to be working for your company in a senior position.

LESSON 3.5 RECORDING 3.7

S = Student, C = Counsellor

S: I know you usually send a covering letter with a CV. But … what is it exactly?
C: Well, really it's a letter telling an employer why you're interested in their company or organisation. You can tell them about your special skills and qualities and why you want to work with them. It gives you an opportunity to sell yourself to the employer.
S: I see. Erm … how long should it be?
C: It depends. But generally I'd say a covering letter should be short, say four to five paragraphs. And the tone should be enthusiastic and professional.
S: Right. Could you give me a little more detail about what to put in each paragraph?
C: OK, I'll suggest a structure, a way to organise the paragraphs, if you like.
S: Thank you.
C: Right. The first paragraph is your introduction. You say who you are, why you're writing and where you saw the position advertised.
S: OK, I've got that.
C: In paragraph two, tell the employer why you want the job – in other words, say what attracted you to the organisation. Show that you're enthusiastic and motivated.
S: Right.
C: The third paragraph is really important. This is where you sell yourself. Here you mention your qualities, erm … skills and experience that match what they are probably looking for. You tell them what you can contribute to their organisation. OK? Now we come to the final paragraph. Say when you're available for interview. And end on a positive note. For example, say you look forward to hearing from them soon, or something like that. OK, that's about it.
S: Thanks, that's really helpful.

LESSON 3.5 RECORDING 3.8

1 I think you should put as much as possible in a CV so the employer gets a complete picture of your qualities and skills and qualifications. If you don't do that, they may not call you for an interview.
2 It's essential to write a personal profile at the beginning of your CV. Everyone's doing it these days. It helps to focus your reader's attention on what you really have to offer their organisation. It's where you can sell yourself as a candidate.
3 If you're sending out CVs to lots of companies at one time, I mean if you're just seeing if there's any interest, not replying to an ad for a job, then I think your CV should be really short, just one side of an A4 sheet.
4 I try to write as much as possible in the work experience section. I start with my first job then put my most recent job last – that's the order I prefer. I had a period of six months when I was unemployed, but I never show that on my CV.
5 I only apply for jobs online. I use the Job Boards for my industry and if I see an interesting position, I fill in an online application. Sometimes I have to send a covering letter by email as well. Online adverts are the best way to find a new job. You get a quick reply from employers when you apply online. I always keep my CV up to date and I use a spellcheck to make sure there are no spelling mistakes.
6 To be honest, I think the covering letter's much more important than your CV. If they like what they read in your letter, they'll look at your CV. But if your letter's no good, they'll throw your CV in the bin right away.

LESSON 4.2 RECORDING 4.1

H = Henri, F = Fabio

H: Hello.
F: Oh hi, Henri. It's Fabio here.
H: Fabio, hi. Have you finished the essay on the differences between British and American English yet?
F: No, not yet. I'm going to finish it tonight. What about you?
H: I'm finding it quite tough especially when it comes to idioms. In Bill Bryson's book … it's quite funny actually … he says it can take years for an American to master British idioms and the other way round … but I'm definitely going to finish it by tomorrow's class. I want it out of the way!
F: Henri, I'm just phoning to ask – James and I are going to the cinema on Thursday evening. Do you want to come?
H: No, I can't. I'm giving my presentation to the language seminar group on Friday.
F: Oh, of course.
H: So I have to prepare that. I'm doing it on the growth of Arabic. I read something recently that said that Arabic is the fastest growing of the world languages.
F: Yeah, I saw something that said international agencies like Al Jazeera will provide a standard model … almost like the BBC. I saw an article about it in the paper the other day. I'll find it for you.
H: Thanks, that'd be great. When's your presentation?
F: It isn't till the end of next week.
H: Do you know what you're doing?
F: Yeah, I'm probably doing mine on spelling and how important it is.
H: That's interesting. I saw a film a while ago on spelling competitions in America. They're really popular there. Anyway, I'd better get on with the essay. I'll see you at the lecture tomorrow.
F: Great, and I'll text you when I find that paper.
H: Thanks. Bye.
F: Bye.

LESSON 4.3 RECORDING 4.3

I = Interviewer, R = Richard Falvey

I: What kind of work do you do, and is using correct and appropriate language important in your work?
R: I work for The British Council, an international charity that develops cultural relations between Britain and the rest of the world through our work in the Arts, Education and Society and English. My focus is developing partnerships with other charities and NGOs, or 'non-governmental organisations', educational institutions, businesses and governments in order to help students, young people and professionals and develop relationships with people from other countries and backgrounds.
So we're building trusting relations at all levels across different societies and key to building trust are effective communication and appropriate language – especially as most of our work is carried out in English. Having said that, few of the people we collaborate with have English as their first language. If you get your language wrong, you create confusion, and you can lose the trust you have been working to build up.

LESSON 4.3 RECORDING 4.4

I = Interviewer, R = Richard Falvey

I: What advice would you have for young people using social media?
R: Most of the principles are the same as face-to-face conversation – your language has to be appropriate to the context. We need to look at four things. Firstly, who's your audience? Secondly, how well do you know them? Thirdly, how much do they know about the topic? And finally, what is the effect you want? What do you want them to do as a result of your message? With social media you also need to remember that you can't see how people are reacting as you're speaking, so if you're not being understood or you're beginning to offend people, you can't see their face or body language. Also, think about the medium – text, email, Facebook, Twitter, YouTube, etc., and what effect this has. For example, who will see the message or picture, and will it be a permanent record?

LESSON 4.3 RECORDING 4.5

I = Interviewer, R = Richard Falvey

I: Can you be a bit more specific? Can you give some tips?
R: OK, so thinking about those points I just mentioned, and the ones specific to social media, it's a question of finding the right balance. For example, between being formal and informal and giving enough, but not too much detail.
So, let's look at three areas: how to avoid confusion, how to avoid losing trust and how to get the register right.
To avoid confusion, keep your language simple, use short sentences. Show the message to a 'non-knower', that is somebody who does not already know what the message is about. If they can understand it, then the person you're sending the message to, who already has some context, will also understand it.
To avoid losing trust, think about your

167

audience and make sure that you are 'reading' the message through their eyes. And don't post late at night, when you are in a rush or feeling emotional and might use inappropriate language.

To get the register right … and let me begin by defining register. By register, I mean a way of speaking or writing which you use when you're in a particular situation. That way of speaking or writing could, for example, be formal or informal or humorous or polite or familiar. So, to get the register right, use the right medium for the message. For example, you might text or use instant messaging to a tutor or business partner that you are friendly with, using abbreviations and textspeak to say thanks for a meeting. But in a business situation with someone you're not close to, or when submitting an assignment or asking for feedback, use email or a forum and use more formal language. So for students, what I'm basically saying is don't transfer the language you use with your close friends on Facebook and other social media sites to the language you use when you email your lecturers.

LESSON 4.4 RECORDING 4.6

C = Claire, F = Frank, S = Sophia

C: OK, let's talk about the directors and senior staff first. After that, we've got to discuss whether we want the training to focus on British English or American English. And if we have time, we'll consider the needs of our biggest group, the admin staff. OK?
F/S: Fine/Yeah.
C: OK, the directors and senior staff. They're our top priority. How about sending some of them, the weaker ones, on a crash course to England or the US? It'd be a quick way to improve their English. What do you think, Frank?
F: Mmm, I don't know about that. Let's think this through.
C: OK? What's the problem?
F: If we do that, what will happen? In my opinion, it'll have a bad effect on our work. We don't want to lose a lot of our top staff just like that. Who'd run the charity?
S: You know, Frank, I think you're right. It'd create a lot of problems for us. Why don't we send just one or two directors to Britain or the US and a few senior staff? We can offer the others one-to-one classes at Head Office. What do you think, Claire?
C: Mmm, one-to-one classes, in company time? Some companies do it, but I'm told the classes are quite difficult to organise. Teachers always seem to want to give the lessons at the wrong time. You know, when staff are really busy, and at the moment we're all up to our ears in work.
S: Mmm, maybe you're right, Claire. Let's do some research. Find out a bit more about one-to-one classes. I have some good contacts I can ask.
C: OK, good idea. Let's move on. What about British English or American English? Some of our staff will probably prefer American English, the ones working closely with our US partners. Frank, what do you think?
F: I think you're right, Claire. Some staff will want to learn American English. But, you know, there's an easy solution – we could hire two teachers to teach classes at Head Office, one English and one American.
S: That's a great idea. What do you think, Claire?
C: Mmm, well, yes, if we do decide to have English classes here, at Head Office, because it's a cheap option, then it's certainly worth considering. But I think most staff will want British English. We need to get more information about this. Do some more research. I hope it won't be a big problem for us. OK, we need to think now about the admin staff. There are a lot of them and they'll want to improve their English. They'll have to improve to do their job properly. We'll need to set up classes for them pretty soon as well.
F: I'm not sure about that, Claire. They're not a priority …
C: Maybe, but think of the consequences if we leave them out. It won't help to create good staff relations.
F: That's a good point. We'll need to provide some English classes for them, but keep the cost down.
C/S: Right.

LESSON 5.1 RECORDING 5.2

1 I remember a really eye-catching advert for a Ford car. It showed the car starting, then being driven out of a car park and through the city. And it started all the lights in the surrounding buildings. In the country it powered the overhead power lines and the electricity seemed to follow the car along the road. It really was an attention-grabbing ad. It is difficult to be original with car adverts but I thought this was quite creative. It also had a catchy slogan: 'Feel the power. Ford. We have ignition.' You could also see the recognisable Ford 'blue oval' logo. It must have been an effective ad because I've actually remembered that it was a Ford car. It was also quite persuasive as I would consider buying a Ford next time.

2 I normally like humorous ads. But the ad that sticks in my mind was really inspirational. The music was really lively and it was set in different exotic locations. Everyone was drinking this soft drink, but I can't remember which one it was, and the camerawork was really creative. It made you want to be there, drinking that soft drink, having fun.

3 I saw this really dull advert for washing powder on the television recently that I'd really like to forget. But it had this really catchy jingle that I can't get out of my head. It's so irritating. It was informative – it gave you lots of information about the product but I can't even remember what the brand was.

LESSON 5.2 RECORDING 5.3

L = Leon, D = Dita, S = Simone

L: OK. So, you are based in Cairns, and where do you cover?
D: Well, Leon, we cover all of North Queensland so we can get stunning wedding shots of the bride and groom standing in front of vibrant, green rainforests and white sandy beaches. We've got the luscious rainforests of North Queensland with all their waterfalls and rivers.
S: And then we've got the amazing Great Barrier Reef.
L: As a web designer, can I just say that you've got some excellent photos in some stunning locations. In fact, we're spoilt for choice. Makes my job so much easier.
S: I think we've got all the shots we need now, haven't we Dita? Although, if we get an invitation to a ceremony in Papua New Guinea, we'll go there right away for a great shoot.
D: Too right.
L: OK and why do you want a website now?
D: Well, to be honest, we'd design the website ourselves if we had enough time. But we don't and we think we are losing out to our competitors who have websites.
L: Don't worry. If we act quickly, we'll limit the damage and catch up with your competitors. And your photos are stunning. This is such a great shot. The bride is beautiful and we won't need to do any airbrushing. And I love all the colours. If we make the sea bluer, the picture will look even better. If I were you, I'd use this photo as your main image.
S: Yes, we're very proud of that shot. Actually, if I had the couple's number on me, I could give them a call now to ask for permission to use it, but I've left all my contact details at home.
L: OK. We can get it tomorrow. Let's look at what you would ideally like and then look at all the different options. So, what would you do if you had an unlimited budget?

LESSON 5.4 RECORDING 5.4

A = Amy Chen, L = Larissa Klein

A: There are several points I'd like your team to cover in their presentation.
L: OK.
A: Well, for a start, we can't agree on a name for the drink. We've had lots of suggestions but none of them have been very exciting, so could you come up with some new ideas for names, please?
L: Certainly, no problem.
A: We need a good slogan too, something that's easy to remember and original. One of our staff wanted to call the drink 'Krakkle'; she came up with the slogan 'Kool kids drink Krakkle', but no one really liked that one. We'd also like your ideas for the design of the packaging. Should it be a can or bottle, or something different? Nothing too detailed, just … oh I don't know, design, colour, shape – that sort of thing.
L: OK, what else do you want us to look at?
A: Well, we've talked quite a lot about the kind of advertising we should use. Should we have a TV commercial during children's television in the afternoon? Or maybe early in the evening? How about advertising in children's magazines? Should we use the internet as well? Another question is, do we want just one TV commercial, with different languages for the various markets, or should we have a different one for each country?
L: Interesting. What about radio spots?
A: Ah yes, I forgot to mention that. Do you think we should advertise on radio? If we do, what time of the day should we choose for a radio spot, and what sort of programme could we sponsor?
L: Is that everything?
A: I think so. … Oh yes, one other thing, if your team have any interesting ideas for special promotions, let us have them. I mean, would it be a good idea to give out free cans in schools? Or offer cheap T-shirts with the logo on them. That sort of thing.
L: Fine. I'm sure we can come up with some

AUDIO SCRIPTS

good ideas for you. We'd certainly like to be your agency for the campaign.

A: Well, if we like your presentation, you'll have a good chance of winning the contract.

L: That's good enough for me.

LESSON 5.4 RECORDING 5.5

Larissa Klein:

Good morning, I'm Larissa Klein, head of Klein Benson Advertising. I'd like to introduce my colleagues, Emilio Sanchez on my left, and next to him, Karl Reiner.

Our purpose today is to present some ideas for your new product. We'll also suggest how to advertise and promote it.

Our presentation is divided into three parts. First, I'll talk to you about our ideas for the name of the soft drink and a suitable slogan. After that, Emilio will give you our ideas about the can – he's an expert on packaging – and finally Karl will tell you our ideas about how to advertise and promote the drink. If you have any questions, we'll be pleased to answer them at the end of our presentation.

LESSON 5.4 RECORDING 5.6

Emilio Sanchez:

Moving on now to the design of the can. We asked a group of young people about this. We showed them ten different designs. Please look at the screen. As you see, we've numbered the designs one to ten. If we now look at the table of results, it's very clear. Over 80% of the group preferred design 6, the blue can with the yellow stripe.

LESSON 5.4 RECORDING 5.7

K = Karl Reiner, L = Larissa Klein

K: Well, I've given you our ideas for advertising and promoting the drink. I hope you've found them interesting. Now, let me summarise our main points. Larissa gave you three possible names and mentioned the one we prefer. She told you what slogan we liked, with her reasons. Emilio showed you the design for the can that we recommend. Finally, I talked about ways of advertising the drink and told you about our ideas for special promotions.

L: Thank you very much everyone for your attention. Are there any questions?

LESSON 5.5 RECORDING 5.8

OK, what is critical thinking? Very simply, it's a way of thinking about a subject or problem. It's a skill you use to decide whether a statement or opinion is always true. So, critical thinkers make judgments based on evidence and clear thinking. They look at problems in a thoughtful way and try to solve them.

It's an important skill for academic studies. Teachers and lecturers expect students to think critically when they do essays and reports, and carry out research. Students need to show the ability to analyse information, question statements and opinions, and identify key points in a text.

But most of all, critical thinking is an important skill for everyone. It encourages you to ask questions about what you see, hear and read, and not accept ideas and opinions uncritically. So, critical thinkers are curious about life, and they form their own values and beliefs.

LESSON 6.1 RECORDING 6.1

1 Well, I'm not sure really. I think it's important to go to university and get a degree, but it isn't an easy experience. It was hard to get a place, and I wasn't sure what to do. I worried about going just to study any subject, maybe not the right one. It can be hard to get a good result in a lot of subjects. You can fail a course, like I did. I seem to be revising for, or sitting exams all the time! There are a lot of lectures and we have to go and speak in seminars every week. If I can get good grades, I will finish next year. To be honest, it has been a good experience, although I can't wait to graduate from university and get away from exams!

2 School was a waste of time for me. Handing in essays, doing homework and all that stuff. It just wasn't useful. I only wanted to do sports. I couldn't study for exams, so when I did any exams I failed them. I just made too many mistakes. Maybe I didn't have the right system for revising subjects. When I retook the exams, I failed again. My friends did a lot better. I just wasn't interested. It was a great day for me when I could leave secondary school!

3 I always tried to do well at school, you know, handing in assignments on time, trying to get good grades and doing my coursework so I could go to college. I liked school a lot. I think it is about doing your best, but this is more than just passing exams and studying for tests. I think it's about making progress generally. It's also a social experience, how to get on with other people. I still have many friends from my school days. Yes, I had a great time at school.

LESSON 6.2 RECORDING 6.2

We had a teacher called Mr Rojas and he taught us Chemistry. He was an excellent teacher, but we couldn't say that we actually liked him. He wasn't friendly or easy-going – the opposite in fact. He was different from the teachers we normally liked. In fact, he often criticised us. He treated us all equally – well, criticised all of us equally. He didn't treat us like unique individuals, so it was funny that we all respected him. He was very strict and always punctual – I don't think he was ever late, and neither were we! He gave us lots of tests and lots of homework, and his formal approach to teaching seemed to work. He explained things very clearly and was very good at answering all our questions. He was always very well prepared and his lessons were always interesting. He always varied things, changed the pace of the lesson, and used different methods to teach us. The chemistry laboratory was a strange environment to be in, but we all enjoyed the classes. In the end, we all passed the Chemistry exam and Chemistry became my favourite subject on the curriculum.

LESSON 6.3 RECORDING 6.3

1 I'm an American, and I can tell you, a college degree in the US puts you way ahead of people who don't have one. If you want to work in cities like Boston, New York or San Francisco, your starting salary will be much higher than guys who don't have a degree, and you certainly need a good salary to afford an apartment in those cities. I think I'll get about $50,000 as a starting salary once I graduate, and I'll get a lot of fringe benefits too, like life insurance and a retirement plan.

2 I love sports. I love playing sports and being outside. Like most of my school friends, I went to university. I did Sports Science, but it wasn't really for me. I liked the practical bits and enjoyed playing for the university sports teams, but I hated the academic side. I left after a year and had to pay off some university loans. I did work experience after that and then got a job as a sports coach and personal trainer. I think university was a waste of time for me.

3 I did my degree at Cambridge University – it was a three-year course. I don't like the idea that you study for a degree for what it gets you later in life. You should go to university because you're really interested in the subject you choose. I don't think my degree helped me to get a job. OK, it may have given me an edge over non-graduates for getting interviews, I suppose. But I really enjoyed studying French literature, and don't regret it at all. When I left, I applied for lots of jobs, and I think employers liked the fact that I was confident and had good people skills. I'm now a computer programmer, nothing to do with literature.

4 I graduated from university a few years ago. I did enjoy my time at university, and maybe that's the problem. I did well at school, so it was logical to go to university. I guess I just enjoyed myself too much. Without the discipline of school, I didn't study as hard as I should, so I only just got a degree. A lot of my friends got jobs straight from school and are now doing really well. There are a lot of unemployed graduates around these days. I don't regret my time at university – I learnt quite a lot about people, and I did a lot of sport. I'm not sure it really helped my career though.

LESSON 6.4 RECORDING 6.4

M = Marie Laforêt, P = Pablo, MC = May Cheng

M: OK, I've noted what you've told me about the library. We can discuss the matter at our next committee meeting. Now what about the parties, you say some students in the halls of residence have been complaining about the noise?

P: Yes, it's a real problem. There are lots more parties at the moment in people's rooms, especially late-night parties. They're really noisy, music blasting out late at night, everyone talking at the top of their voices. They really annoy people who want to study.

M: Mmm, that's not fair, is it? A lot of students like to study in the evenings and even at night in their rooms. They must have some peace and quiet.

P/MC: Exactly/Right.

M: Let's see, there are several ways to deal with this. Let's look at our options. Erm, we could agree to ban parties in rooms, or we could only allow parties after the exams … What do you think, May Cheng?

MC: Well, the good thing is that it's fair to everyone, but the bad thing is, it wouldn't be very popular. I mean, everyone likes parties, don't they? It's part of our education.

P: Could I make a suggestion, Marie?

M: Sure, go ahead.

AUDIO SCRIPTS

P: Supposing we let each floor of the hall have one party per semester. That'd reduce the number of parties a lot.
M: Maybe, but there would still be quite a lot of noise when each floor had their party. No, I don't think that's the right thing to do. Let's see, what other options do we have?
MC: I've got an idea. How about letting the students book a room in the main building for parties? You could charge a small fee, and tell them that they have to book, say, four weeks in advance. I think most people would accept that.
M: Yes, good idea. That's the best solution, I think. OK, Pablo?
P: I don't know. I'd like to discuss it with the other reps first. They may come up with some other ideas.
M: All right, I know there are other things you want to talk about. The best way is to discuss the matters at our Management Committee meeting. Why don't you send me notes on all the problems and I'll include them in the agenda?
P: Right, we'll do that.

LESSON 7.2 RECORDING 7.2

A: Let's brainstorm some ideas for our new project, the folding chair. So first, who exactly is our target consumer?
B: Well, we need to reach as many people as possible. The chair could be useful for all kinds of people, you know, people going camping or fishing, or even going to outdoor concerts. In fact, it could be suitable for anyone who has to sit outside for a long time.
A: OK, what about the materials for making it?
B: Well, it must be light and easy to carry if we want to gain market share. We can't use steel – that's too heavy. We can use aluminium for the frame and canvas for the seat. And to keep costs down, maybe we should make it in just three colours.
A: Yes, that's important. Also, it must be cheap if we want to be competitive. There are one or two chairs on the market that sell at under €50. We can produce something similar – it doesn't have to be very different for this market. But we can have a second more expensive model too, if that's what people want.
B: Mmm. Good point. OK, another thing: the rules say it has to be strong enough to support a heavy person.
A: Absolutely. OK, in terms of timing we don't need to rush, but we could launch it just before the summer – there'll be a big demand for it then. In fact, we really mustn't miss this opportunity.
B: You're right, but we shouldn't launch it until we're really ready. Look, I think we should wait for the results of our market research before making any decisions.

LESSON 7.3 RECORDING 7.3

1 A = Anna, B = Becs
A: Wow, look at that. What is it?
B: It's a drawing. I think it's a sort of flying machine.
A: Yes, it could be that. Who do you think it's by?
B: Mmm, it might be by da Vinci, I believe he did that sort of thing. Have a look at the sign. What does it say?

A: Erm … yes, you're right, it is da Vinci.
B: Goodness! It's in very good condition … it says here he was born in 1452, so it must be over 500 years old.
A: Yes, and it's an amazing drawing.
B: Yeah, I read somewhere he was fascinated by birds and flying. Perhaps that's where he got his ideas for the drawing.
A: Yeah, you're probably right.

2 P = Pablo, I = Irina
P: Oh look at that, Irina. That must be the famous Anna G. corkscrew.
I: Yes, it can't be anything else. Oh look, there's a full range with all the different colours. How long have they been around for?
P: I think since the early 1990s.
I: No, they can't be that old. What does it say here? Oh, you're right. It first appeared in 1994.
P: Mmm, it was a classic design. I think you can still buy them in the Alessi shop.

3 G = George, S = Sally
G: What's that?
S: I've no idea. What could it be?
G: It might be a spaceship. Well, a toy spaceship. It's the right shape.
S: No, I'm certain that it's not that. It wouldn't really be in a museum of design.
G: Mmm, I see what you mean. And maybe it's too heavy to be a toy. What else could it be?
S: Mmm, I don't know really. What does it say on the notice?
G: It says it's a lemon squeezer. Apparently it's the designer Philippe Starck's best-known design.
S: OK, I see it now. Would you like something like that?
G: No way! It just doesn't look practical.

LESSON 7.4 RECORDING 7.4

I think this is by far the best entry. It's a lightweight travel jacket, designed by an Italian student, Antonia Moretti. As you can see, it looks very modern and stylish. In my opinion, it's aimed at young people. It will appeal to people who are on the move, people who want to carry lots of things on them when they make trips abroad or go to sports events or music festivals. They're the kind of people who would love this jacket. But it's also suitable for students and for people commuting to work. It has several special features. There are three extra-large pockets for carrying clothes, shoes, and other items like that, and four smaller pockets. All of them zip up for extra security. One of the jacket's best qualities, I'd say, is that the zips have a lifetime guarantee, so they must be very sturdy.
The jacket has two unique features. Firstly, it's made from a new material which is very strong, waterproof and heat resistant. And secondly, it's got a pocket with a lock, so you can keep money and valuables in it safely. Not even a pickpocket could open it! Another strong point is the logo on the sleeve – a unique, one-off design by the famous street artist, Miki Panos – so it looks really cool.
OK, this is the design that gets my vote. The jacket's durable, functional, easy to use and, above all, innovative. I think we should give it our first prize.

LESSON 7.5 RECORDING 7.5

L = Lecturer, E = Erika
L: So, you'd like me to give you some advice on editing your work, Erika?
E: Yes, if you could give me a few tips, it would be very helpful. I know I need to check my written work more carefully.
L: OK. I'll try to keep it simple. What are the most common mistakes students make when they write? These are the sort of things you should be looking for. And everyone should think about them when they check their written work.
E: Exactly.
L: OK. I'll give you five or six points to think about. First of all, check your spelling and punctuation carefully. If you've typed your work, don't forget to use a spell-checker.
E: Oh, yes. Good idea.
L: Of course, you'll make mistakes with difficult words, like, oh, erm … 'accommodation' or 'receive', but students often make mistakes with simple words, like spelling 'writing' with two Ts! And of course you need to punctuate your work correctly. Many students seem to forget that we use full stops when we write English!
E: I know what you mean. My teacher is always telling me to use a full stop instead of a comma!
L: Right. And don't forget about capitals. Check your written work to make sure that you have used capital letters where they're appropriate.
E: OK. Got that.
L: My next tip is to check your work for grammatical errors. In particular, check your verb tenses and verb forms. Make sure you've used the right tense or form. You have problems using the present perfect tense. Think carefully before you use that tense. It's easy to make a mistake with a verb form, especially with the past tenses of irregular verbs. Don't use 'gone' when you mean 'went' and don't use 'catched' when it should be 'caught'. OK?
E: Right. I often make mistakes with irregular verbs – they're very difficult to learn and then I write the wrong form in an essay.
L: Yes, they're difficult and so are prepositions. Check that you've written the correct preposition after an adjective or verb. For example, don't write 'depend of' when it should be 'depend on'. So many students make that error, you wouldn't believe it.
E: OK. Be careful with prepositions. I'll check them in a dictionary if I'm not sure.
L: Good. Word order is important, too. Check that you've used the right word order in your sentences. That's especially important for you.
E: Yes, that's true – I often make mistakes with word order. It's a real problem for me.
L: My final piece of advice is, after you've written something, always ask yourself the questions 'Is my meaning clear?' and 'Will someone reading my work understand what I'm trying to say?' That's it, really, I hope my tips will help you.
E: I'm sure they will. I'll put them into practice when I write my next essay.

AUDIO SCRIPTS

LESSON 8.1 RECORDING 8.1

I = Interviewer, A = Allan Smith

I: Tonight, we're focusing on starting your own business. I have with me Allan Smith, an accountant and business adviser. Good evening, Allan – thanks for joining us.
A: Good evening, John – it's a pleasure.
I: Allan, could I start by asking you to give us the most important tips for someone setting up a business?
A: Certainly. First of all, I'd say you must understand you'll never know everything there is to know about running a business – it's as simple as that. So, you'll need help in certain areas – maybe with finances and tax, or perhaps with selling and marketing. Once you know the areas where you need help, you can train yourself, or bring in an employee who has the skill you need. Another way is to get advice from an expert or a friend who has their own business. OK?
I: Right, very useful. Anything else?
A: Yes, my second tip is all about marketing. You need to be sure that your product will sell in sufficient numbers, at a price that covers your costs. In other words, it must give you a return on your money; it's got to make a profit. To do this you must be clear about how you price your product – for example, are you going to price it above, the same as or below your competitors? Then, you must also think about how you'll promote it. I mean, how are you going to let people know about the product, so that they become aware of it? That's important. And, you know, you may have to market it in a different way to different people. That could be the key to success.
I: OK, so good marketing is essential when you start your own business.
A: Exactly.

LESSON 8.1 RECORDING 8.2

I: You spent many years, Allan, working in accountancy firms with businesses that failed, that went bankrupt. Why did most of them fail?
A: Erm … I think there were three reasons really. Firstly, some failed because the market had moved on and the business was left behind. It was using old equipment that just wasn't up to date, wasn't efficient – the printing trade is a good example of that. Another reason was that some of them depended too much on one main customer, and then if the customer decides they don't need you any more … And the third reason, well … it could be a number of things, poor planning, cash flow problems, bad debts, erm … not dealing with tax properly, that sort of thing – just not managing the business properly.

LESSON 8.1 RECORDING 8.3

I: A final question – what do you think about business plans?
A: Oh, they're vital. You should think of them as a map which'll take you from today to how the business will be in a few years' time. The business plan will set out your objectives, how you are going to get there, to achieve them and how you're going to measure your progress. Too many people say their plan is in their head, but when that happens, they often can't deal with unexpected things, like, erm … sales that are lower than they hoped, or rising costs. You should get your forecasts down in writing. Check how you're getting on and use your plan to help you succeed in the business. Oh, yes, one other thing – don't expect to get the forecasts right straight away. You'll improve later when you have more experience.
I: Thanks very much, Allan. Some good advice there for people starting up a business.

LESSON 8.1 RECORDING 8.4

A: I think a car washing business is a good idea. We'll need to research the market a bit first. Maybe the supermarkets will allow us to wash customers' cars in the car park.
B: Yes, good idea.
A: Also, how about contacting a local taxi firm? They have a lot of cars which always seem to be dirty. There could be a cleaning service for the inside of the cars as well. We wouldn't need much equipment, but we should have a good name – how about something like KarKlean, with a K – you know, K-A-R K-L-E-A-N?
B: Yeah, good idea. We could give people a discount to start with and print a few leaflets to advertise the business.
A: Yes, I don't think it'd cost much to set up the business and we could make quite a lot of money.

LESSON 8.4 RECORDING 8.6

V = Vanessa, B = Bob

V: Could I speak to Bob, please?
B: Yes, speaking. How can I help you?
V: Hi Bob, it's Vanessa from Domino in Italy here.
B: Hi Vanessa. How are things?
V: Fine. Did you get my email?
B: Yes, I did, but I've been really busy – sorry I haven't replied. You want to order some sunglasses from us.
V: Well, yes … maybe. Thanks for the samples you sent us, Bob, they certainly look good.
B: They sure are Vanessa, they're selling really well. OK, how many would you like to order?
V: Mmm, well, we're thinking of placing quite a large order, about 50,000, at the price you gave us in the email.
B: Great!
V: Yeah, but it's really important that you can deliver to us in August.
B: Oh, I'm afraid that would be a bit difficult, Vanessa, we've already still got quite a few summer orders to deal with. Maybe in September – that should be OK.
V: What about if we pay earlier? Will you be able to deliver in August?
B: Vanessa, let me check if I understand you, do you mean payment on delivery, in August? Well, that would be good …
V: No, we couldn't pay that soon. I was thinking of paying after 60 days. How do you feel about that?
B: Sorry Vanessa, I don't think we can wait that long. How about 30?
V: I'm not sure about that. OK, Bob, look … I'll think it over and maybe get back to you.
B: That sounds fine. Well … I hope to hear from you soon.
V: Right, Bob, thanks a lot. Bye for now.
B: Bye.

LESSON 9.1 RECORDING 9.1

I = Interviewer, L = Lindsey Barone

I: For our next guest on *A Woman's World*, I'd like to welcome to the programme Lindsey Barone, head of engineering at Swift Aerospace – a very good example of a woman in a man's world.
L: Good morning everyone.
I: Lindsey, you're an engineer, but why did you become one? What got you interested?
L: Well, from a young age I was always interested in how things work. I chose engineering as a career because I wanted to make things better. Engineering isn't just about testing theories and building models. It's about designing new products and finding new uses for old products. I suppose at its most basic it's about how to solve problems. It's great when you make a breakthrough and improve the way the world works!
I: Mmm, interesting. And could you tell me a bit about your training?
L: Well, I studied engineering at university. I was the only woman in the mechanical engineering department!
I: So, how was that?
L: Well, at first I felt a bit uncomfortable, but after a while it didn't bother me. People got used to me and I was treated like anyone else. In fact sometimes it was a bit of an advantage because people liked to have me in their team!
I: You're head of engineering now. How did you get to where you are today?
L: Well, I started in a test lab for aeroplanes. I did stress and safety tests there. Basically, I broke things! Doing that sort of research is very important as it tells you what loads the structures can carry. Then I went into aeroplane design. I worked on all areas of commercial planes before moving into project management in the aircraft industry.
I: Now you're head of department and I guess in charge of a lot of men. How do you find that?
L: Well, it wasn't too easy at first. I had to prove myself. It's true, it's a very male environment. When they could see that I had good practical experience and ability and could meet my deadlines, everything was fine.
I: I suppose that's true of anyone who's in charge. OK, Lindsey, finally – what's the best thing about being an engineer?
L: Oh, that's an easy one to answer. I love the challenge of finding solutions to problems. I hope that what I do improves people's lives. For me, engineering is fun, exciting and satisfying. We really need more women coming into the profession!
I: Thanks very much, Lindsey. Now, our next guest is someone who …

LESSON 9.3 RECORDING 9.2

1 He's an engineer.
2 I work for a big bank.
3 She's the Chief Executive.
4 Rachel's the head of department.
5 She goes to the University of Oxford.

LESSON 9.4 RECORDING 9.3

Some exciting news now from the Minister of the Environment, Susan Lau, which should please all the engineers in our country.

AUDIO SCRIPTS

The government has announced that it is considering the possibility of building the tallest city in the world – a vertical city located just on the edge of our capital, which would bring new life to the city, as well as boosting tourism. It will be over 1,500 metres high – at least that's the idea – with a width of about 500 metres at its base. The idea is that about 40,000 people will live there, and over 100,000 will work in the city during the day. The vertical city, which is being called at present the 'Mega Project', will have apartments, a hotel, an international conference centre, offices, food outlets, and entertainment and leisure facilities. And, just like any other city, there'll be green spaces, fountains, parks and gardens.

At the moment, it's just an idea, but an exciting one – it would really put the country on the map, no doubt about that. The minister plans to contact engineering departments in universities and invite new angles and discussion of the idea.

LESSON 9.4 RECORDING 9.4

A: Hey, did you see the news on TV last night? There was something about building a new, vertical city?

B: Yeah, I saw the interview. Really interesting. I think it's a great project, building a new city. It'd create a lot of publicity and attract foreign businesspeople. That's just what we need, isn't it?

A: Yeah – I like the idea a lot. It's really exciting, a big project like that. It'd certainly help to solve the housing problem, that'd be a big advantage, and it'd probably reduce crime in the area. Also, it'd create lots of jobs and really boost the economy.

B: Yes, exactly. I suppose the people working there would also live there. That's probably what they have in mind. People would walk to work instead of driving, so there'd be fewer traffic jams and a lot less stress for people.

A: Mmm, I must say, a vertical city sounds like a really good idea. I think it'd be a good way of using the land in the area. A good use of resources, I mean, putting a lot of people in a small space. That makes sense to me. I just hope the government approves the project. Do you think they will?

B: I suppose it depends on a lot of things. Erm, you know, will it be popular with the public? Are there any strong arguments against it? Can we actually do it? Where will the money come from? Have you thought about that one?

LESSON 9.4 RECORDING 9.5

A: What about calling it Mega City? It's easy to remember.

B: Mmm, it's a possible solution, I suppose, but there are other possibilities. How about Hope City? It's a really good name because it'll provide a lot of housing for poor people. Give them hope for the future.

C: Yeah, Hope City. It sounds good to me, I must say. But what other names can we think of?

A: Well, one option would be to call it Tower City. That's exactly what it would be – a towering city, one of the highest in the world.

B: I don't know, I'm not too keen on that name. We have one other option, you know. If we called it Paradise City, I think most people would like that name. It suggests the city would be a wonderful place to live and work in. That's what we all want, don't we?

C: Mmm, nice idea, I really like the name.

A: Me too. OK, we all seem to like it. Are we all agreed then? Have we reached a decision? It'll be Paradise City.

B/C: Yeah. Agreed.

A: OK then. I'll recommend the name to the minister. We're all agreed. It's the best name.

LESSON 9.5 VIDEO RECORDING 9

J = Jake, D = Davide, S = Sheeba, V = Valerie

J: … I think I agree, Sheeba. With an engineering degree, OK, maybe you can get a position on a team or become a project manager. But you don't have the skills to start your own company or become head of a company, a CEO. So maybe management qualifications are really important for engineers.

D: Can I come in here, please? Sheeba, are you saying all engineers must do a management course?

S: No, that's not what I think at all. Let me explain my point of view. I'm saying that technical ability isn't enough if you want to get to the top of your career – that's all.

V: Can I make a quick point, please? It's just not true you can't get to the top without management training. There are lots of heads of big companies who've never been to university. They have leadership qualities …

S: OK, but the point is …

V: Hang on, let me finish what I want to say.

S: Yes, sorry.

V: And they have other abilities, really good communication and interpersonal skills. Some are very charismatic.

S: OK, true, but most of these skills can be taught on a management course – that's my point. Davide, you want to say something?

D: Yes, in my opinion, most engineers will make good managers, even if they haven't studied management.

S: Really, what makes you say that?

D: When you study engineering, you learn the skills you need to be a good manager. Like, erm, analysing things, evaluating risks, being creative and innovative, dealing with figures, working in teams, those kind of things. You don't need to do an MBA to learn those things, you know them already. I think you agree with me, don't you, Valerie?

V: Yes, I agree completely. I'd like to ask Sheeba and Jake a question, if I may.

S/J: Yeah/OK.

V: Do you think all engineers want to get to top positions in industry?

S: No, of course not. Let me clarify … let me explain. I'm saying most engineers will get better jobs and earn more money if they have the management skills as well as the technical ones.

J: Perhaps that's true. But many engineers study management for the wrong reasons. Let me explain. They've been in the same job for a long time and they just get bored. They haven't got a promotion so they think, oh well, I'd better do some management studies. You see, they don't really have a career plan, they just can't think of anything better to do.

D: Can I just say something here? In my opinion, it's better for most engineers to work in a technical field, in an area where they can use the knowledge they've gained during their engineering studies.

J: Absolutely, Davide. When I leave here, I want to do research and use my engineering skills. I didn't come here to learn to be a manager. When I leave here with a degree, I want to do something fantastic, build a new bridge or a dam or invent a new system of communication, that's what really motivates me. For me, management studies is a total waste of time – right now. Later, maybe …

LESSON 9.5 RECORDING 9.6

Most people are effective in group discussion when they've had a lot of practice. It's normal to be nervous, of course, if you're taking part in a group discussion, a tutorial or seminar, for example, for the first time. There are, however a few Dos and Don'ts when it comes to group discussions. I hope you'll find my advice useful.

A golden rule, I'd say, is to listen carefully to the opinion and advice of other speakers. That shows that you respect their opinions, even if you don't agree with them. If you disagree, you can do so politely. You can say things like, 'That's a good point, but …', or 'I see what you're getting at, but …', or even 'I'm afraid I don't agree with you.' Above all, don't use strong language like, 'That's nonsense, rubbish, really stupid.' Other speakers may have different opinions from you. They may not be wrong, just different.

If you are nervous about making a contribution, start with something small. For example, agree with what someone says, ask for an example or prepare a question you want to ask. Try to speak clearly, even if you're uncertain about your ideas or language.

A very important point now. Don't speak while someone else is speaking, in other words, don't talk over another person. It's very rude to do that. Also, don't speak a lot more than everyone else in the discussion. Give other people a chance to have their say. So, try not to interrupt speakers, let them finish what they're saying. If you feel you have to interrupt a speaker because your point is really important, how about saying, 'Could I just say something please', and use a bit of body language as well, like a small movement of the hand to attract attention.

Finally, pay attention to your body language. Try to look relaxed and friendly. Don't make aggressive gestures, like pointing your finger or banging the table. And if you ask a question, make sure you don't sound aggressive. Use polite language like 'Could I ask a question, please?' or 'Could you expand on that, please?'

LESSON 10.2 RECORDING 10.1

M = Manager, C = Chloe

M: Hello Chloe, good to see you. We've got a little time before my next meeting, so … how are things going?

C: Very well, thanks. I've really enjoyed my first week here. I've talked to a lot of the trainees and served a few customers.

M: No problems, I hope?

C: Not really. There were just a couple of customers who were a bit difficult, but they were OK in the end.

M: Good. Let me give you one or two tips while I have the time. First of all, many

AUDIO SCRIPTS

trainees think they don't need to know anything about the rest of the store, but we've found the best sales staff are not just fashion specialists, they also find out about the rest of the store so they can help customers when they're looking for other sections. So don't forget, you'll need to answer questions about other departments, especially cosmetics and jewellery.

C: Right, that's good advice. By the way, I've noticed no one wears any kind of uniform in this department. Most of the assistants seem to be wearing designer labels. Is that your policy then?

M: Yes. We have no rules about uniforms. Staff can wear some of our fashions. You see, you and your colleagues are models for our fashions as well as advisers. We picked up this idea last year in Milan during their fashion show. We visited a few of the top stores in Milan and learnt a lot from them.

C: So you travel abroad?

M: Yes. I used to do all the trips on my own with no help, but last year I took some of the assistants along with me. It's good training for them.

C: Wow! I didn't realise you did that. No wonder you keep your staff for years!

M: We believe in treating staff well, it's very important. Actually, we need to start thinking about next year's fashion shows – but we've got plenty of ideas and we'll get some information from the organisers soon.

C: Do you have any other tips for me, like how to approach customers? I don't have a lot of sales experience.

M: I know, but you've got the right personality. Look, the best piece of advice I can give you is to give customers enough time to make up their minds without any pressure. Give them a lot of attention and plenty of advice, but only when they need it. It's your job to judge the right moment. OK? Never oversell or put too much pressure on a customer. We have enough sales assistants to do the job properly.

C: Thanks very much. That's very helpful.

M: Good, well Chloe, I must be off to my meeting. I've enjoyed chatting to you. Well done, you've had a very good first week.

LESSON 10.3 RECORDING 10.2

1 These days I only buy records. Why? The quality of the sound is better than the sound of digital music.

2 I haven't bought any music in ages. I mainly listen to music on YouTube, Pandora and other streaming services. It's free.

3 I get all my music from iTunes and download to my iPod. I love making my own playlists of songs for parties, jogging or driving. And I can carry my ipod anywhere.

4 I get all my music free from the internet. I don't see why anyone would pay for it when you can download it all for free.

5 Well, I'm 40 and over my life I've bought records, cassettes, CDs and now I buy my songs from iTunes. I love being able to carry my iPhone around, but for sound quality I think vinyl is best.

6 I buy my music from Amazon as a CD. I hardly ever download free music off the internet. I love playing CDs in my bedroom. I also like the CD packaging with the artwork, and also reading lyrics from the booklet.

LESSON 10.4 RECORDING 10.4

C = Claire Maxwell, M = Michael Harvey, B = Brenda Fisher, P = Patrick Riley, D = David Jenkins

C: OK, our first caller is on the line – Brenda Fisher.

M: Go ahead, Brenda. What would you like to ask me?

B: Good evening, Mr Harvey. I want to talk about the parking problem. I'm very unhappy about it. I use my car a lot in the city and it always take ages to find a space. I go round and round searching, it's a nightmare. And if I do get a space, and go just a little over the time limit, some guy rushes up and sticks a huge parking fine on my window. And you know, your parking attendants, they're awful people, so rude. They seem to enjoy giving us fines.

M: Mmm, I understand how you feel, Brenda. It's true, a lot of motorists are unhappy about the parking facilities. It's a serious problem and we're looking at various ways of dealing with it. Thanks very much for your comment.

C: Thanks Brenda. Now a call from Patrick Riley.

P: Evening, Mr Harvey. It's about the noise and awful behaviour of young people on Friday and Saturday nights. You see, I finish work late at night. I have to walk through the centre of town to get back home. I can tell you, it's not a nice experience. These youngsters come out of the bars and clubs after midnight. They make a tremendous noise, singing, shouting, screaming, some of them get into fights. I tell you, I wouldn't want to be a police officer in this town. What are you going to do about it, Mr Harvey?

M: Mmm, I have to agree, our city is becoming a bit like New York these days. Young people just don't want to go to bed at the weekends. We're very concerned about this problem. We're taking it seriously and thinking about various options to deal with it. We'll be considering solutions at our next council meeting.

C: OK, time for one more call before we have the news report. David Jenkins, you want to talk to our mayor about air pollution in the town, I believe?

D: Hello, Mr Harvey. Good evening. Perhaps I should say 'Goodbye'!

M: Oh?

D: I want to talk to you about pollution. I'm moving away from here pretty soon. The air is so polluted, it's really bad for my health. You know, I've been here over thirty years, but recently I've been in very bad health, it's all because of the bad air, too many fumes from the cars, I think. Anyway, I'm getting out, I've had enough.

M: Well, I don't know what to say to you, David. I'm sorry that you're thinking of leaving our city because of your health. I can tell you, our environment officer is preparing a report on reducing pollution levels. I'll make sure you get a copy.

D: Thank you. I hope you publish it soon.

M: Could I just say, Claire, before our break? We're having a public meeting in the town hall next week. Anyone is welcome to come and raise any issue that's bothering them. I'll be there and also a colleague from the council. We want to have an open discussion and decide what our priorities are.

We can't change everything immediately, we need to think about what the most important issues are.

LESSON 10.4 RECORDING 10.5

M = Marilyn, F = Frieda

M: So, what are you going to ask about at the meeting, Frieda?

F: Well, there are plenty of things I'm not happy about, but it's the beaches that really bother me. I want to know what they're gonna do to clean them up and keep them clean.

M: Yeah, know what you mean. There's always loads of plastic rubbish on them, bags, cups, empty bottles, it's really disgusting.

F: Exactly. Why do they allow dogs on the beaches? And let people have barbecues on them. I've seen families have picnics on the beach and not clear anything away. I want to get some answers from the mayor and the council. Not just, 'OK, I'll look into it', that's what he usually says, and then does nothing. How about you? What are you going to ask about?

M: I'm really angry, well, that's putting it mildly, about the development they're proposing at Sandy Cove.

F: Sandy Cove? That lovely little beach where we used to go at lunchtime to have a quick swim?

M: Yeah, but it won't be lovely much longer. They're planning to develop the area there. Didn't you read about it in the paper?

F: No I missed that. Tell me about it.

M: Well, they want to use most of the beach to build a two-storey restaurant and a big amusement arcade. And at the side, they want to put a car park.

F: Really?

M: Yeah, the development will ruin the area. No one will want to go to the beach because there won't be much of it left. I'm so angry about it. And I'm not the only one. But the mayor and council think it's a great idea. There are even reports about it in the national press, I believe. The mayor will be on national TV next, with a big smile on his face, no doubt.

F: Oh, another thing I'm unhappy about is student accommodation. My son would like to move out and live with some of his college friends, but they can't find any flats at the right price. Everything's just too expensive. I don't think the council is doing enough to keep rents low for students.

M: I agree, it's a really serious problem. Something needs to be done for them. But you know, the council isn't doing much about it.

F: Does it surprise you? I'd like to see a lot more action to solve our problems, but I'm not holding my breath.

M: Mmm, well, let's see what happens at the meeting. It'll give us a chance to tell the mayor how we feel.

LESSON 10.5 RECORDING 10.6

1 I like to test myself by putting new vocabulary I want to learn onto cards. I put an example sentence with the word or phrase missing on one side of the card. On the other side I put the word or phrase. I often test myself when I'm on the train.

2 I like to organise new vocabulary under topic areas, for example, verbs, nouns and idioms connected to a subject, like crime,

173

AUDIO SCRIPTS

so I can concentrate on learning vocabulary on the same theme.
3 I like to have word families in my vocabulary book. I test myself by starting with a verb or noun and then try to remember adverbs or adjectives, and synonyms and opposites.
4 For difficult vocabulary I try to make a link with my own language, so I try to think of a word that sounds the same, and I remember the new word that way.
5 I have a great vocabulary app on my phone. It lets me record and test my pronunciation, and gives me random tests of vocabulary meanings as well.
6 I try to note down five new words each day and learn their meaning. What I do is write them on post-it notes and stick them on a board in my office.

LESSON 11.1 RECORDING 11.1

4 Good morning listeners. Last night, I attended the first live recording of a new radio comedy series *It's a Laugh*, which is going out on Comedy FM. It'll be on every Monday evening for six weeks. I'm pleased to report that the series lives up to its name. It's hilarious. Some of the jokes don't always work, but overall I really recommend it. You'll enjoy yourselves.
5 Even though you're probably fans of his, I'm sorry to tell you all that there's no real plot. It's meant to be a gripping thriller, but nobody seems to have a reason for doing anything. I couldn't relate to any of the characters. This is the worst novel I have read recently. I found the first few chapters very heavy going. I know his first novel was excellent, but this was a huge disappointment.
6 Good evening, viewers. The first of the old films we're discussing tonight is *Dracula*, the 1931 version. It's a classic example of the horror genre and I'm sure it'll keep you on the edge of your seats. It made Bela Lugosi an international star and its dark atmosphere is truly frightening.

LESSON 11.3 RECORDING 11.2

N = Nura, R = Richard

N: Hi, Richard. How did you get on in the interview? Did it go well?
R: I don't know really. I think so.
N: So, what kind of questions did they ask you?
R: Well, the editor of the newspaper did most of the talking. She asked me why I wanted to be a foreign correspondent and obviously I was expecting that. I said that I'd studied journalism at university and that I'd been the editor of the student newspaper. I also said I had worked for the local newspaper for five years and a national newspaper for three years and now wanted a new challenge as a foreign correspondent for a national newspaper. Then she wanted to know what parts of the world I was interested in.
N: Mmm, what did you say?
R: Well, all the Arab countries and South America. I told her that I also knew Brazil and Argentina well, so they would be interesting to report on.
N: Oh, I see. What else did she ask you? Those questions don't sound too difficult.
R: No, they weren't really. Well, the subject of languages came up. She asked if I spoke any foreign languages.
N: Ha! That was an easy one for you!
R: Yeah, I told her I was bilingual in English and Arabic and that I spoke Spanish and Portuguese fluently. She seemed pretty impressed.
N: I'm sure she was. Did she offer you the job on the spot?
R: Not quite. She wanted to know where I'd gone to university and if I'd taken any further qualifications. I told her I'd taken extra qualifications in IT and new digital technologies and a Masters in Media. She also wanted to know what articles I'd written and so on. There was only one difficult question really …
N: Oh yeah?
R: Mmm, she asked me what qualities a journalist needed to be a foreign correspondent. I wasn't sure how to answer that one.
N: How did you handle it?
R: Well, I said, obviously, I'd never done the job, but I had thought about it. I said that foreign correspondents had to be able to make decisions without waiting for people to tell you what to do. So, they needed to show initiative when they were reporting in a foreign country. They also needed to be digitally literate and aware of all the new digital technologies.
N: I think that's a really good answer. Was she pleased?
R: She seemed to be. Anyway, there were a few more questions. Then at the end, she asked if I was physically fit.
N: Funny question, but I suppose it's important if you travel a lot in your job.
R: Yes, true. Anyway, I said that I went to the gym three times a week and go jogging twice a week, so I should be.
N: Good answer. Do you think you'll get the job?
R: I've got a good chance, I think, but I wasn't the only candidate. I'll just keep my fingers crossed and hope for the best.

LESSON 11.4 RECORDING 11.3

A = Amy, B = Bob

A: Well Bob, you know I think that this is a great opportunity for the company, but it's very different from the kind of things we've done in the past. We could make a lot of money, but we could also lose a lot.
B: Amy, don't worry too much. It's the same as TV really, just everything's bigger.
A: I hope you're right. I just want a safe investment, something which is quite similar to the sort of stuff we usually make. I think some kind of mystery is the sort of thing most people really like.
B: Now, that's where we disagree again. I think this is a great opportunity to do something very different – you know, a proper big-budget film, something which will really sell around the world and something much better than what we've been doing recently. You know, those rather sad mini-series about unhappy housewives. Having said that, I don't think the genre is that important really. It could be action, adventure, or even a musical. It just has to be different!
A: I see your point Bob, but we need to be sure exactly what we want. What are our main criteria for investing?
B: Well, for me it has to be down to the originality of the idea. That's what'll get people interested and help sell it.
A: Yes, I understand that, but I also think the experience of the director is important. They can make or break a film and they make a difference to its sales.
B: True. Actually, I think the director is less important than the location. I think we need plenty of locations around the world so people see places they've been to or would like to visit. So the film becomes aspirational and means something to people.
A: Mmm, good point, They are both important, and a variety of locations will help to sell the film in different places. On the one hand, it'll have more international appeal, but on the other hand if we choose a film like that it'll be much more expensive, don't forget. We have to think about cost.
B: Yes, we do, but if we want a big hit, we'll need to spend more.
A: Maybe I'm being too careful, but I don't want to spend millions and find we have something a lot worse than our usual TV series.
B: Yes, you are a careful person Amy. Maybe that's why you're successful. But film-making is always a big risk, whether for TV or cinema.

LESSON 12.2 RECORDING 12.1

1 It's no surprise I'm in prison. I'm just like my dad. He was a big man and he had a very quick temper. He was violent at home, always hitting me and my mum, and he was violent outside the home, always picking arguments and fighting with people. So he was in and out of prison all the time. I'm the same. That's why I'm in jail at the moment. Me and some mates, we went to a club, someone said something I didn't like and I hit him. Really hard, so he was badly injured. The police came and took me off to the station. In the corridor of the police station, I did something really stupid. I lost my temper with a police officer and attacked him. I'm sorry now, of course. If I had learnt to control my temper when I was a kid, I wouldn't have hit the police officer. You just can't do that. In prison, I attend a class on how to control your anger. I'm learning a lot from the instructor and the other people in the class. I think it'll be useful when I come out of prison – I'll be able to control my temper better. Actually, all I want to do now is keep out of trouble, settle down and lead a normal life.
2 The newspapers called me 'Mr Big'. I liked that, but I didn't like the sentence I got – 20 years in prison. I didn't expect to be caught. You see, I plan crimes, but I don't actually commit them. I get other people to do that. I know I'm very intelligent, everyone says so. If I had wanted to, I could have become a top businessman or maybe a lawyer. But early on, I decided to follow a life of crime. It was an easy way to make money. And later, I started planning really big robberies. That's what I really enjoyed. I organised some big robberies and we made lots of money. But then I planned a robbery at the airport – gold bullion, worth over £10 million. Unfortunately, my team of

174

AUDIO SCRIPTS

robbers made a mistake. They stayed at the airport too long. If they had done the job more quickly, they would have left in time and the police wouldn't have caught them. One of my gang gave my name to the police and I was arrested. I'm 51 now. When I get out of prison, I'll buy a villa in Spain and retire there. Plenty of my friends are already over there.

3 My parents didn't have much money, but they were good to me. We lived in a poor area in Glasgow. A lot of people were unemployed and the crime rate was high. When I was about eight years old, I joined a gang of girls and we used to go shoplifting – you know, stealing things from shops and stores. It was great fun, until we got caught. I'll never forget my mum's face when the police officer came to our door.
Then, when I was a teenager, I started stealing from houses and when they caught me, I was sent to reform school. That's where they put young people who commit crimes. When I came out, I couldn't get a job and I was unemployed for over a year. So what choice did I have? If I hadn't have been unemployed, I wouldn't have started robbing cash machines. I was sent to prison for two years. I'm 21 now and I don't want to go back to prison. I think I've been so unlucky in my life. I might have tried harder to lead an honest life if I hadn't been unemployed. Anyway, now I'm going to move out of the area and make a new start somewhere else.

LESSON 12.3 RECORDING 12.2

1 They took so much money that everyone in this country and in Europe will be aware of it, and they might have wanted to use the money in Europe.
2 They shouldn't have stolen such a large amount of money. Someone found a huge bag of cash the other day and the first thing they thought was, 'Could it have come from that Stockholm job?'
3 Basically, they can't have planned it properly. They should have involved fewer people. And you know, the more people involved, the greater the chance a friend or relative will tell the police.
4 The £2 million reward might have got some informers and other criminals interested. The culture of not informing on other criminals no longer exists. People will do anything to get their hands on that much money.
5 Banks have become much better at tracking bank notes, so there is a possibility that they might have traced some of the cash.
6 The police think someone with inside knowledge could have been involved – someone who works there – and, if so, that person will be the most likely one to offer up information when they are questioned by the police. They won't be used to police questioning and they could be the weakest link.
7 The security people must have been very careless. The robbers could have been caught easily if the security people were doing their jobs properly.
8 Well, in one sense it couldn't have been more successful. They got away with £50 million.

LESSON 12.4 RECORDING 12.3

D = Mr Davis, C = Ms Cornish, T = Mrs Taylor

D: You can look at it in two ways, I think. Do you believe the witness who said he was definitely stealing the books, or do you believe the man himself? He said he was just borrowing the books for half an hour to read, then he was going to return them. But he didn't get the chance to do it. It seems to me that he's innocent because the manager didn't give him a chance to explain before calling the police. He appears to be an honest person to me. What do you think, Ms Cornish?

C: Mmm, it's a difficult one, Mr Davis. On the one hand, he may look honest, but on the other hand, there's some evidence from one witness to suggest he was stealing the books. Personally, I'm not certain he's guilty because I think he acted on impulse, without really thinking. What do you think, Mrs Taylor?

T: Well, I've made up my mind. I'm certain he's guilty. He didn't look honest to me. No, he didn't fool me for one minute. There's very little doubt, as far as I'm concerned.

C: You seem very certain, but you presume a lot. I don't think it's a case of trying to fool us. We need to be sure that he really is guilty. My perception is that he is probably innocent. Really, it's obvious to me that he didn't intend to steal the books.

D: Well, I'm not sure it's as clear cut as that. I mean he had money to pay for one of the books, and he didn't leave the shop. Are people likely to steal if they have money to pay for things? Is that really the case?

T: Well, actually they do. Most shoplifters tend to have money with them when they steal things.

D: Really, I didn't know that. Well, let's have another look at the statements and try to come to some agreement.

LESSON 12.5 RECORDING 12.4

Good morning. I'm Police Constable Martin Wilkes and today I am going to talk to you about simple home security. How can we improve security in the home and how can we protect ourselves? In the first part of my talk I'm going to mention simple precautions that don't cost anything. In the second part, I'll talk about devices you can buy to help with home security.

You might think I'm stating the obvious, but in my experience failing to follow these simple steps leads to most security problems. First, always remember to close the doors and windows at the front of your house or apartment when you are at the back of the building or in the garden, especially in warm weather. Leaving your windows open creates a target and an opportunity for burglars. Second, don't leave signs that you are not at home, such as leaving a note on the front door saying you've just gone to the shops and you'll be back soon. Another simple precaution is to ask for identification from any visitors who claim they are from the gas, electricity or water companies.

Now for the second part of my advice. An easy way of improving security is to buy and fit locks for your windows. Window locks are cheap to buy and easy to fit. A further simple and cheap device is a safety chain. This allows you to open the front door just a little. You can then see who is calling and talk to them. The advantage of the safety chain is that no one can push the door open and come into the house. You mightn't believe it but many people who have safety chains forget to put them on when opening the door to strangers. A more expensive security method is to fit improved locks to all your doors. These locks are difficult to force open so they keep your property safe. An even more expensive method is to fit a burglar alarm for when you're away from home. Alarms are a very effective way of deterring burglars. If you use all these methods you'll find that you can make it very difficult for thieves to burgle your home.

LESSON 12.5 RECORDING 12.5

Good morning. Today I'm going to talk about two main topics. The first is car security. That means keeping your car secure. The second is security in the car. That means keeping yourself safe and secure in the car.

If you have a car or if you're a passenger in a car there are some simple tips that will help you to protect your goods. The first tip is always to lock the car, even if you're just going to be away from it for a few moments. Secondly, never leave anything valuable where it can be seen, even if the car is locked. If you can't take your valuable goods with you, make sure they are locked in the boot of the car. Radios, DVD players and satellite navigation systems are expensive. Remove them from the car when you park. Nowadays, a lot of drivers use car immobilisers, which prevents thieves from starting the car, and tracking devices that help the police track the position of your stolen car. Finally, if your car is old and doesn't have an alarm, put one in.

Now, let's switch to security in the car – your personal security. The first thing to do is to lock your car doors as soon as you get in. A common trick for thieves is to wait for a driver to get in the car, then to open the passenger door and steal a bag on the passenger seat, for example. But there is one point to always remember – release the locks when travelling at high speed. This helps you get out of the car quickly in case of an accident.

My next point concerns protecting yourself when you're stationary. If you see any crowds or if someone on the street shouts at you, lock all the doors and close all the windows. This is a simple precaution to prevent theft from the car. My mother once nearly had her bag snatched as she sat in the car at some traffic lights on a busy street. Fortunately, she was very quick-thinking and managed to hold the thief's fingers, bending them backwards and forcing him to drop the bag in the car. She then closed the windows, checked that the doors were locked and drove away. She was lucky. But unless you follow my advice you mightn't be so lucky. Of course, you shouldn't really leave your bag or briefcase in the front with you – it's much safer in the back, with the doors locked. Finally, worse than this is carjacking – someone jumping in at traffic lights and stealing your car with you in it. This is less likely to happen if your doors are locked.

So, remember, car security is not only the security of your car and of things in it, but also your security in the car. Follow my advice and stay safe. Thank you.

ABOUT THE AUTHORS

Far left: Simon Kent
Centre left: David Falvey
Centre: Gareth Rees
Centre right: Ian Lebeau
Far right: David Cotton

Elementary, Pre-intermediate and Advanced levels

Gareth Rees studied Natural Sciences at the University of Cambridge. Having taught in Spain and China, he currently teaches at the University of the Arts, London. As well as teaching English, he is an academic English course leader, and unit leader on courses in cross-cultural communication for the London College of Fashion. He has also developed English language materials for the BBC World Service Learning English section, and he makes films which appear in festivals and on British television.

Ian Lebeau studied Modern Languages at the University of Cambridge and did his MA in Applied Linguistics at the University of Reading. He has thirty-five years' experience in ELT – mainly in higher education – and has taught in Spain, Italy and Japan. He is currently Senior Lecturer in English as a Foreign Language at London Metropolitan University.

Intermediate, Upper Intermediate and Advanced levels

David Cotton studied Economics at the University of Reading and did an MA in French Language and Literature at the University of Toronto. He has over forty-four years teaching and training experience, and is co-author of the successful *Market Leader* and *Business Class* course books. He has taught in Canada, France and England, and has been visiting lecturer in many universities overseas. Previously, he was Senior Lecturer at London Metropolitan University. He frequently gives talks at EFL conferences.

David Falvey studied Politics, Philosophy and Economics at the University of Oxford and did his MA in TEFL at the University of Birmingham. He has lived in Africa and the Middle East and has teaching, training and managerial experience in the UK and Asia, including working as a teacher trainer at the British Council in Tokyo. He was previously Head of the English Language Centre at London Metropolitan University. David is co-author of the successful business English course *Market Leader*.

Simon Kent studied History at the University of Sheffield, and also has an M.A in History and Cultural Studies. He has over twenty-five years' teaching experience including three years in Berlin at the time of German reunification. Simon is co-author of the successful business English course *Market Leader*. He is currently Senior Lecturer in English as a Foreign Language at London Metropolitan University.

SHEFFIELD UNIVERSITY RESOURCES

ONLINE LEARNING RESOURCES
why not have a look at these useful websites to help you improve your English?

ELTC's favourite sites
http://eltc-students.group.shef.ac.uk/

News and information about social activities, competitions, as well as useful guides about Sheffield and the UK and lists of useful websites and apps.

BBC Learning English
http://www.bbc.co.uk/learningenglish/

BBC Learning English has been teaching global audiences since 1943, offering free audio, video and text materials.

British Council - Learn English
http://learnenglish.britishcouncil.org/en/

A website with lots of different English learning activities.

ELTC Support Hub
http://eltc-support-hub.group.shef.ac.uk/

A website with useful academic materials and online seminars to watch. You will need your university username and password to log on.

Quizlet
https://quizlet.com

Learn vocabulary quicker by creating digital flashcards and revising and testing yourself using your mobile phone.

Box of Broadcasts
https://learningonscreen.ac.uk/ondemand

Access a huge library of British television and radio to practise your listening and reading skills. You will need your university username and password to log on.

DICTIONARIES AND REFERENCE MATERIALS

Longman Dictionary of Contemporary English
http://www.ldoceonline.com

An excellent dictionary.

Academic PhraseBank
http://www.phrasebank.manchester.ac.uk/

Produced by the University of Manchester, this site gives a wide range of commonly used phrases and their usage.

Flax: interactive language learning
http://flax.nzdl.org/greenstone3/flax

Learn about collocations, words that commonly go together in English. This can really help you improve your accuracy in speaking and writing.